LOCAL HEROES

THE VILLAGERS OF WRITTLE WHO GAVE THEIR LIVES IN THE GREAT WAR

JOHN W. TRUSLER LL.B (HONS)

Dedicated to my grandfather
Edwin ("Ted") Alfred Hare
(2nd Battalion, Scots Guards
25th November 1914 to 4th June 1917
Honourable discharge from wounds)

who made it through

and to my great uncles

Edward Arthur King
(Royal Canadian Horse Artillery
23rd September 1914 - 2nd September 1916)

James Charles Bender M.M.
(Canadian Infantry, 2nd Central Ontario Regiment
--- - 26th August 1918)

and

Edgar William Hare
(8th Battalion Queen's Own Royal West Kent Regiment
9th September 1914 - 8th November 1915)

who did not

_____

In Memory of
Benjamin James Trusler
31st July 1975 - 20th September 1975

Published by John. W. Trusler 2008
jwtrusler@btinternet.com
©copyright J.W.Trusler 2008

Published in Great Britain by

Print Wright Ltd
6 Boss Hall Business Park
Ipswich, Suffolk, IP1 5BN
www.printwright.com

ISBN 9780956043702

Contents

Index of Names

*Names marked with an asterisk were born or lived in Writtle but are not named on the War Memorial

Bibliography

Under the Devil's Eye – Alan Wakefield and Simon Moody; The Essex Regiment – John Wm. Burrows; The First World War – A J P Taylor; Most Unfavourable Ground – Niall Cherry; Cowan's War – Geoffrey Bennett; Army Service Corps 1902 – 1918 – Michael Young; Somme – Lyn McDonald; Writtle, Village of Distinction – Geoff Owen; The Mobbs Own – David Woodall; Queens Own West Kent Regiment – C T Atkinson; Men of Essex – Essex Branch of the Western Front Association; The Royal Fusiliers in the Great War – H C O'Neil; The Die-Hards in the Great War – Everard Wyrall; Topography of Armageddon - Peter Chasseaud.

And numerous source books from which I have gleaned information over the years.

Acknowledgements

Grateful thanks for assistance from Writtle Archives; Imperial War Museum; Essex Chronicle; Essex Weekly News; Essex Record Office; Kew Archives; the Writtle Society; Chelmsford Library; Essex Branch of Western Front Association and in particular Karen Dennis; Kate Brett Curator of the Naval Historical Branch of the Ministry of Defence; Orkney Museums and Heritage; those Regimental Museums who were able to assist; the Commonwealth War Graves Commission; Ian Hook and Essex Regiment Museum; the Estate of Siegfried Sassoon; Kevin Northover of Oxfordshire Branch of the Western Front Association for many of the Ox and Bucks pictures; the War Graves Photographic Project www.twgpp.org and in particular Steve Rogers; Patrick Roberts of Print Wright Ltd for his invaluable advice.

The poem on (viii) taken from "If you want the Old Battalion". The magazine of the Essex Branch of the Western Front Association.

Many pictures have been taken from long defunct publications such as The Sphere and The Daily Sketch. I believe that I have obtained permissions where necessary or have used works which are out of copyright but if I have inadvertently breached any copyright my apologies.

My business partner, Bob Wolny and all my colleagues at Weight Wolny & Trusler Solicitors of 81 Moulsham Street Chelmsford Essex CM2 0JD and in particular Pat Smeets, Carole Smith and especially Michael Jones without whose computer skills this project would never have come to fruition.

Hilary Cooper for reading through the manuscript and for that most elusive thing, the title.

My wife Rosemary for all her support and help in every way and for traipsing round cemeteries!; my son Daniel for navigating me and finally my grandson Benjamin for providing the essential ending for this book.

Introduction

This project to honour those from Writtle who died in the First World War started out life some years ago and has continued slowly ever since with other commitments hampering progress. It was originally intended to be just a brief account of the names on the Writtle War Memorial accompanied by whatever information could be gleaned. Personal detail has in fact been hard to obtain, perhaps hardly surprising given the passage of years

As time went by the project has acquired a momentum of its own and the gap caused by lack of personal information has been filled with detail about the regiments in which they served and then where they died. In turn that lead to finding out more about surrounding events. Information has been patchy. In some cases I have found out more than others. It also proved very difficult to find anything at all about some of the names but eventually I was able to trace all of them with the exception of Richard Beckett where the only Becketts appear to have no likely connection with Writtle. So "Rest in Peace" Richard Beckett whose only record appears to be a name on our Memorial.

I could have carried on delving into family and regimental history for ever but had to call a halt somewhere and the 90th Anniversary of the Armistice this year was as good a place as any.

My apologies therefore if I have missed anything obvious and also my apologies for any errors in family relationships. The project is not intended as a serious historical work and if my brief accounts of the events leading to the deaths of our men – and woman – contain any factual errors then again my apologies in advance.

The First World War continues to exert a strong influence upon us today. Interest which had waned has of late been revived but with it the danger that the Western Front is becoming over-commercialised, just another tourist attraction and a soft option for hard pressed teachers. Fortunately these tours tend to stick to the same few major sites and there are plenty of places where it is easy to capture the sense of the past. But there is a danger of "Disneyfication" and visitors to the Western Front should approach it as pilgrims not as tourists. Simply putting the War in the examination syllabus and sending coachloads of children off to France and Belgium may be a very nice break for all concerned but is no way to foster a genuine sense of remembrance.

There is also another threat to what I would describe as the integrity of remembrance so far as the War is concerned. This comes ironically enough from those who are in fact ardent enthusiasts of the Great War and indeed comprise many of today's historians and teachers. In turn they pass their message on to their students which, in a nut shell, is that on the whole the generals did a pretty good job and that the War was not as bad as depicted. These are what are called revisionist historians and just as there are trends in fashion so there are trends in history and what we see is a desire to find something new to say about the War. And of course once a movement starts then others jump on the band-wagon.

Their attempts to relieve the generals of responsibility for the horrendous number of casualties are wrong. On the whole, especially in the earlier years, the politicians of all nations felt inhibited about criticising the military and gave them a free hand. Field Marshall Kitchener saw matters clearly when he wrote to Sir John French, then Commander of the British Expeditionary Force, on 2nd January 1915 "The German lines in France may be looked upon as a fortress that cannot be carried by assault and also cannot be completely invested". Unfortunately he then forgot this and, by and large, the military top brass never even subscribed to this point of view. And so the same tactics of men against shell and machine gun fire were repeated again and again with the inevitable consequences. Not until the latter part of the War could it be said that lessons had been learned. This is not to detract from the individual bravery of many senior officers, a high percentage of whom were killed.

Of course there were exceptions but it is a fact that there was a fairly slow appreciation of the changes and challenges of mechanised warfare. It is not as if there were no precedents. The American Civil War had shown how improvements in rifles and field guns had created a situation where armaments would prevail against mere flesh and blood. And during the War itself it seems that the lessons of Battles such as Festubert and Loos were not really learned. Those in charge of policy and tactics may have been trying to do their best but in so many cases their best was just not good enough and was paid for in men's lives.

The revisionists are also very keen on challenging what they consider to be the myths of the Great War. They deplore all the popular images surrounding the War, blind to the fact that these images were in fact harsh reality. And how they hate popular shows such as "Oh What a Lovely War" and "Blackadder", completely overlooking the fact that whilst classics such as these may exaggerate for effect, nonetheless their basic premise is true.

The Great War poets had it right – a terrible war, in many ways poorly managed and impacting on just about every family in the country.

Paradoxically however the sheer horror of the trenches did not mean the soldiers' lot was a miserable one. Especially in the early days, volunteers flocked to join up, overwhelming the recruiting offices. And why not? If you were a farm labourer or a factory worker or a clerk this gave the chance of swapping a hard or boring lifestyle for some adventure. Who would not choose to be a soldier when the whole of the nation was applauding. And for those higher up the social strata it was a positive duty to enlist and serve one's country.

In addition there was perhaps less cynicism in those days. Today we despair at the way we are governed; politicians back then were no different but their actions impinged less on people because there was less regulation and less interference in their day to day lives. No worrying about which dustbin to put one's rubbish in! So ordinary men and women were prepared to answer their country's call.

No doubt once in the Army or Navy or, for women, the factory or hospital, it was a rude awakening and that sense of adventure was replaced with other emotions. But it is quite clear that although much in their new lives was unpleasant , not to say downright lethal, there were compensations, the chief of which was the comradeship forged through undergoing the same life changing experiences. Indeed a common theme with many who participate in a war is that the rest of their lives become something of an anti-climax.

Despite all the dangers and hardships it was not all doom and gloom and much of this was due to the sense of community engendered by a common experience. Perhaps that is what villages in Britain had which we have largely lost today, a sense of community, of all pulling together. That is not to romanticise the past; the Good Old Days – I don't think so. We are immensely better off nowadays in just about every way possible.

And yet; we dare not leave home without setting our alarms and double locking our doors; we are wary of strangers and often with good reason; our town centres are all too often given over to rowdy drunks; our politicians of every persuasion have taught us to take their utterances with a very large pinch of salt; our Christian values are disappearing to be replaced with who can say what; we are bullied by self-righteous Greens; we do not want ever increasing over crowding but no one is listening when we say enough.

It does seem, as a generalisation, that we have no more control over the events that govern our lives than a labourer would have had back in the Writtle of 1914/18. However one difference appropriate to this project does stand out. Recently our politicians took us to war on a lie; in 1914 the country went to war for a righteous cause. We had given Belgium a guarantee and when the German invaders trampled on that country we honoured that guarantee. The men, and the woman, of Writtle gave their lives in a just cause.

> But ye shall die like men,
> and fall like one of the princes.
> Psalm 82

The Names

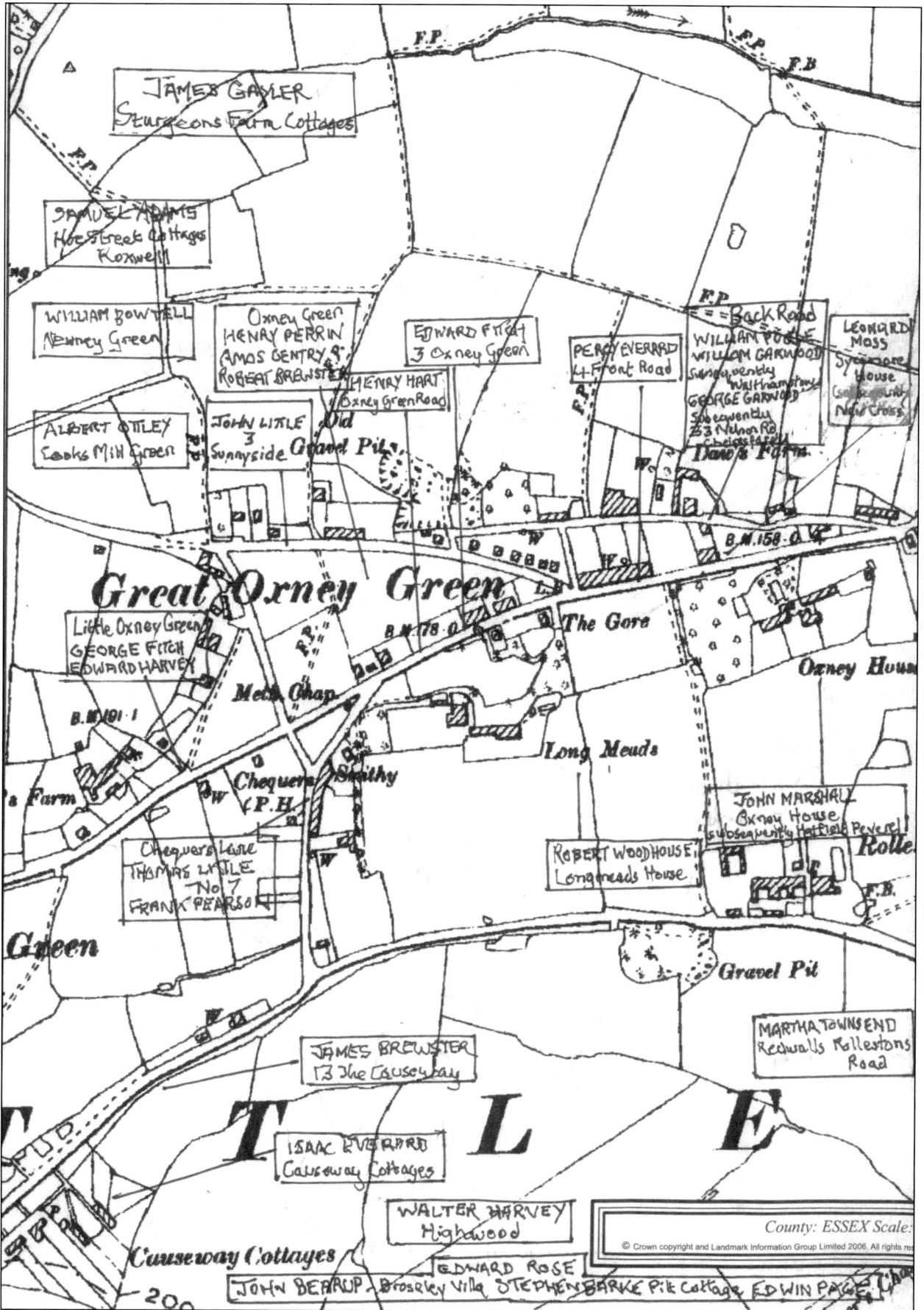

James Gasler
Sturgeons Farm Cottages

Samuel Adams
Hoe Street Cottages
Roxwell

William Bowtell
Newney Green

Oxney Green
Henry Perrin
Amos Gentry &
Robert Brewster

Edward Fitch
3 Oxney Green

Percy Everard
4 Front Road

Back Road
William Poole
William Garwood
subsequently
Walthamstow
George Garwood
subsequently
23 Nelson Rd
Chelmsford
Dand's Farm

Leonard Moss
Sycamore House
Cooksmill Green
New Cross

Albert Otley
Cooks Mill Green

John Little
3
Sunnyside

Henry Hart
Oxney Green Road

Old
Gravel Pit

Great Oxney Green

Little Oxney Green
George Fitch
Edward Harvey

B.M. 78·0

The Gore

Oxney House

Meth. Chap.

B.M. 191·1

Long Meads

's Farm

Chequers
P.H.

Smithy

John Marshall
Oxney House
subsequently Hatfield Peverel

Rolle

Chequers Lane
Thomas Little
No 1
Frank Pearson

Robert Woodhouse
Longmeads House

Green

Gravel Pit

Martha Townsend
Redwalls Rollestons
Road

James Brewster
13 The Causeway

T T L E

Isaac Everard
Causeway Cottages

Walter Harvey
Highwood

Causeway Cottages

Edward Rose
John Bearup Brosley Villa Stephen Barke Pit Cottage Edwin Page

(vi)

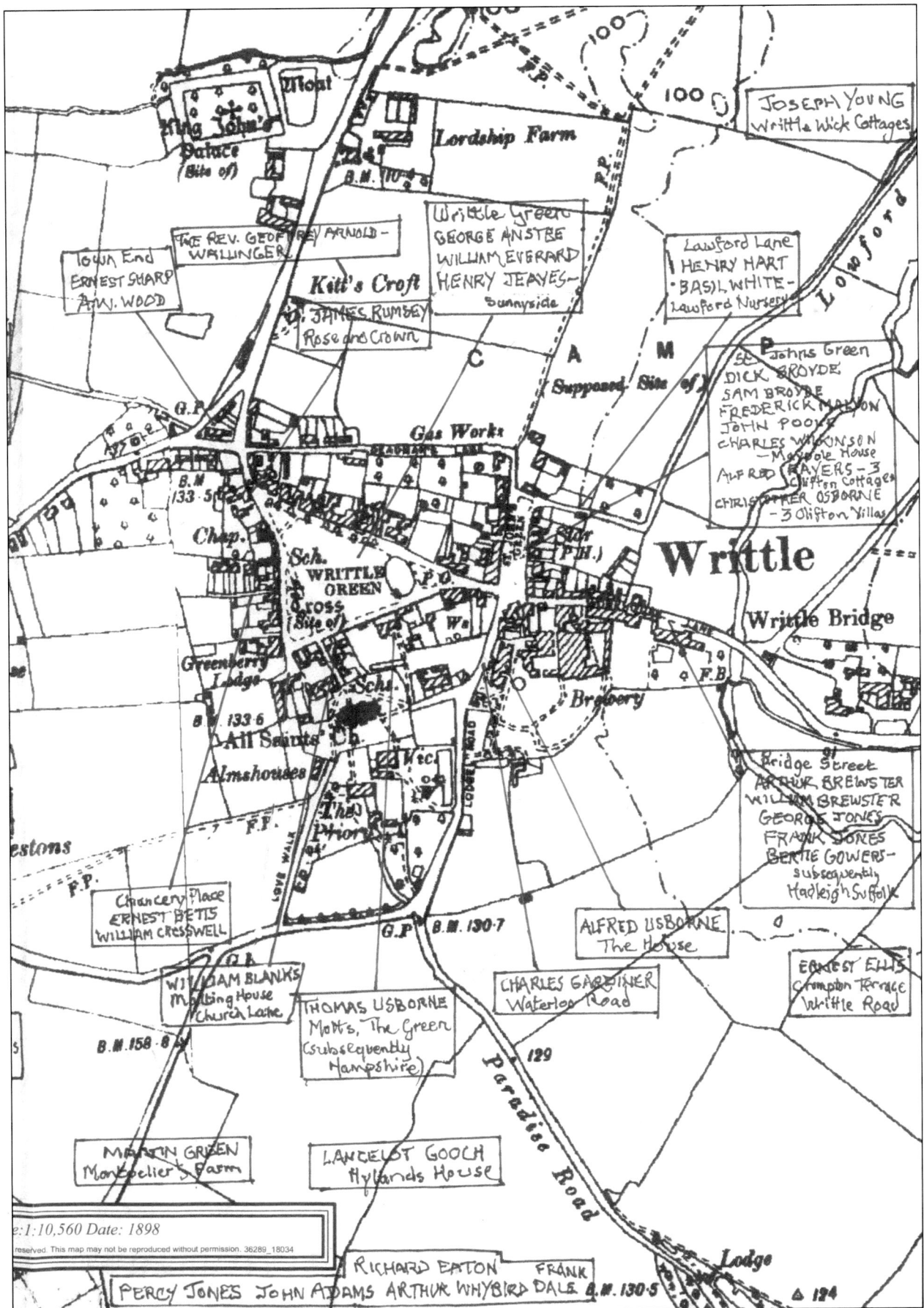

King John's Palace (Site of)

Moat

Lordship Farm

JOSEPH YOUNG
Writtle Wick Cottages

THE REV. GEOFFREY WALLINGER

REV ARNOLD —

Writtle Green
GEORGE ANSTEE
WILLIAM EVERARD
HENRY JEAYES —
Sunnyside

Lawford Lane
HENRY HART
BASIL WHITE —
Lawford Nursery

Lawford

Town End
ERNEST SHARP
A.W. WOOD

Kitt's Croft

J. JAMES RUMSEY
Rose and Crown

C A M

St Johns Green
DICK BROYDE
SAM BROYDE
FREDERICK MALYON
JOHN POOLE
CHARLES WILKINSON
— Maypole House

ALFRED RAYERS — 3
Clifton Cottages

CHRISTOPHER OSBORNE
— 3 Clifton Villas

Supposed Site of

G.P.

Gas Works

B.M. 133.5

Chap.

Sch. WRITTLE GREEN

P.O.

Star P.H.)

Writtle

Writtle Bridge

Cross (Site of)

Wa

Greenberry Lodge

Sch.

B.M. 133.6

All Saints Ch.

Brewery

F.B.

Almshouses

Vic.

The Priors

Bridge Street
ARTHUR BREWSTER
WILLIAM BREWSTER
GEORGE JONES
FRANK JONES
BERTIE GOWERS —
subsequently
Hadleigh Suffolk

Westons

F.P.

F.P.

Chancery Place
ERNEST BETTS
WILLIAM CRESSWELL

G.P. B.M. 130.7

ALFRED USBORNE
The House

ERNEST ELLIS
Crompton Terrace
Writtle Road

WILLIAM BLANKS
Malting House
Church Lane

THOMAS USBORNE
Moats, The Green
(subsequently
Hampshire)

CHARLES GARDINER
Waterloo Road

B.M. 158.8

129

Paradise Road

MARTIN GREEN
Montpelier's Farm

LANCELOT GOOCH
Hylands House

Scale: 1:10,560 Date: 1898

reserved. This map may not be reproduced without permission. 36289_18034

Lodge

RICHARD EATON
FRANK

PERCY JONES JOHN ADAMS ARTHUR WHYBIRD DALE B.M. 130.5

△ 124

They are speaking, best beloved, of erecting you a shrine
That your death may live for ever there, immortal son of mine.
They will deck your name with laurels for the price that you have paid
To deliver us for freedom – for the sacrifice you made.

For you went out in the darkness, smiling gaily from the train.
We did our best for you, and hoped to see you soon again.
Sadly home we went without you, all your chances to review
While you entered that mad maelstrom, made by others, not by you.

And we waited – waited – waited - for the scanty news that came
While your bed and chair were empty and the home was not the same.
The blow fell soon and swiftly, for we learned that you had died;
But you knew then how we sorrowed – you were with us as we cried.

Though the days to years are turning, you we never can forget,
And the heavy aching sorrow in our hearts is living yet,
But we feel that in the spirit you are with us once again,
Telling us our earthly loss is to your eternal gain.

They are speaking, best beloved, of erecting you a shrine,
That your death may live, forever there, immortal son o'mine;
And in all the future ages when we see you near to God,
Men will read your name and bless you, for the narrow path you trod.

The British Soldier in a conquered enemy trench: Quiet and steadfast and in triumph merciful

As illustrated in a contemporary magazine...

"Well, if you knows of a better 'ole, go to it."

...And as more irreverently portrayed by Bruce Bairnsfather, artist and soldier, and the creator of "Old Bill" the archetypal "old Soldier"

The reality…

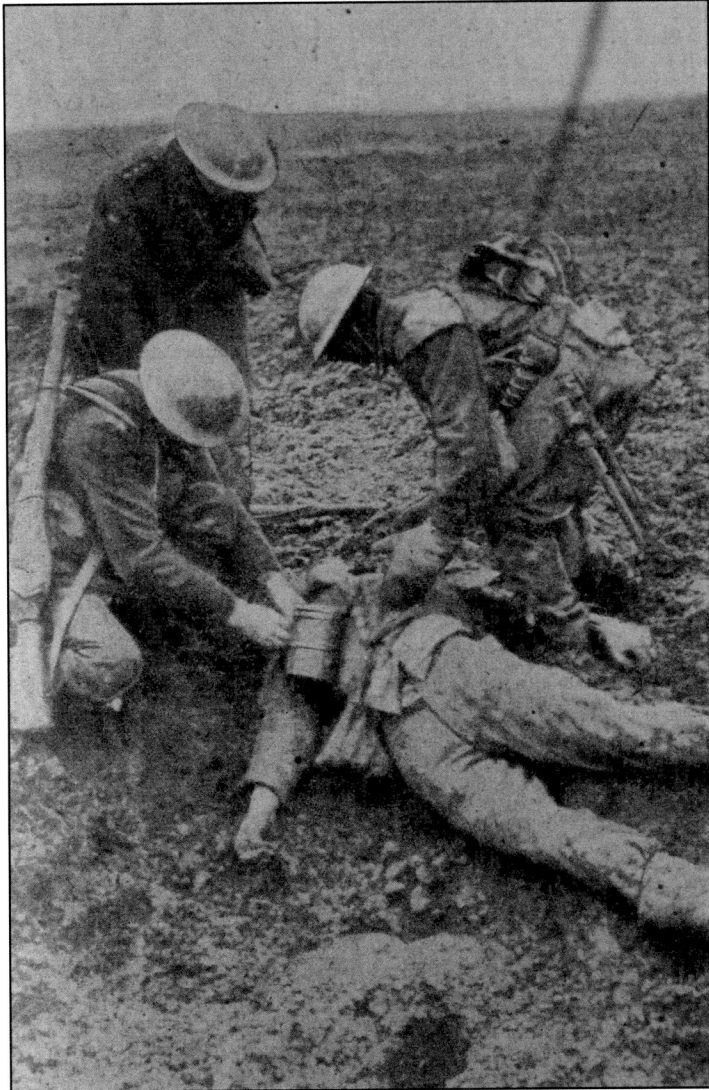

... and the reality of War

CHAPTER 1 - 1914

The Writtle of 1914

Writtle, in the years leading up to the Great War, had at the last count, in 1911, a population of 2649.

Many of the men worked in agriculture. The village was surrounded by farms. The chief landowners were the Lord of the Manor, Lord Petre; Sir Daniel Fulthorpe Gooch, Bart of Hylands House; and Wadham College, Oxford. Wadham College had been a major land owner in Writtle for centuries; in the reign of Edward I a Charter granting Montpeliers Farm to the College was issued on the 24th October 1285. The total acreage of Writtle was 8427 land, 21 of water. About a quarter of the land, 2440 acres, was farmed.

The centre of the village is in many respects quite similar today as it was in 1914, but possibly a lot smarter now. Many of today's expensive houses were just ordinary working-men's cottages. The working class was, as a generalisation, poor in the material sense.

Religion occupied an important place in the community. The Church of England Church was All Saints. The Parish of Writtle is a peculiar of New College, Oxford. The Sexton was John Poole. Other Churches were the Congregational Chapel and the Weslyan Methodist Chapel at Oxney Green. The Congregational Chapel was founded in 1672 and was rebuilt in 1885 at a cost of £500; it seated 200. The Weslyan Chapel seated 120.

One of the other village centres was the Attwood Village Hall, built in 1909 at a cost of £850.

Behind All Saints was Hawkins Almshouses providing housing for six poor women of the Parish.

The main educational establishment was the Public Elementary School with 450 children. Thomas Williams was the headmaster, Miss Frost the headmistress and Miss Spink the infants' mistress. The Chelmsford Union House for Boys was opened in 1905 for 35 boys.

George Hurrell was the village policeman and Alfred Hunt the sub-postmaster.

For an account of the by-gone commercial life of Writtle one cannot do better than the Writtle Archives' publications of "Writtle Shops" and "Writtle Inns and Pubs". And for a tour around past Writtle "The Writtle we've loved" by Pam Marden and Barbara Trevor.

It is conjecture as to the views of villagers about events brewing up on the Continent in the summer of 1914. Probably they had more to worry about in terms of earning enough to keep the family than international storms but one thing was certain. For many Writtle families the next few years would turn their world upside down.

The First World War may have been triggered by the assassination by Serbs of Arch Duke Franz Ferdinand of Austro-Hungary and his wife on the 28th June 1914 but from a practical point of view railway timetables ensured that once troops started moving there was no going back.

Following the assassinations the Austrians, allied to Germany, presented the Serbs with a harsh, even unreasonable, ultimatum. But the protector of the Serbs was Russia. Troops could be moved relatively speedily and efficiently by train rather than marching as in previous wars but the Austrians discovered that their train timetables would permit mobilisation against Serbia but they could not then mobilise against Russia. And in turn the Russians realised that if they mobilised just against Austro-Hungary they would be defenceless against Germany. So rather than mobilise in any one particular direction general mobilisation was the order of the day. Germany had but one plan – the Schlieffen Plan involving a swift knock out blow against France, the ally of Russia, before the Russians could get going in any strength. But the Schlieffen Plan involved an advance through Belgium and Belgium's neutrality had been guaranteed by Great Britain.

On the 28th July Austria declared war on Serbia; on 1st August Germany declared war on Russia; on 3rd August Germany declared war on France; on 4th August Great Britain declared war on Germany.

Of course the causes were in fact many and complex but it could be said that the First World War had begun "imposed on the statesmen of Europe by railway timetables. It was an unexpected climax to the railway age" (A J P Taylor)

And so in August 1914 the Great Nations marched enthusiastically to war. In Essex "The Essex County Chronicle" (now the "Essex Chronicle") produced a somewhat subdued editorial in their issue on the 7th August 1914.

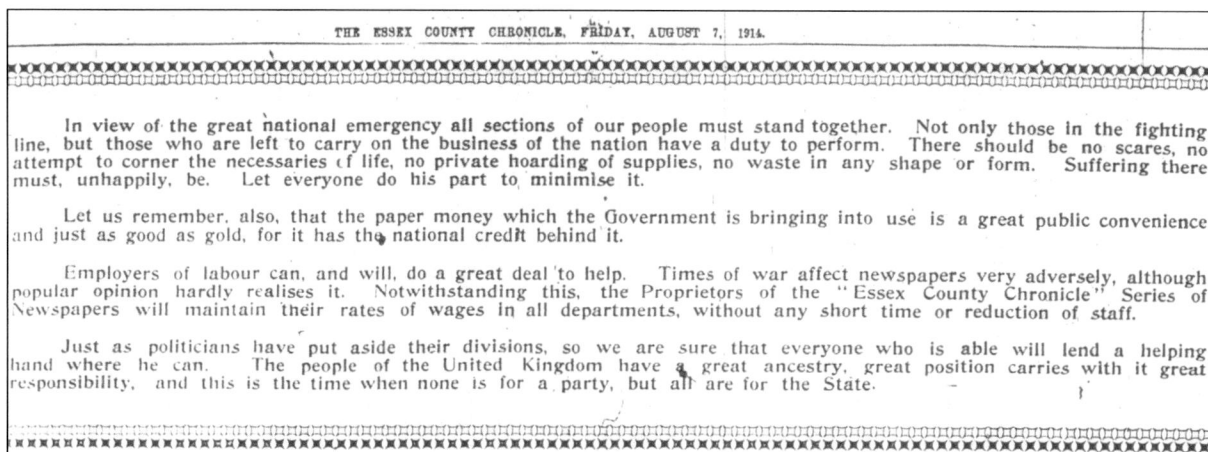

THE ESSEX COUNTY CHRONICLE, FRIDAY, AUGUST 7, 1914.

In view of the great national emergency all sections of our people must stand together. Not only those in the fighting line, but those who are left to carry on the business of the nation have a duty to perform. There should be no scares, no attempt to corner the necessaries of life, no private hoarding of supplies, no waste in any shape or form. Suffering there must, unhappily, be. Let everyone do his part to minimise it.

Let us remember, also, that the paper money which the Government is bringing into use is a great public convenience and just as good as gold, for it has the national credit behind it.

Employers of labour can, and will, do a great deal to help. Times of war affect newspapers very adversely, although popular opinion hardly realises it. Notwithstanding this, the Proprietors of the "Essex County Chronicle" Series of Newspapers will maintain their rates of wages in all departments, without any short time or reduction of staff.

Just as politicians have put aside their divisions, so we are sure that everyone who is able will lend a helping hand where he can. The people of the United Kingdom have a great ancestry, great position carries with it great responsibility, and this is the time when none is for a party, but all are for the State.

The Chronicle Editorial, 7th August

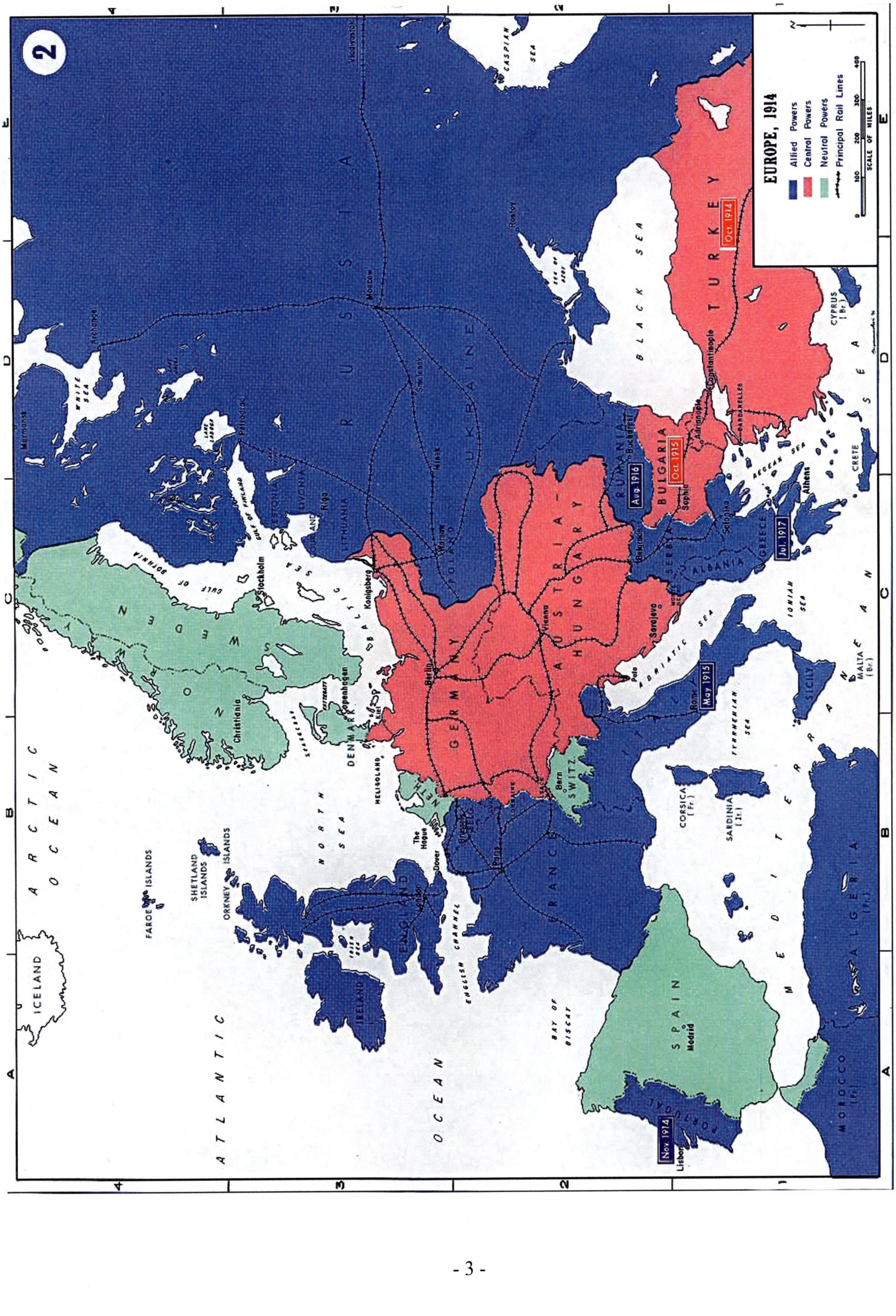

EUROPE, 1914

Allied Powers
Central Powers
Neutral Powers
Principal Rail Lines

SCALE OF MILES
0 100 200 300 400

ARCTIC OCEAN

ICELAND

ATLANTIC OCEAN

FAROE ISLANDS
SHETLAND ISLANDS
ORKNEY ISLANDS

IRELAND

ENGLAND
London
Dover
ENGLISH CHANNEL

NORTH SEA

The Hague
Brussels
BELG.
LUX.

FRANCE

Paris

BAY OF BISCAY

SPAIN
Madrid

PORTUGAL
Lisbon | Nov. 1914

MOROCCO (Fr.)

ALGERIA (Fr.)

MEDITERRANEAN

CORSICA (Fr.)
SARDINIA (It.)

ITALY
Rome | May 1915

TYRRHENIAN SEA

SICILY
MALTA (Br.)

SWEDEN
NORWAY
Christiania
Stockholm

GULF OF BOTHNIA

DENMARK
Copenhagen
Kiel
HELIGOLAND
KATTEGAT
SKAGERRAK

BALTIC SEA

GERMANY
Berlin
Königsberg

FINLAND
GULF OF FINLAND
Petrograd
LAKE LADOGA

ESTONIA
LIVONIA
Riga
LITHUANIA

POLAND
Warsaw

AUSTRIA-HUNGARY
Vienna
Sarajevo
Prague
Munich

SWITZ.
Bern

ADRIATIC SEA
Pola
Trieste

RUSSIA
Moscow
Minsk
Smolensk
Tula

UKRAINE
Rostov

WHITE SEA
Murmansk
Archangel

CASPIAN SEA

BLACK SEA

SEA OF AZOV

RUMANIA | Aug. 1916
Bucharest

BULGARIA | Oct. 1915
Sofia

SERBIA
Belgrade
MONTENEGRO

ALBANIA

GREECE | Jul. 1917
Athens

TURKEY | Oct. 1914
Constantinople
Adrianople
Dardanelles

AEGEAN SEA
Saloniki
CRETE

IONIAN SEA

CYPRUS (Br.)

Vladivostok

The Essex Weekly News carried a Call to Arms for men aged 19 to 30. By the beginning of September the upper age limit was raised to 35. Later, the lower limit was often ignored and the upper limit effectively disappeared.

YOUR KING AND COUNTRY NEED YOU.

CALL TO ARMS.

YOUNG MEN ARE WANTED

For Three Years or During the War

FOR THE ARMY

Age from 19 to 30.

- ALSO -

BAKERS, GROOMS, AND TRANSPORT DRIVERS.

APPLY AT

THE RECRUITING OFFICE,

DRILL HALL, CHELMSFORD.

Rail Fares will be Repaid from Outlying Towns and Villages.

GOD SAVE THE KING!

On Wednesday 14th October His Majesty King George V inspected some 15,000 troops in Hylands Park.

LOYAL WRITTLE.

Following the review of the troops at Hylands King George motored through Writtle on his way to Col. Lockwood's. The inhabitants lined the road through the village, and greeted his Majesty with cheers and the waving of hats. Many school children and Territorials took up a position on the village green and waved flags. His Majesty thoughtfully acknowledged the compliment.

The enthusiasm of the world generally for the War was matched in Writtle. The Chronicle reported on the 11ᵗʰ September a meeting on The Green on the previous Friday evening. A fairly typical appeal by local bigwigs to get men to enlist.

NO POLTROONS AT WRITTLE.

Col. the Hon. Alwyne Greville, M.V.O., chairman of the Chelmsford District Committee of the Essex Territorial Force Association, presided on Friday evening at a meeting on Writtle village green, and announced the necessity of England sending out every possible man.

Mr. W. Clement Wells, C.C., said there was no reason why we should not get a million men. We wanted the spirit of self-sacrifice. It was the first duty of every citizen to fight for his country if it needed him. Essex had always been a loyal county, and it would not fail to-day. (Hear, hear). A cousin of his in the 15th Hussars said the British Army in France was overborne by numbers, but man for man they could lick the enemy's heads off. (Cheers). If they got the men they could do it. (Cheers). Our hearths and homes were at stake in this matter. Our very existence was threatened. We were dealing with an unscrupulous enemy, who were committing the most barbarous atrocities that ever stained an uncivilised nation, let alone a civilised. (Hear, hear). The mother of an officer in one of the Essex Regiments was condoled with in her anxiety about her son. Her reply was, "I wish I had twelve sons to send for our country." (Cheers). That was the spirit of the women, who could do a great deal to help. Let those who had sweethearts tell them what they thought of them if they skulked at home when their country needed them. (Cheers).

Col. W. N. Tufnell, D.L., said that for recruits they did not want the loafer from the taproom; they wanted men whom they could trust. (Hear, hear). The little British Army in France had done glorious deeds. They were the finest trained troops anywhere on the Continent. Never had the Germans broken through them. (Cheers). Their shooting had been most excellent—quite different from that of the Germans, whose rifle fire was described as almost contemptible. He (the Colonel) was glad to see that football was to receive little attention in England. (Hear, hear). Let the boys give themselves for King and country, and let the "nuts" avoid the taunts of the girls, who at Folkestone had gone up to them as they sucked their cigars, and put white feathers in their hats. (Laughter).

Capt. Charlie Russell announced that Writtle had already sent in 73 men to the colours. (Cheers). Mr. James Usborne, of the R.F.A., who resigned his commission to be a doctor, had rejoined his regiment. (Hear, hear). All who went up would return with broader shoulders and enjoying more respect from the girls. (Hear, hear). If they did not do their duty they would be like the charity dog—ashamed to show themselves and only too pleased to hide their tails. (Laughter). But Writtle would do herself justice. Already, among others, Ginger Lingard, Cooney Perry, Perce Jones, and the three Gardiner boys had set a noble example, and the Gardiner boys' father had volunteered as a farrier. (Applause).

Mr. R. Woodhouse, jun., said they would never look back from the moment they had taken the oath. When the South African War came he forgot how old he was—(laughter)—and went out. In the first year he was unlucky. He was a prisoner for eleven weeks, but things went better. General French—(applause)—came along, and he was released, and put on the General's staff. No finer soldier ever existed than General French. (Cheers). He (Mr. Woodhouse) enlisted as a farrier, and at the end of the first year he was a captain. (Hear, hear). He then had a squadron from the district (Oxford and Banbury) whence the Territorials now in Writtle came. (Hear, hear). And excellent fellows they were, too. (Applause). Now the men of Essex and the men of Kent had led the van of the British Army. (Cheers). Were they degenerate now? ("No.") Would they at Writtle not take their share? He could not believe that they would not. They were not poltroons; they were only a little diffident. Let them get rid of that diffidence and go now, for they were wanted. "Mothers," concluded Mr. Woodhouse, "it is better that your sons should die if they have to die than that you should have brought forth poltroons." (Applause).

A goodly number of recruits then gave in their names.

Many men from the village had already volunteered and others came forward at the meeting.

By all accounts, a lot of young men saw enlistment as an adventure and for many it was an escape from the drudgery of labouring. And, again from accounts, their families were proud of them. But the horrific casualty lists had yet to come in.

In the meantime the remaining months of 1914 saw events proceeding much as before.

On the 7th August the Weekly News reported the Diamond Wedding of Mr & Mrs George White of Musa, Lordship Road and the death of Mrs Rutter of Romans Place, a most respected lady who for many years had ministered to the needs of the occupants of the almshouses. The wedding took place of Major Frederick Schofield to Miss Winifred Osborne.

Just two weeks after the outbreak of war Bates of Maldon could be said not to have missed a trick. The advertisement read "Have your horses been commandeered? Replace them with a Ford car or van". The next month they advertised a Ford ambulance "Full Ford equipment but without speedometer £125".

In October the death of another well known parishioner was reported, that of James Pamplin at the home of his son Mr F. Pamplin of St Johns Green. The late Mr Pamplin was in business in Writtle for 40 years as a general smith and as engineer to Writtle Gas Company. He was a member of the first Parish Council and umpired for Writtle Cricket Club.

Also in October details were given of the Harvest Festival at All Saints and entertainments at the Village Hall. Now we start to see the War making an impact on village life. Soldiers of the 4th Battalion the Oxford and Bucks Light Infantry were present and the proceeds of the entertainments were on behalf of Writtle and Widford Nursing Association and Belgian Refugees.

And amongst the six men named at the meeting on The Green, two of them, Percy Jones and Charles Gardener, would not return. And Robert Woodhouse, the local JP, who had wound up the meeting by saying "Mothers, it is better that your sons should die if they have to die than that you should have brought forth poltroons", was, within less than a year, mourning the death of his own grandson, Robert.

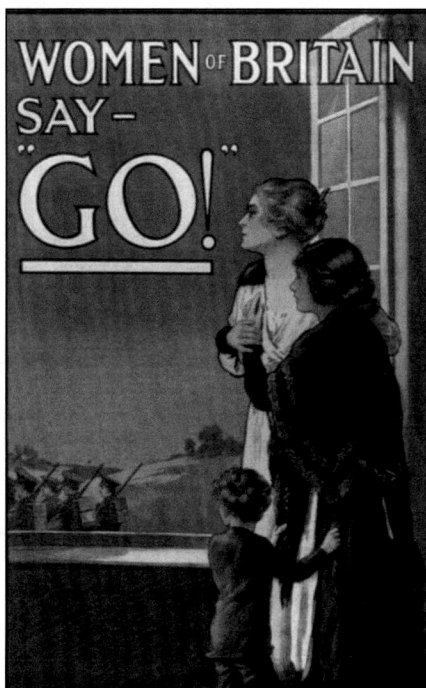

September - the Marne and the Aisne

In 1914 the British Expeditionary Force comprised some 160,000 men. By comparison with the vast conscript armies of Europe it was small but it was the most professional in the world. And the Army was backed up by the supremely powerful Royal Navy – for years the policy had been to ensure that the Royal Navy could out match the next two largest navies put together.

In August the British Expeditionary Force crossed the Channel and joined the left wing of the French Fifth Army. The British moved up to Mons in expectation of forming part of the offensive but the speed and strength of the German advance forced the Allies to retreat. However the retreat from Mons was not a rout but a relatively ordered retirement.

On 26th August the 2nd Corps made a stand at Le Cateau, a delaying tactic to gain time to allow the bulk of the Army to withdraw safely, albeit for the loss of 8000 men.

And so on 5th September began the Battle of the Marne when the Allies were in a position to halt the German advance. This was aided by a change in German tactics brought about by a loss of nerve on the part of their Commanders. Whether the Schlieffen Plan would have worked is a matter of conjecture but when the German High Command departed from its essential features then the aim of encircling Paris and achieving a knock out blow against the French disappeared. And so the seemingly unstoppable advance faltered and then was halted.

As a consequence the Germans fell back but regrouped. The Allies moved onto the offensive and the armies clashed again in September at the Battle of the Aisne. The month was spent in numerous attacks with no clear cut results and became bogged down in stalemate, a forerunner of the years to come.

Writtle suffered its first losses at the Marne and the Aisne. John Adams was killed on the 9th September and Walter Harvey on the 12th September.

John William Adams is not commemorated on the Writtle War Memorial. There may be a number of reasons for this. Sometimes the family did not want it. Some times it was a pure oversight. Or by the time the memorial was erected the family may have moved away. However his records indicate that he was born and lived in Writtle. He became a regular soldier having enlisted in the Norfolk Regiment in 1908/09. The 1st Battalion landed in France in August 1914 and was immediately in action on the 24th August at Mons.

At the beginning of September the German advance had been halted. The two wings of their Army had separated and on the 8th September orders were given for the British to cross the Marne and move against the left flank of the German First Army.

On the 9th September the weather broke and the heat of the previous days gave way to a downpour accompanied by a chilly breeze. But despite the change in the weather the British were in buoyant mood as they were now going to advance. They forced the Germans back across the Marne and although the British progress was slow in places, enabling the Germans to organise defensive positions, nonetheless the day was a success.

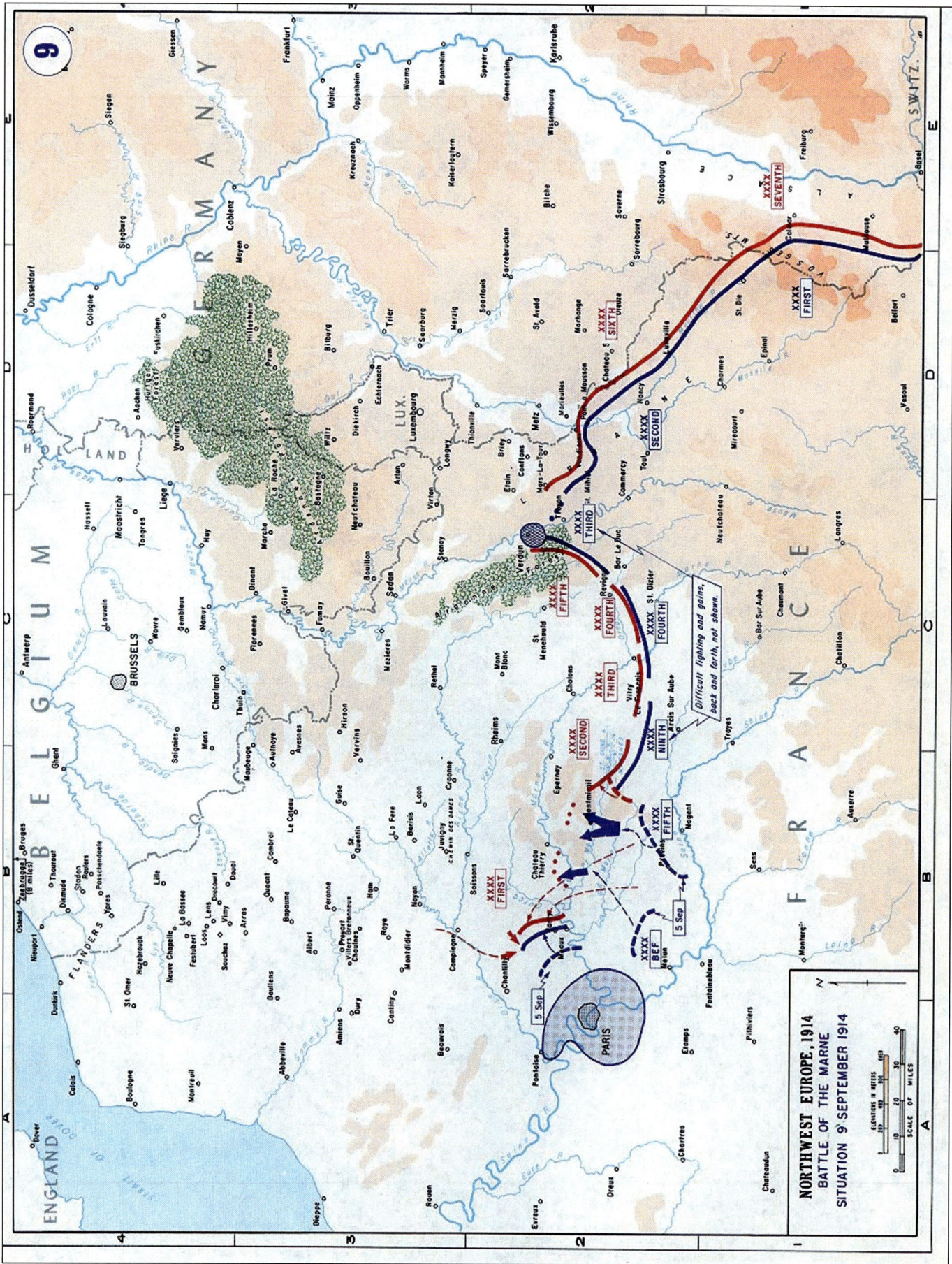

NORTHWEST EUROPE, 1914
BATTLE OF THE MARNE
SITUATION 9 SEPTEMBER 1914

During the advance John Adams was one of the casualties. He was killed at Hill 189 south east of Montreuil aux Lions and just to the north of the River Marne. He has no known grave and is commemorated on the La Ferte-sous-Jouarre Memorial, a Memorial to the Missing - the 4,000 officers and men of the British Expeditionary Force who died in August, September and early October 1914 and who have no known grave.

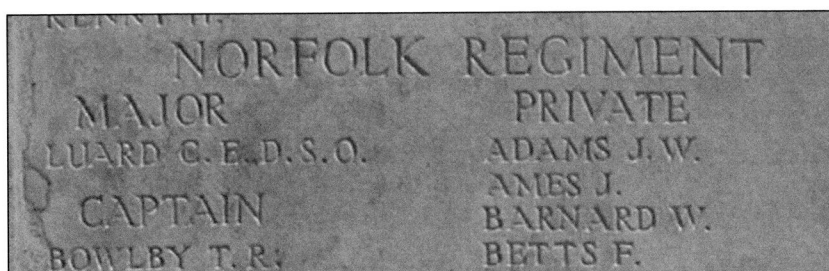

John's name on the Memorial

Walter Harry Harvey was born in Messing and lived in Highwood. His death is recorded as being on the 12th September although there is some confusion on this and it may have been the 15th. He was a private in the 16th (The Queens) Lancers. The Commonwealth War Graves Commission records show that he died on the 12th September whereas the Lancers' records state that he was killed in action on the 15th September.

The British Commander, Sir John French, did not wait for instructions from the French, who were in overall charge of the Allies, but gave orders for the Germans to be pursued. On the 10th September the British moved off at 5 am. At 11 am the Division came up to a German rearguard and captured a large number of their wagons. After this no further contact was made and they stayed the night at Breny and Roset.

Next day the pursuit continued north-westward. Some German wounded and stragglers were picked up but the British reached their positions without fighting. In the evening instructions did then come from the French with General Joffre wanting the pursuit to continue on the front Bazoches-Soissons, the advance being supported by the French who would endeavour to outflank the German right wing. Sir John French was to seize the bridges over the River Aisne and to occupy the high ground north of the river.

It had rained heavily the whole of the 11th and the 12th was even worse. The roads were, in consequence, in a terrible condition. Despite the difficulty in obtaining accurate information there were signs that the German fall back was nearing its end and that masses of troops were concentrating on the line of the Aisne.

The British Brigades moved forward. The 3rd and 5th Brigades crossed by the bridge at Chassemy. From there troops advanced to Condé but found this strongly held. Whilst this was occurring the 5th and the 16th Lancers clashed with two companies of German infantry moving south from Brenelle and killed some 70 of the enemy and captured about 100.

The weather and the bad condition of the roads delayed further movement and the troops were obliged to halt on a line from Longueval - Chassemy - Buzancy. The 16th had two casualties on the 12th - 1 killed, and 1 wounded. If the War Graves Commission is right the soldier who lost his life that day was Walter Harvey. But Regimental records clearly show his date of death as the 15th September.

The geography of the valley of the Aisne favoured the German defenders and their guns swept the whole extent of the valley. The spur at Chivres was the key to the German position dominating Condé and its bridge and giving flanking fire along the river. On this spur the Germans placed eighteen heavy guns and it was the failure to take this position which decided the Battle of the Aisne.

The Allies carried out a number of attacks the next day, successful in some places, less so in others. Meanwhile the 16th Lancers had been left at Ciry but were shelled out of it, sustaining just one wounded, and took cover at a nearby farm.

The 14th September was a day of hard fighting and great disappointment. Unknown to the Allies, fresh German troops had arrived to fill the gap between the 1st and 2nd Armies, a gap which the British and French had intended exploiting. As it was, only part of the Allied force achieved any success and that was at great cost, some 3500 casualties. For the remainder, their attacks failed completely.

In the evening the 16th Lancers moved into billets at Lime. It is at this point that again records are unclear. The Lancers' casualty list shows Walter Harvey as having died on 15th September whereas the Regimental History states that he was killed in the fighting on the 14th. In the confusion of battle it is perhaps not surprising that there are discrepancies.

Walter has no known grave. Records indicate that his name is on the La Ferte-Sous-Jouarre Memorial but in fact it appears to have been omitted from the section for the Lancers.

The bridge over the Aisne where British troops crossed in September 1914
(Photo by kind permission of the Imperial War Museum)

La-Ferte-Sous-Jouarre Memorial

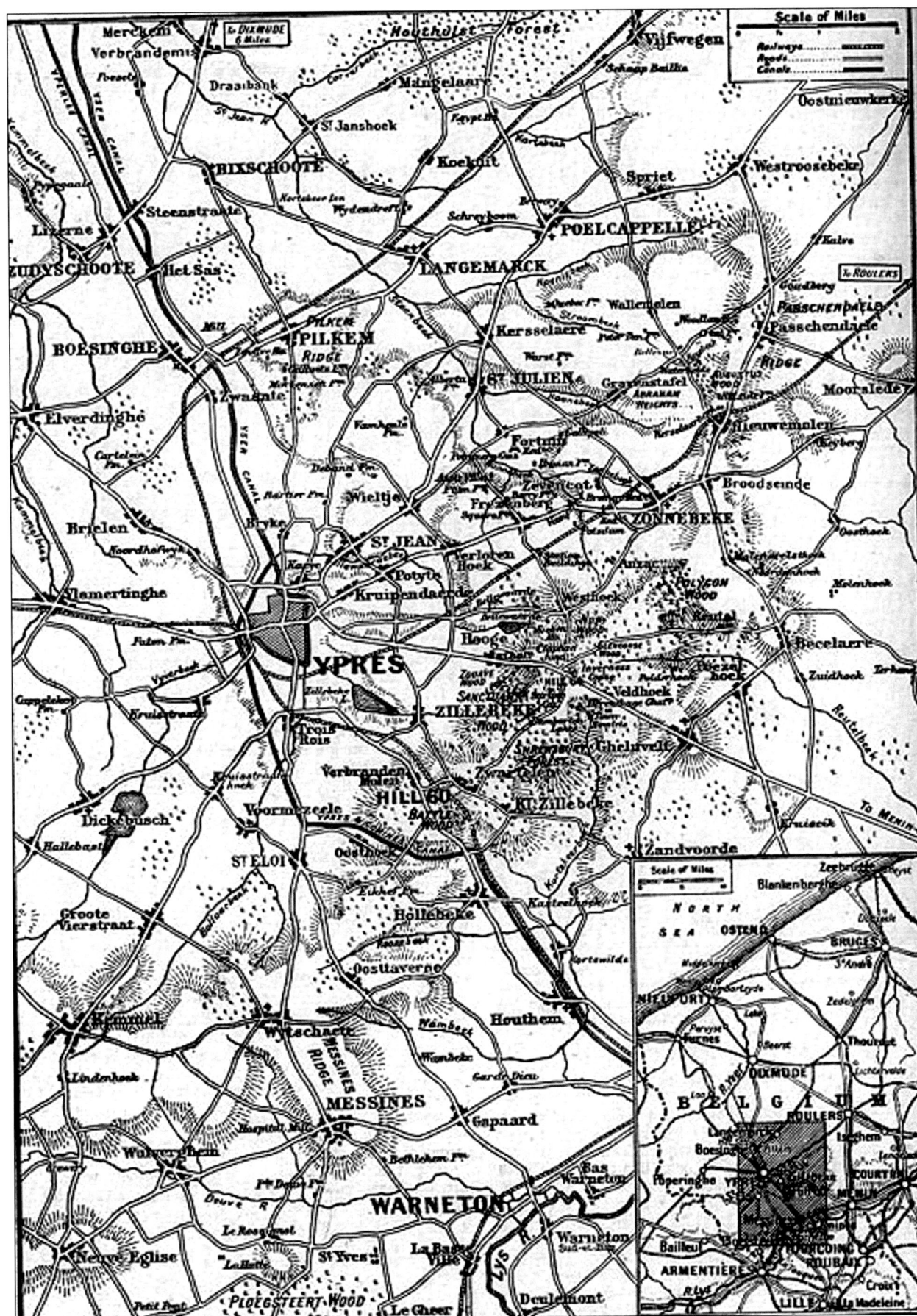

Only after the enforced retreat to the Aisne did the Germans appreciate the importance of the Channel ports, ignored in the original plan. And so began the race to the sea with each side attempting to outflank the other. The Belgian Army was ill equipped to resist the Germans but its resistance was instrumental in holding up the invaders. The British transferred to Flanders and as a result the Belgians were able to make an orderly retreat along the coast.

The next object of the German attack was the capture of Ypres. The town stood on the Flanders plain between a ridge of low hills. These hills sloped down from Wytschaete, from Gheluveldt and from Passchendaele. If the Germans could gain possession of the high ground and the town they could drive a wedge between the Allies and that could then lead to them seizing the coastal plain and ports. And so began the battle known as First Ypres.

During October and November the Germans unleashed a series of onslaughts, slowly pushing back the French in the north and the British in the centre and south of the Menin Road. The Germans had overwhelming strength but, using their last reserves, the British halted them in front of Ypres.

Reproduction Interdite

Photo ANTONY, Ypres

Visé Paris N° 221114-16

Incendie des Halles, le 22 novembre 1914.
Fire of the Halles.

Ypres; the Cloth Hall on fire 22nd November 1914

Thus was formed the Ypres salient, the arena for a constant struggle for the whole of the War. Both sides then created a complex line of trenches stretching from the North Sea to the Swiss frontier.

But halting the German advance came at a heavy cost. In October and November losses amounted to some 58,000 men. In all from the outbreak of the war to 30th November the total losses were nearly 90,000. It meant the virtual destruction of Britain's small professional army.

James Gayler came from a family of farmworkers. The 1901 Census shows that living at Sturgeons Farm Cottage was his father James, the farm stockman, and his wife Louisa and their four children, James then aged 19 and his sisters Ellen, Lucy and Mary. Later James moved from agriculture to working at Hoffmans. When war broke out he enlisted as a private in the 2nd Battalion, the Essex Regiment.

During October the 2nd Battalion had moved north and on the 14th were billeted in a convent in Bailleul where they were treated very well and were able to have a wash. The following day they secured the bridges over the River Lys. The next task was to hold the road at Ploegsteert and so on the 20th October 1914 the Essex were in trenches around Perenchies. The Germans were pushing hard and the Essex men were distributed along the line.

Ploegsteert and its wood lay some 10 miles south of Ypres. Just south of the Wood was the road between Ploegsteert and Warneton. Crossing the road leading south to Armentieres and north to the Wood was the crossroads at Le Gheer.

At 5.15 on 21st October, in the early morning mist, part of the German XIX Corps attacked and forced back the 2nd battalion on the left for a quarter of a mile to le Gheer. A counter attack was ordered with 2 platoons of the Essex, some East Lancs and the Somersets.

Numbers 13 and 15 platoons of D company moved to the road junction north of le Gheer at 6am. Emerging from Ploegsteert Wood, Sgt Barton with No 13 caught the enemy by surprise. No.15 went to the other side of the road and in doing so their senior officer, Major Moffitt, was wounded. Both 13 and 15 lost heavily from machine gun fire but were both in the charge at 9 o'clock which recovered le Gheer. In the charge 15 went with the 9th Lancers and 13 with the East Lancs. The village was taken. Three counter attacks were launched by the Germans but each one was beaten off. 14 and 16 platoons were on the left flank of the Kings Own to the east of le Gheer. In the course of heavy fighting many men were killed including their commanding officer Lt. Vance.

D company's losses for the day were 1 officer killed, 1 wounded and one taken prisoner together with 66 other ranks killed, wounded or missing.

Amongst those killed was James Gayler who has no known grave and is commemorated on the Ploegsteert Memorial which has on it the names of more than 11,000 British and Empire troops who died in this sector and have no known grave.

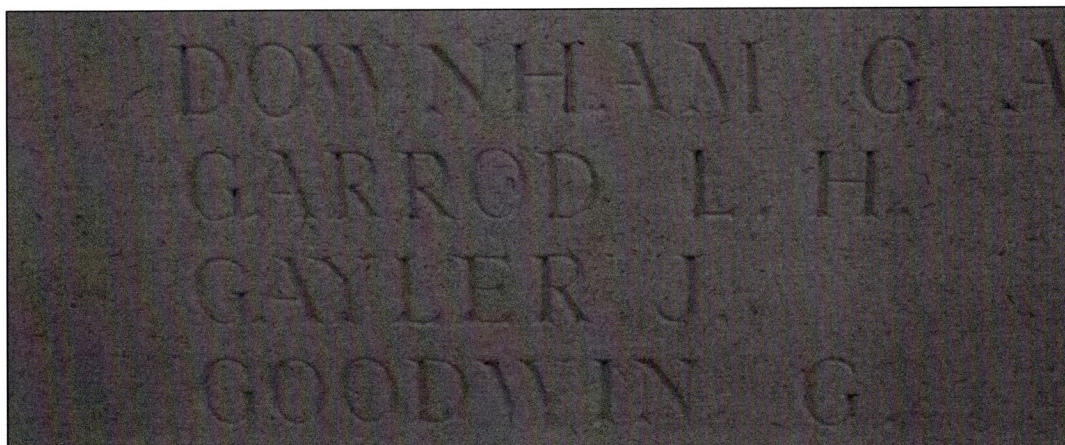

James Gayler's name on the Ploegsteert Memorial

le Gheer Crossroads 2008

Ploegsteert Memorial
Records 11,447 missing who fell in battles in the south of the Ypres Sector

One of the lions guarding the Ploegsteert Memorial

Arthur Brewster was a private in the 2nd Battalion Grenadier Guards. In the 1901 Census he is shown as aged 15, a gardener, living at Bridge Street with his father Thomas, a widower, and his brothers, Joseph aged 18 and William aged 10. Their mother Martha had died sometime prior to 1901. Arthur joined the Grenadier Guards on the 11th December 1906 having enlisted under the false name of Arthur Watson. He was transferred to the Reserve on 5th July 1914 but was remobilised on the 5th August.

Grenadier Guards Reservists reporting at Wellington Barracks

On 1st November 1914 the 2nd Battalion of the Grenadier Guards was sent to clear the wood near Klein Zillebeke and the War Diary records that this was completed successfully albeit with 47 killed, wounded or missing.

On the 2nd November the Germans countered with intermittent attacks and shelling throughout the day. The most serious attack was noted at dusk which was driven off but at the cost of 4 killed along with 12 wounded and 1 missing.

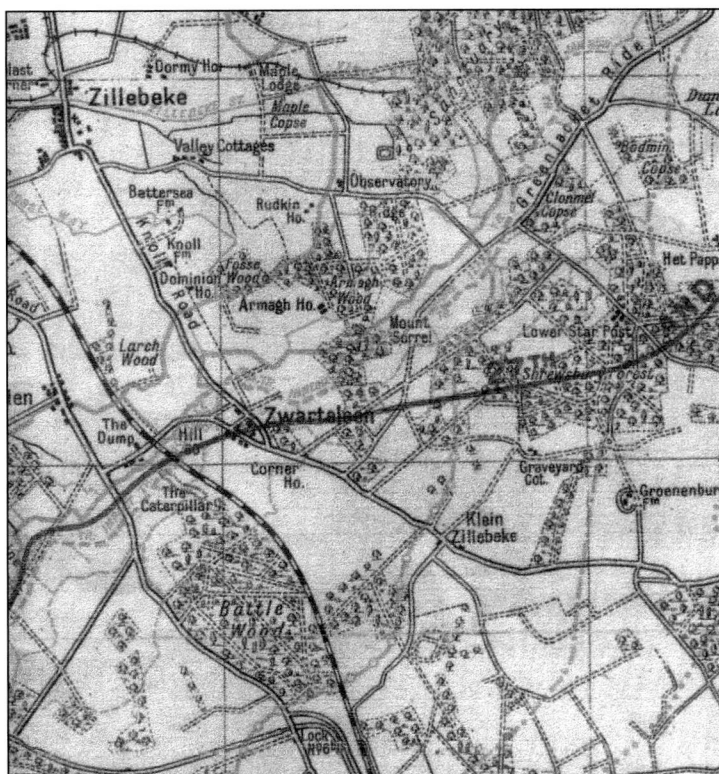

Klein Zillebeke; bottom line, middle square

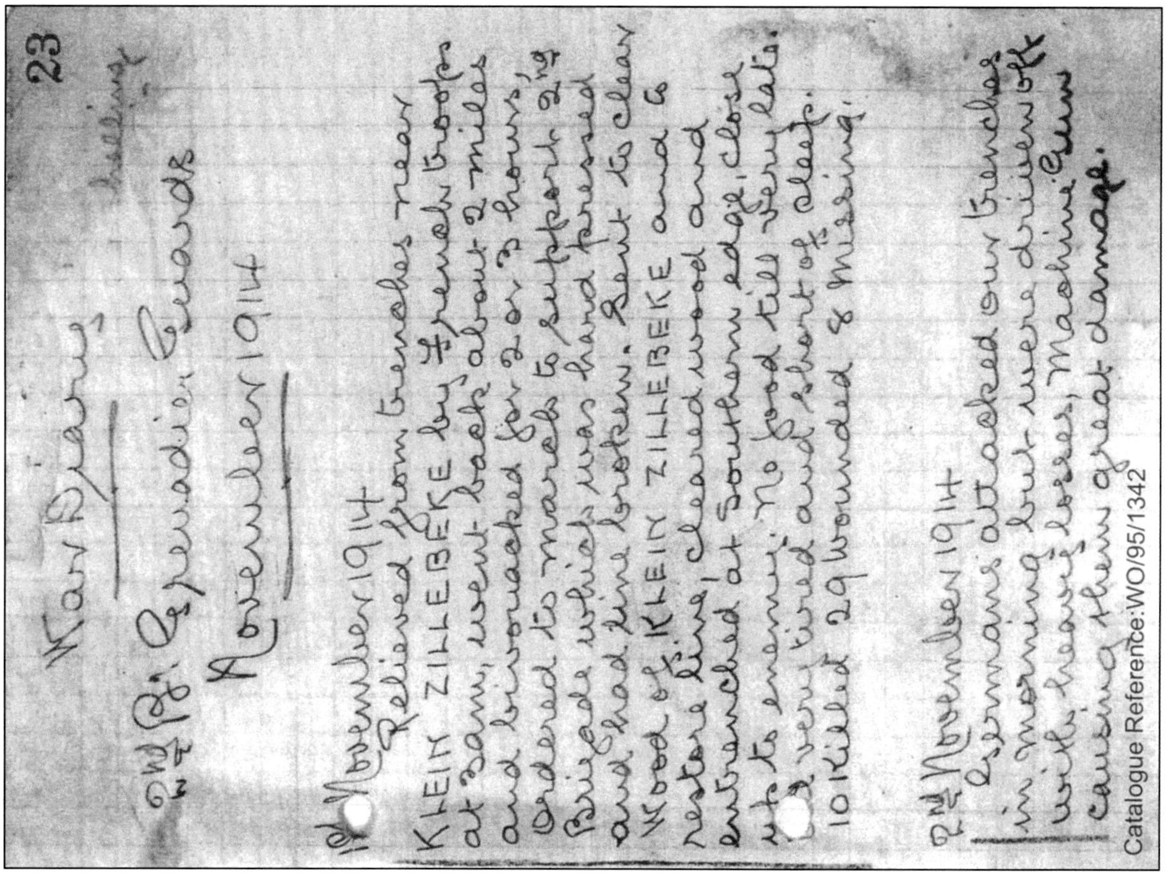

23

War Diary

shelling

2nd Bn. Grenadier Guards

November 1914

1st November 1914
Relieved from trenches near KLEIN ZILLEBEKE by French troops at 3am, went back about 2 miles and bivouacked for 2 or 3 hours, ordered to march to support 2nd Brigade which was hard pressed and had line broken. Sent to clear Wood of KLEIN ZILLEBEKE and to restore line, cleared wood and entrenched at Southern edge, close up to enemy. No food till very late. [illegible] very tired and short of sleep.
10 Killed 29 Wounded 8 Missing.

2nd November 1914
Germans attacked our trenches in morning but were driven off with heavy losses, Machine Gun causing them great damage.

Catalogue Reference:WO/95/1342

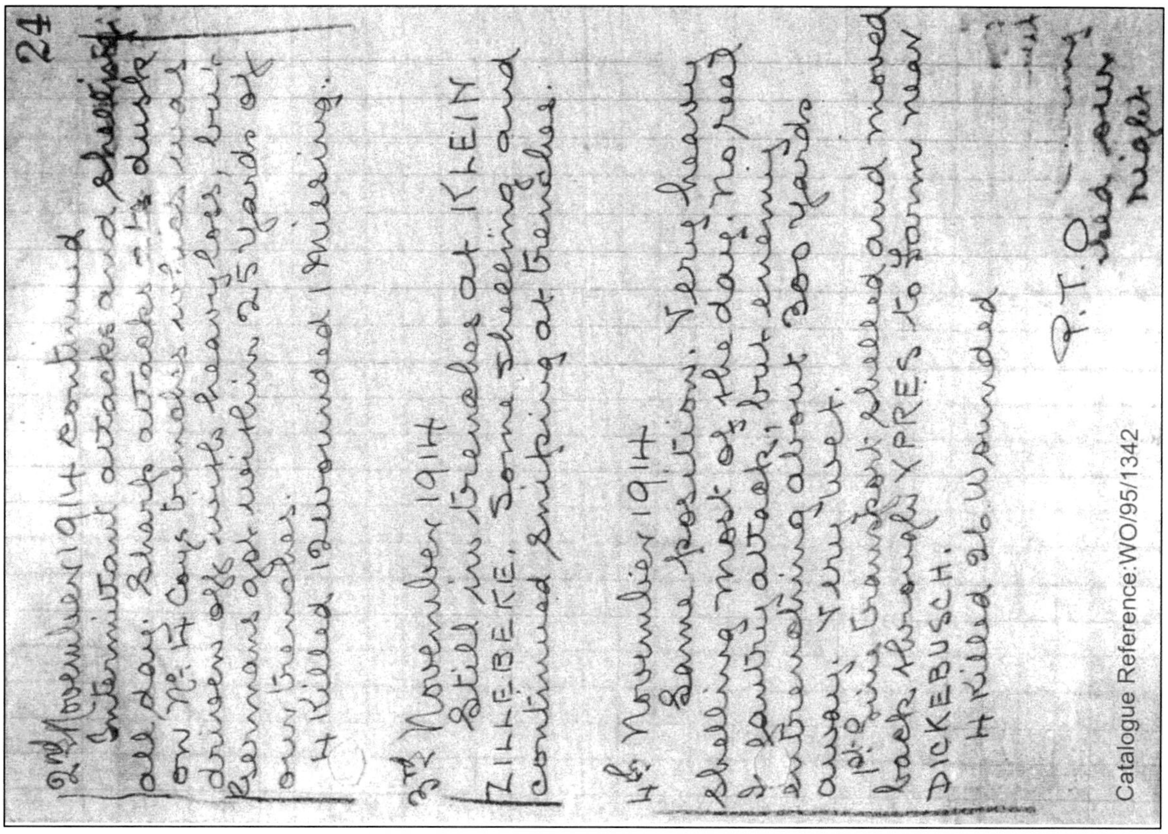

24

2nd November 1914 continued
Intermittent attacks and shelling all day. Sharp attacks at dusk on No. 4 Coys trenches which was driven off with heavy loss, but Germans got within 25 yards of our trenches.
4 Killed 12 Wounded 1 Missing.

3rd November 1914
Still in trenches at KLEIN ZILLEBEKE. Some shelling and continued sniping at trenches.

4th November 1914
Same position. Very heavy shelling most of the day. No real infantry attack, but enemy entrenching about 300 yards away. Very wet.
1st Line Transport shelled and moved back through YPRES to Farm near DICKEBUSCH.
4 Killed 26 Wounded

P.T.O.

[illegible] road our night

Catalogue Reference:WO/95/1342

The War Diary of the 2nd Battalion Grenadier Guards, 1st and 2nd November 1914

Arthur was one of those killed. He has no known grave and is commemorated on the Menin Gate at Ypres. The Menin Gate bears the names of approximately 54,000 men who died in the Ypres Salient up to August 1917 and who have no known grave.

STOKER T.	BEARD G. W.	MASTERS E.
STONE P. V.	BEDNALL O.	MATEHAM E
STONE S. A.	BEEKS C.	MATHER J.
STONEMAN A.G.	BENNETT A. T.	MELIA J.
STRATFORD W.	BILBIE C.	MENDORF A
SUTHERLAND J. E.	BINDING C.	MILLS T.
SWAINSTON W.	BONFIELD R. W.	MITCHELL S
TAYLOR J. H.	BOULTON F.	MIZON G.
TELFORD T.	BOURKE W.	MOORE T.
THOMAS A.L.	BOWES J.	MORGAN P.
THOMPSON J. M.	BREWSTER A	MORRIS A.
THOMSON J.	BROOKS W. A.	MORRIS E.
THORN W. J.	BROWN D.	MORSEY C.
THORNTON W.	BROWN H.	MURTAGH
TULETT H.	BROWN J.	NE'AL F. A
TURNER H.	BROWN R.	NEWMAN
TALLELY J.	BUGGS A.	NICKOLLS
ANSTONE E.G.	BUNNETT H. A.	NOUTCH
	BURGE	OAKLEY

Arthur's name on the Menin Gate

The Menin Gate

And so the year drew to an end. There had been predictions that "it would all be over by Christmas". Mrs Leworthy of St. Johns Green received a post card from her son, Driver William Leworthy of the Royal Field Artillery, "Dear Mother - we are just having a rest after four days of fighting. I am quite all right and quite well. I have seen C. Johnson. He is quite alright. We have had no sleep for three nights so we are enjoying our rest. Get Christmas dinner ready for me".

However this was just the first of four Christmases.

At home Christmas was marked by appeals for comforts for the troops. Typical of these was the Chronicle's Christmas box of cigarettes and tobacco "a smoke is all that is wanted to keep him cheerful".

The Soldiers' Christmas Box.

How our Readers can send a Christmas Box of Tobacco, Cigarettes, Pipe, Pouch and Matches to our brave Soldiers in the Trenches.

A Gift that will Gladden their Hearts on Christmas Day.

No one deserves a Christmas-box more than "Tommy," and our readers will, we feel sure, be glad to know that we have now made arrangements to despatch to our heroic soldiers on Active Service a Christmas Tobacco-box, which will make them as happy as sandboys on Christmas-Day.

From the hundreds of letters we have received we know there is nothing that can take the place of tobacco and cigarettes. In nearly every letter written home we hear how much it is wanted; that every cigarette is "as good as a reinforcement"; that "a smoke is all that is wanted to keep him cheerful."

OUR CHRISTMAS-BOX OF SMOKES.

Our Fund is doing very well, and the response has been generous, but for Christmas we want to do something more—we want to send a Special Christmas-box to every soldier that we can—and we appeal to our readers to make their subscriptions a little more and so help us to do this. When Christmas-Day comes we want him to know that he will be in our thoughts, and that we wish him as jolly a day as the rigours of war permit.

Our Christmas Tobacco-box is the very thing the soldiers are longing for—it will include:

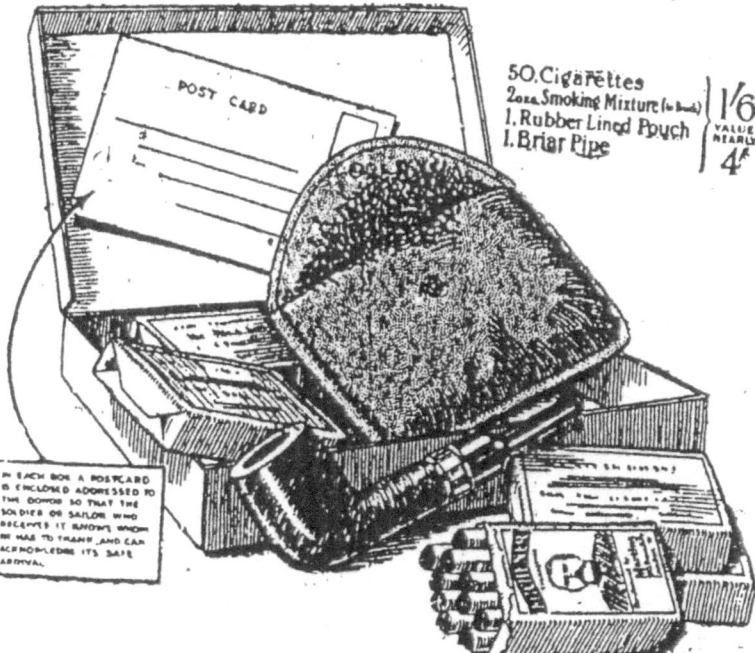

50. Cigarettes
2oz. Smoking Mixture (in tin)
1. Rubber Lined Pouch
1. Briar Pipe

1/6
VALUE NEARLY 4/-

POST CARD

IN EACH BOX A POSTCARD IS ENCLOSED ADDRESSED TO THE DONOR SO THAT THE SOLDIER OR SAILOR WHO RECEIVES IT KNOWS WHOM HE HAS TO THANK AND CAN ACKNOWLEDGE ITS SAFE ARRIVAL.

Tobacco was an important part of the soldier's life, a fact recognised by Princess Mary who was instrumental in the provision of a brass tin for every soldier and sailor containing for smokers, amongst other things, cigarettes, or for pipe smokers, tobacco.

Princess Mary's Christmas Tin

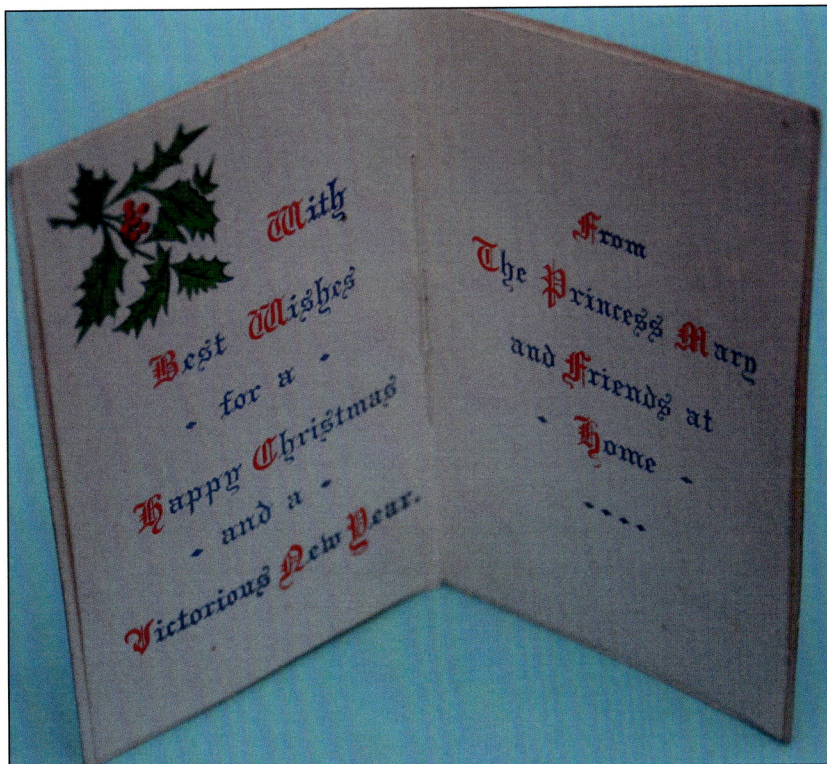

The Christmas Card from Princess Mary

And in France and Belgium a Christmas truce between the men of the opposing armies took place spontaneously, and most definitely unofficially, at many places along the Front.

"Wipers"

The one constant throughout the War was Ypres – or "Wipers" as it was called by the troops. There were four main battles designated First, Second, Third and Fourth Ypres. However the Front here was rarely quiet.

The Ypres Salient formed a bulge in the line. It was created when the German advance of 1914 was halted a few miles before Ypres. In 1915 the Germans advanced still further and held the high ground – basically a series of gentle ridges – to the east, south and north of Ypres, thus the town could be bombarded from three sides. It would have made sense from a military point of view to have withdrawn from Ypres and straighten the line but the town had become a symbol of resistance to the German invader so withdrawal was out of the question.

Prior to the War Ypres was a thriving and prosperous town. The surrounding land was farmland with Ypres in the centre. Weekly markets were held in the town square. There was a garrison in the town and a riding academy. The many fine houses bore witness to the wealth of many of its citizens. Ypres also attracted many tourists drawn by the Cloth Hall in particular – the largest non-religious Gothic building in Europe.

All this was to change in the Autumn of 1914 when Ypres became the focal point of the Salient. From the 18th November the town was systematically bombarded by German artillery fire. On the 22nd November the Cloth Hall and St Martin's Church were set ablaze.

Many of the citizens were reluctant to leave, taking to their cellars. There were those who died in the town, killed by the shelling or succumbing to typhus brought about by the increasingly awful living conditions. In April 1915, with the Germans even closer to the town, the remaining residents had no choice but to leave the shattered ruins. After May it was populated only by soldiers and rats. A popular billet was the prison with its thick walls giving considerable protection. Many civic paintings also found a temporary home there for safe keeping.

The town was a staging post for the troops going to and from the front lines. South through the Lille Gate, north alongside the canal and, notably, east through the Menin Gate and then by way of Hellfire Corner on to the front line. Coming back, the troops would take the rail journey, or walk if necessary, to the rest centre of Poperinghe – although even here they were not safe from the German long range guns. The countryside surrounding Ypres had been pounded into desolation, countless shell holes overlapping each other and villages reduced to nothing.

One who was there – H Quigley – described the Ypres Salient thus:-
> "The country resembles a sewage heap more than anything
> else, pitted with shell holes of every conceivable size and
> filled to the brim with green slimy water, above which a
> blackened arm or leg might project. It becomes a matter of
> great skill picking a way across such a network of death-
> traps, for drowning is almost certain in one of them"
> ("Flanders Then and Now" – John Giles)

The Battle of Third Ypres saw the British push forward, at tremendous cost, to Passchendaele only for the Germans to re-take all the land again in Spring 1918. However they were stopped about a mile from Ypres, at Hellfire Corner, and so were never able to take the town.

Demarcation Stone at Hellfire Corner (these stones marked the limit of the German advance)

Over the years Ypres was destroyed until by 1918 a man on horseback could see right across the town. Only a few buildings survived in any recognisable form, for the most part it was knee high rubble.

Once the Armistice had been signed people began to return. In 1919 temporary huts were provided but an argument raged over the future of Ypres. In Britain there was a strong movement, headed by Winston Churchill, that the ruins be preserved as "Holy Ground", a symbol of the War and the British sacrifice. The return of townspeople made this impractical. Another proposal was to create a totally modernistic city. But it was the plan of the city architect, Jules Coomans, backed by Burgomaster Colaert, that prevailed, namely to rebuild and retain the Flemish, medieval and renaissance appearance.

There was still strong British pressure for the preservation of some part of the ruins but ultimately those plans were conceded in favour of a substantial monument – the Menin Gate.

At first it was a case of simply clearing rubble. From 1920 builders were able to start work. The roads and utilities were repaired and at the same time small local industries sprang up. Tourism became a lasting source of income. The moment the War was over people came to see the battlefields and find where loved ones were buried.

Ten years after the Armistice, quite remarkably, a good part of the town looked as if it had never been witness to any war. The unveiling of the rebuilt Belfry in 1934 represented more or less the completion of the reconstruction. However as late as 1990 the restoration of the ramparts was still being financed by German war damage reparations.

For many, Ypres remains a place of pilgrimage with the Menin Gate as its focus. It bears the names of some 54,000 men who died in the Ypres Salient between 1914 and August 1917 and who have no known grave. Every night, with a brief interruption in the Second World War, the traffic is stopped at 8pm and buglers from the Ypres Fire Brigade play the Last Post.

The inscription on the Menin Gate reads:-

TO THE ARMIES OF THE BRITISH EMPIRE
WHO STOOD HERE FROM 1914 TO 1918 AND
TO THOSE OF THEIR DEAD WHO
HAVE NO KNOWN GRAVE

The Cloth Hall 1918

The Cloth Hall 2008

St Martins Cathedral 1918

St Martins Cathedral 2008

La Rue au Beurre 1916
(Butter Street)

Boterstraat 2008
(Butter Street)

Lille Street 1916

Rijselsestraat 2008

English Cemetery on the Ramparts 1918

Ramparts Cemetery 2008

St Nicholas Church 1918

St Nicholas Church 2008

Cloth Hall

St Martin's Cathedral (centre)

Floral Tributes

The Fire Brigade Buglers

Veterans' Parade

The Ox and Bucks in Writtle

The 4th Battalion of the Oxfordshire and Buckinghamshire Regiment ("the Ox and Bucks") was a Territorial Battalion and in 1914 was off to its annual training camp. They left Oxford at midday on the 2nd August heading for Marlow and picking up detachments at stations along the line.

Next morning to everyone's surprise, Reveille sounded between 2.30 and 3am and the Battalion was ordered back to Oxford. At 9am headquarters was reached and three hours later the men were dismissed with orders to hold themselves in readiness to mobilise at a moment's notice.

The order for their mobilisation reached Oxford on the 4th August and the men assembled at 7am next day. By the evening the Battalion was ready to move. Rapid mobilisation was made easier by the fact that it had come when the Battalion had already assembled for annual training. Over the next few days parades and drills were held. On Sunday 9th August after Church parades they left Oxford by train for Swindon.

It was in August that the Battalion arrived in Writtle and made camp. Here they underwent training. Some of the men were under canvas whilst others were billeted in homes in the village. The Battalion Headquarters was in Maypole House, St. Johns Green.

By early September, four-fifths of the men having volunteered for foreign service, the Battalion became a Foreign Service Battalion and a recruiting campaign soon brought it up to full strength. By the end of September the strength of the Battalion had reached 1300 although some were then transferred to the Reserve Battalion. This influx must have had a considerable impact on the village but it seems that both soldiers and villagers got along with each other well enough.

On the 14th October the Ox and Bucks paraded in full marching order in Hylands Park for inspection by His Majesty King George V.

In order to improve the physique of the men, all spare time during the winter was set aside for football, hockey, boxing and cross country running. The first cross country run was held on the 29th November when about 800 men took part. In the Brigade run at the end of December the 4th Battalion was placed third although they did have the first man home. In January extensive training commenced in musketry and night entrenching.

By this time command of the Battalion had passed to Colonel Schofield. The Battalion was re-organised into four companies under the command of Captains Conybeare, Fortescue, Rose and Hadden respectively.

In February the Division was inspected by General Sir Ian Hamilton. The 4th Ox and Bucks training was coming to an end and soon it would be time to embark for France.

On the 2nd April Mr Charles Russell, the manager of the Writtle Brewery, on behalf of the village, thanked the officers and men for the way the troops had behaved.

In reply, Colonel Schofield thanked the residents for their kindness.

Many of the following photographs are from the Usborne Collection

The arrival of the 4ᵗʰ Battalion Oxfordshire and Buckinghamshire Light Infantry
August 25ᵗʰ 1914

The above photographs and those that follow on Pages 28, 29, 30, 36 and 37 are from the Usborne Collection and are reproduced by courtesy of the Writtle Society and Essex Record Office.

August 25ᵗʰ 1914

Going to their billets August 25ᵗʰ 1914

Marching to Church, August 30ᵗʰ 1914

The Band, August 30ᵗʰ 1914

Church Parade, September 6ᵗʰ 1914

Ox and Bucks Officers September 6ᵗʰ 1914
Col. Stockton, Capt. Ballard Adj., Capts. Fortescue
Haddon, W. Tubbs? Hon L Fionnes?

Gun Carriages belonging to the Ox & Bucks, outside "White Bears" St John's Green

Practising trench digging

Route march

Lunch

Rifle drill. Some look very young · one wonders what happened to them all. These photos came originally from the Compton family. Two Compton brothers served with the 1st/4th Ox & Bucks and it is believed they are shown here · William was killed in 1917

Three Collett brothers, William in glasses (the eldest), was billeted in St. John's House, married Florrie. Frank, on William's right, and Sidney were billeted together in the village. Frank kept a diary of the Battalion's stay in Writtle; before they were sent to France, he married Ada. Sidney, the youngest, was killed in action.

A group from the 4th battalion of the Oxford and Bucks Light Infantry outside the Rose and Crown during the Great War.

A group from the 4th Battalion outside the Rose and Crown

Ox & Bucks outside their Mess in Ongar Road. 1915

Outside The Maltings, dinner cooking, March 22ⁿᵈ 1915

Cooking quarters

March 22nd 1915

Bayonet Practice

'At Play'

March 22nd 1915

Giving out new kit

Y.M.C.A. Hut in Ongar Road

Souvenir of the Great War 1914-1918

The Western Front

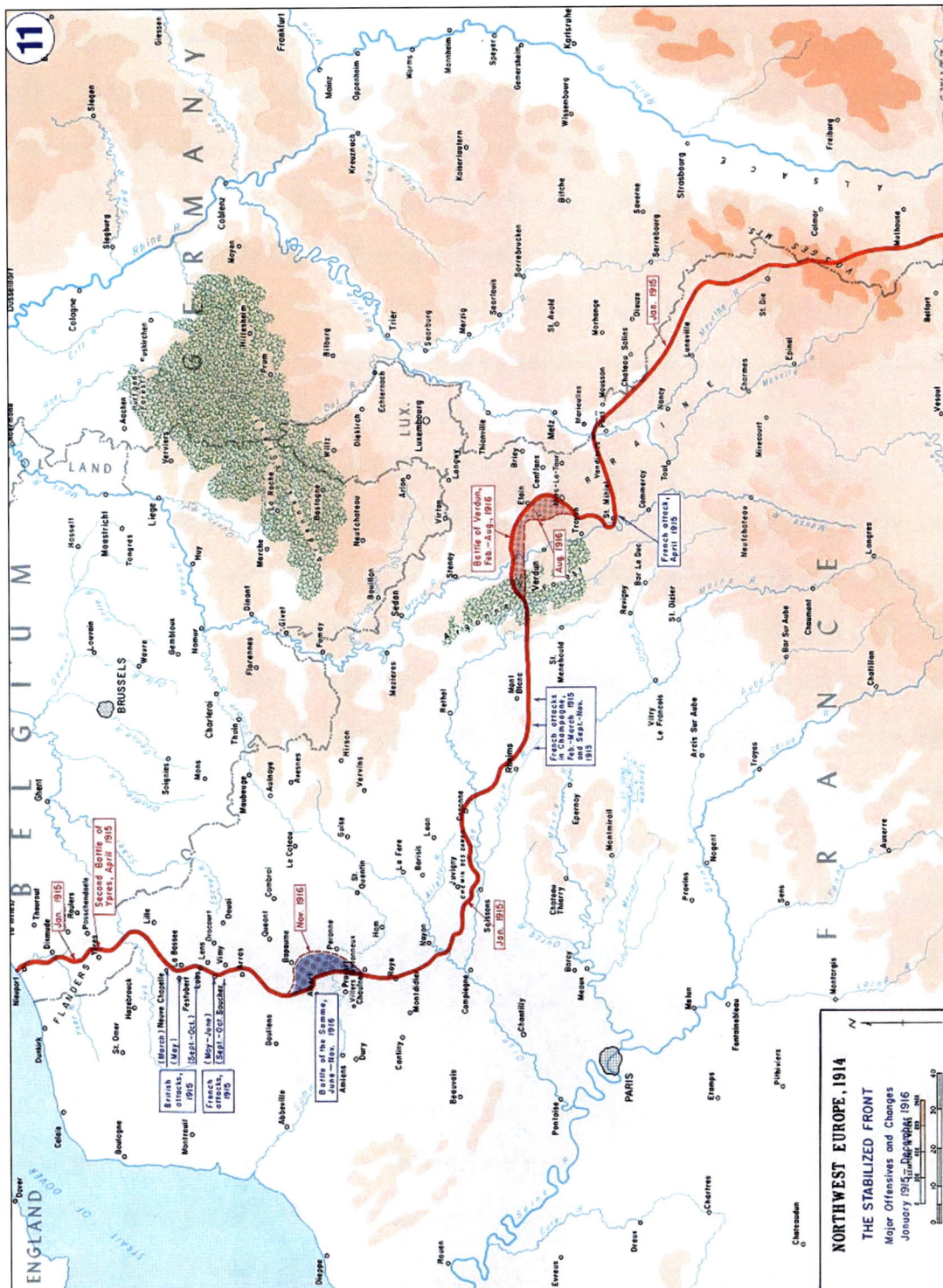

The end of 1914 and the opening of 1915 saw the Front settle into a shape it retained for much of the war

1915 saw choices facing the Allies. To try and beat the Germans in France and Belgium or look at alternatives. British policy was to a large extent dictated by the French who wanted the Germans off French soil. And so it was agreed that there would be offensives on the Western Front but also an attack on Germany's ally, Turkey. An attempt to please everyone ended up largely failing in all aspects.

Because the British Army was still small compared to that of the French, Field Marshall Kitchener felt, despite his misgivings, that he had to go along with what Joffre, the French commander-in-chief, wanted. Joffre concealed his plans from the Russians who, in turn, failed to keep their allies informed. Civilian ministers, notwithstanding their doubts about the ability of the generals, felt unable to critise their conduct of military matters. And the generals, although suspicious of each other, were contemptuous of the politicians

At home, there was still enthusiastic optimism. More and more men, both from Britain and the Colonies, were answering Kitchener's call " Your Country Needs You". These men needed training but German offensives and victories over the Russians diverted the resources of the Central Powers to the east giving the Allies in the west something of a breathing space.

The Gallipoli campaign began in April and although the plan was perfectly feasible it was badly executed.

On the Western front the opposing forces faced each other in 500 miles of trenches from the English Channel to Switzerland in a deadlocked war of attrition. The year opened with Allied offensives in Artois and Champagne. The Germans attacked at La Bassee and Soissons. The British made some headway at Neuve Chapelle but further attacks at Aubers Ridge and Festubert and then at Loos were hugely costly in lives but achieved very little. 1915 also added a new dimension to the horrors of warfare, that of poison gas. At the Battle of Second Ypres in April and May the Germans attacked with 5000 cylinders of chlorine gas enabling them to advance still closer to Ypres. In the east the Russians were in full retreat across Poland. To the south the Serbs succumbed to a vastly superior Austro-German force.

At sea the German submarines were making their presence felt, their most notable victim being the "Lusitania" sunk on the 7th May with some 1200 passengers drowned. This caused an outcry, particularly in America.

1915 also saw an Anglo-Indian force attacking Mesopotamia (now Iraq) and the first Zeppelin bombing raids on Great Britain.

But 1915 was also significant for another reason. Despite the best efforts of the Suffragettes, women's position in the work place was still confined to traditional types of employment. Now for the first time we see in substantial numbers women employed in jobs that were normally reserved for men including as ancillaries in the armed forces. It could be said that war advanced women's rights more than any political or social pressure.

The Lusitania

Airship over the North Sea

Suffragette Rally, 16ᵗʰ November 1908
(from the Usborne Collection reproduced by courtesy of the Writtle Society and
Essex Record Office)

Women correcting type face, Piccadilly

A Munitions Factory

First Girl Messengers at the War Office

Tram Conducteresses

Members of the First Aid Nursing Yeomanry Corps

Women manning a London County Council ambulance

A coal delivery

Thames Paper Works at Purfleet; captioned "Some of the young women arriving on their motorcycles"

Women cleaning a Great Eastern train

Operating a polishing machine in a munitions factory

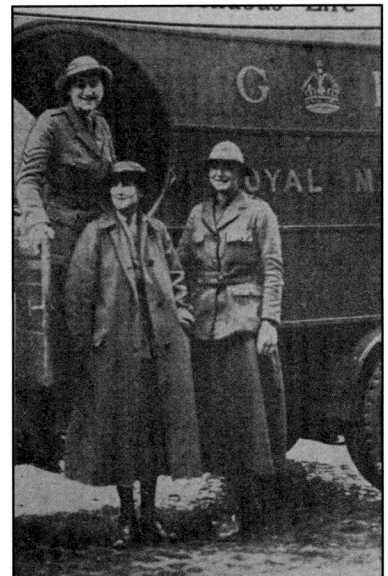
Women Royal Mail van drivers; they received £1.15 shillings (£1.75) a week

Events in Writtle

In Essex the New Year opened with a fierce blizzard, with winds up to 55 mph causing considerable damage. It was reported that the blizzard swept through Writtle strewing the roads with tree branches. Chimneys, slates and roofs were dislodged, large trees uprooted and walls demolished. The YMCA hut was razed to the ground. Low lying districts were flooded and telephone wires were snapped.

In June the funeral took place of one of the most prominent of the villagers, Thomas Usborne of Writtle House (commonly known as just "The House")

Children at play on the lawn at The House 1878

Thomas Usborne was born in Limerick in 1840. His first marriage in 1863 was to Frances Alice, daughter of J A Hardcastle MP. Mr. J A Hardcastle owned Writtle Brewery. The Usbornes lived in The House and also owned three farms. They kept numerous carriages and horses. The 1891 Census records 13 indoor servants and outside there were grooms and gardeners.

Thomas was a stockbroker and a director of Writtle Brewery. He was also chairman of the Anglo-Egyptian Bank, Master of Foxhounds of the Essex Union Hunt and Conservative Member of Parliament for Chelmsford for eleven years.

OUTDOOR STAFF AT "THE HOUSE" 1913/14

F.Poole D.Blanks B.Baker S.Edwards A.Hockley B.Hockley —

? Everard —

Outdoor Staff at The House 1913/14

Dining Room

Drawing Room

Bedroom

Boudoir

Stables

The Lawn

The House
(from the Usborne Collection)

He was a successful financier and well respected in the City. As a Member of Parliament he was perhaps less assiduous. In ten years he spoke only twice in Parliament, on both occasions against the taxation of beer.

Thomas was one of the pioneers of the game of Bridge. He had an extensive collection of stereoscopic plates – a forerunner of modern photography. Those plates which are under the custodianship of the Writtle Society are now housed in the Essex Records Office.

Following the death of his first wife at the age of 56 in 1911, Thomas re-married the next year. His wife was Florence Rose who had a daughter, Phyllis, by her first marriage. Florence had been Thomas' housekeeper.

Captioned "New Renault 1912"   *Mrs Florence Usborne 7th August 1912*
(from the Usborne collection)

During the War The House took in officers to convalesce.

After Thomas' death on the 8th June 1915 a new east window was installed in his memory in All Saints. A peal of bells known as Steadman trebles (5040 changes) had to be abandoned when the tenor rope broke.

Whilst the War impacted greatly on the village, ordinary life went on. So we see the Parish Council investigating the condition of the ditch in Deadmans Lane (now St Johns Road).

The Parish Council held their meeting on the 29th December in the Girls School. The Council resolved that in view of the Military having used the Recreation Ground a good deal without paying Mr Little anything, only a half year's rent would be charged.

On 3rd December Arthur Hitch, dairy farmer from Oxney Green, whilst driving his milk cart past Motts, fell and was concussed and was treated by Dr R Arnold-Wallinger.

Property continued to be bought and sold. The late James Pamplin's Trustees were selling 4 cottages and a building plot in Chancery Lane. Also for sale a shop in Bridge Street producing a rent of £81 per annum. Alfred Darby had a pair of houses for sale at Oxney Green occupied by Mrs Page and Mrs Nottage and producing a rental of £24.14/£24.70p per annum.

But always the war touched all lives. The annual outing of the Writtle Brewery (part of Russell's Brewery) was on a much reduced basis with only elderly men and boys involved as all the others had joined up. Many Writtle events had a military theme or were aimed at helping the war effort such as Empire Day reported on the 28th May.

WRITTLE.

Empire Day was celebrated on Saturday at Writtle with great enthusiasm both by the inhabitants and the military. The committee, augmented by representatives from the 2nd Gloucester R.F.A., organised and smartly carried out a long and enjoyable programme. The proceedings commenced at 1.30 in the afternoon with a parade and march round the village green by the boys, girls, and infants of the Council Schools, headed by the band of the 2nd Gloucester R.F.A. (by kind permission of Col. Metford and officers). At 2 o'clock the flag was broken by Mr. J. E. Brewster (hon. sec.) to the singing of the National Anthem by the company, accompanied by the band. The Boy Scouts and scholars then marched past, the salute being taken by Col. Metford. The children of the schools then entertained the company to the Belgian, Russian, and French National Anthems, the music being rendered by the band, conducted by Mr. T Williams.—The Colonel then addressed the scholars on Empire Day, patriotism, and the duty of Britons.—Mr. C. Russell expressed thanks to Col. Metford and to the band and Gloucester R.F.A. for their able and voluntary assistance, also for the handsome donation toward the fund. (Applause.)—The floral design headdresses by the boys, girls, and infants were in many cases unique, the designs running on military decorations. Miss Hilliard and Miss Christy judged the decorations. During the afternoon a fine programme of races was carried out by the children. At 4.30 the prizes gained by the scholars during the year were distributed by Mrs. Wallinger, Mrs. Christy, and Miss Wallinger. The officials were :—Judges, Messrs. C. Russell, A. P. Lindsell, A. R. Hunt, G. Brown, T. D. Brown, Sec.-Lieut. Unwin, Sec.-Lieut. Morgan; starters and handicappers, Messrs. W. L. White, R. E. Shead, Q.-M.-S. Rice; committee, Messrs. H. Green, T. Williams, H. Pamplin, H. Pearson; hon. sec., Mr. J. E. Brewster. At five o'clock the schoolchildren were served with a bountiful tea. The women of Writtle had tea at separate tables. By kind invitation of Mr. C. Russell the helpers had tea on the lawn at Motts. In the evening the R.F.A. heartily joined with the villagers in the adult sports, which were keenly contested. The band race gave great amusement. The tug-of-war as usual was keenly contested, the military being easily victorious. The proceedings concluded with the National Anthem.

Empire Day in Writtle

Nellie & Dolly Cook, Members of the Order of Rechabites. The Rechabites (a temperance society) held their annual picnic at Ropers Farm

A concert in the YMCA Hut raised £4.10 shillings (£4.50) for the Red Cross Penny Fund.

A stark reminder of the cost of the war to Essex occurred in the middle of the year. Each week the Chronicle carried a Roll of Honour giving the names of all the Essex men killed. But by the 1st August the list was so extensive that the full list could only be printed once a month.

NAVY.

Carter, Lieut. Eccles, Westcliff, H.M.S. Pathfinder.
Robson, Rev. E. G. U., Chaplain, H.M.S. Aboukir.
Westmacott, Lieut. Eric.
Ainger, H., Mistley, H.M.S. Hawke.
Allen, M. C., Berechurch, H.M.S. Hawke.
Ballard, C. H., Great Totham, A.B. H.M.S. Monmouth.
Boarman, W. G., Chelmsford, Leading Seaman, H.M.S. Aboukir.
Brazier, W. E., Blackmore, First Class Stoker.
Buck, F., Mistley, First Class P.O. H.M.S. Pathfinder.
Barnes, H. P., R.F.R., Stoker, H.M.S. Hawke.
Beckwith, P., Tolleshunt D'Arcy, First Class Stoker, Submarine E.5.
Bradley, Pt. R. J., Harlow, R.M.L.I. H.M.S. Hawke.
Clough, A. J., Fingringhoe, Chief Stoker, H.M.S. Pathfinder.
Cox, A., Walthamstow, Wireless Operator, H.M.S. Cressy.
Coolledge, J. H., Hadleigh, Leading Stoker, H.M.S. Cressy.
Cole, G., Great Totham, A.B., H.M.S. Aboukir.
Chiles, S. M., South Benfleet, H.M.S. Aboukir.
Daines, H. A., Leigh, First Class P.O., H.M.S. Aboukir.
Easterbrook, W. T., Canvey Island, A.B., H.M.S. Hogue.
Fisher, V. W., Jr., Ilford, H.M.S. Monmouth.
Gould, A., Wanstead, Chief Yeoman of Signals, H.M.S. Hogue.
Glass, E. G., Witham, First Class Stoker, H.M.S. Good Hope.
Hubbard, W., Chelmsford, First Class Stoker, H.M.S. Cressy.
Hoy, Ilford, Gunner, H.M.S. Hawke.
Hooker, A., Southend, Leading Signalman, H.M.S. Hawke.
Hatcher, G. E., Clacton, Leading Stoker, H.M.S. Hogue.
Hollingsworth, W. G., Barking, First Class Stoker, H.M.S. Bulwark.
Hood, H. L., Thorpe Bay, R.M.L.I. H.M.S. Hawke.
Jennings, A., Canvey Island, First Class Stoker, H.M.S. Aboukir.
Kittle, C. E., Ilford, Signal Boy, H.M.S. Bulwark.
Lofts, J., Saffron Walden, Stoker, P.O., H.M.S. Hawke.
Meadows, J. H., East Ham, Leading Stoker, H.M.S. Aboukir.
Monk, O. F., Althorne, First Class Stoker, H.M.S. Hogue.
Moore, P., Westcliff, Third Officer, s.s. Rohilla.
Nash, H. C., Stanford-le-Hope, Chief Stoker, H.M.S. Hermes.
Norman, E., Saffron Walden, A.B., H.M.S. Hogue.
Oliver, P. F., Braintree, Armourer, H.M.S. Hogue.
Partridge, E. P., St. Osyth, P.O., R.M.L.I. H.M.S. Bulwark.
Peacock, E. D., Brentwood, Leading Carpenter, H.M.S. Cressy.
Prett, J., Harwich, Stoker P.O., H.M.S. Cressy.
Pavitt, S., Bishop Stortford, Stoker, H.M.S. Hawke.
Pavey, C., Stifford, R.F.R., H.M.S. Hogue.
Perkins, A., Saffron Walden, A.B., H.M.S. Cressy.
Page, W. W., Clacton, A.B., H.M.S. Aboukir.
Rudderham, S. W., Halstead, Wireless Operator, H.M.S. Cressy.
Reardon, T. H., Walthamstow, A.B.
Rider, J. A., Dovercourt, First Class Stoker, R.F.R., H.M.S. Hogue.
Skeats, A. W., Dengie, First Class Stoker, H.M.S. Cressy.
Stokes, A. E., Chelmsford, Artificer, H.M.S. Hogue.
Smith, A., Canvey Island, Stoker P.O., H.M.S. Aboukir.
Smith, A. S., Canvey Island, Leading Signalman, H.M.S. Aboukir.
Spooner, C. A. V., Mistley, H.M.S. Hawke.
Stowe, Cressing, A.B., H.M.S. Cressy.
Secker, Pt. G. V., Stansted, R.M.L.I., H.M.S. Hawke.
Sawkins, C. T., Langenhoe, H.M.S. Hawke.
Taylor, E. G., Hockley, Second Class Stoker, H.M.S. Pathfinder.
Watson, W. J. E., Barking, Acting Leading Stoker, H.M.S. Bulwark.
Whybrow, Southend, R.F.R., First Class Stoker, H.M.S. Cressy.
Wigg, E., Shoeburyness, R.F.R., A.B., H.M.S. Aboukir.
Willingale, S. G., Latchingdon, P.O., R.N.S., H.M.S. Aboukir.

ARMY.

Grant-Dalton, Lieut.-Col. A., Colchester.
Marker, Lieut.-Col. R. J., D.S.O., Frinton, 2nd Coldstream Guards.
Chrystie, Major John, R.G.A.
England, Major R., Colchester.
Green, Major A. D., D.S.O.
Ingles, Major A. W., Witham.
Massie, Major, D.S.O., Shoeburyness.
Mercer, Major A. A., 1st Dorsets.
Boone, Capt. C. F. de B., Essex Regt.
Fisher, Capt. H., D.S.O., 1st Manchesters.
Formby, Capt. M. L., Sampford, Wiltshire Regt.
Foy, Capt. M., 1st Batt., Queen's Regt.
Fuller-Maitland, Capt. W. A., Coldstream Guards.
Harden, Capt. A. H., Colchester, Oxon. and Bucks. L.I.
Hogg, Capt. I. D. M., Brentwood, 101st Grenadiers, Indian Army.
Hunt, Capt. F. W., Feering, 19th Bengal Lancers, attached 4th Hussars.
Middleton, Capt. F., Dorset Regt.
Rose, Capt. A. H. P., Essex Regt.
Sybils, Capt. L. A., Wanstead.
Symons, Capt. H. W. K.O. Yorks L.I.
Theobald, Capt. F. G., Great Wigborough.
Tritton, Capt. A. C., Great Leighs, 3rd Coldstream Guards.
Vandeleur, Capt. W. M. C., 2nd Essex.
Waller, Capt. Sir F., 6th Royal Fusiliers.
Whish, Capt. J. K. T.
Chisnall, Lieut. G. H., Prating, 1st Cameron Highlanders.
De Crespigny, Lieut. C. H., Queen's Bays.
Eden, Lieut. J., 12th Lancers.
Maxwell, Lieut. C. W., 2nd Batt. 8th Gurkha Rifles.
Northey, Lieut. A., Worcestershire Regt.
Pearson, Hon. G., third son of Lord Cowdray.
Railston, Lieut. S., 18th King George's Own Lancers (Indian Army).
Round, Lieut. A. H. F., 2nd Essex.
Seabrook, Lieut. J. H., Chelmsford, 5th Cavalry Brigade.
Sewell, Lieut. D. G. C., 1st Royal W. Kent Regt.
Soames, Lieut. H. M., Lexden.
Stone, Lieut. E. R. C., Havering-atte-Bower, Royal Welsh Fusiliers.
Spencer, Lieut. E., Colchester, Wiltshire Regt.
Thompson, Lieut. O. C. W., Wethersfield, West Yorks Regt.
Tufnell, Lieut. C. W., 2nd Grenadier Guards.
Vance, Lieut. J., Essex Regt.
Vandeleur, Lieut. J. B., Leicestershire Regt.
Yalland, Lieut. W. S., Gloucestershire Regt. (formerly in the Borough Surveyor's Department at Southend).
Lockwood, Sec.-Lieut. R. W. M., Coldstream Guards.
Petersen, Sec.-Lieut. W. S., Essex R.H.A.
Thomas Sec.-Lieut. A. C., Westcliff, West Surrey Regt.
Wright, Sec.-Lieut. N. J. R., Westcliff, R.F.A.

ESSEX REGIMENT.

Askham, Sergt. R.
Aylett, Pt. G.
Amos, Pt. W.
Baldwin, Lance-Sergt.
Barton, Corpl. W.
Beaney, Pt. C. T., Castle Hedingham.
Bellis, Pt. T., Braintree.
Burgess, Pt. G.
Beaumont, Pt. R.
Ball, Pt. T.
Bloyce, Pt. A.
Brooks, Pt. G., Halstead.
Burgess, Pt. G., Colchester.
Baker, Pt. A.
Brown, Pt. T.
Carridge, Corpl. R. H.
Cable, Pt. F. J., Leigh.
Cable, Pt. J.
Cliver, Corpl. F., Southend.
Creasey, Pt. C.
Crump, Pt. E.
Cox, Pt. A.
Cable, Pt. J. Rayleigh.
Cox-Brown, Pt. H., Chelmsford.

ESSEX REGIMENT—continued.

Downes, Pt. A.
Cook, Pt. G., Dunmow.
Downham, Pt. G.
Downham, Pt. G., Saffron Walden.
Everitt, Lance-Corpl. R.
Everitt, Pt. W., Great Tey.
Everett, Pt. B., Coggeshall.
Freeman, Pt. A. B., Braintree.
Fitch, Pt. G.
Flack, Pt. A.
Fairbrass, Pt. G.
Gooch, Corpl., Colchester.
Gordon, Lance-Corpl. M., Steeping.
Gingell, Lance-Corpl. H.
Gooch, Lance-Corpl. P.
Groom, Lance-Corpl. A.
Garred, Pt. L.
Goodwin, Pt. G.
Guy, Pt. H. J., Barking.
Graham, Pt. A.
Garnham, Pt. F.
Hallett, Pt. C. J.
Hills, Pt. W., Brentwood.
Harrington, Pt. A.
Head, Pt. J.
Humphreys, Pt. J.
Haley, Pt. W.
Hayden, Pt. J.
Harrington, Pt. A., Halstead.
Haylock, Pt., Bishop Stortford.
Jude, Pt. E. D.
Kirby, Lance-Corpl. F. W., Southchurch.
Ketteridge, Lance-Corpl. W.
Knox, Pt. J.
Lodge, Pt. A. E., Little Baddow.
Loftus, Pt. W.
Linge, Pt. A., Chelmsford.
Lowe, Pt. T.
McCarthy, Acting-Sergt.
Mitchell, Corpl. W.
Miller, Pt. R.
Millbank, Pt. B.
Macey, Pt. U.
Marriott, Pt. C.
Myall, Pt. G.
Miller, Pt. W., Chappel.
Nickolds, Pt. H. W. E., Westcliff.
Oliver, Corpl. F., Southend.
Porter, Pt. A.
Perry, Pt. H.
Payne, Pt. W., Coggeshall.
Porter, Pt. A., Saffron Walden.
Pewter, Pt. B. C., Romford.
Rankin, Lance-Corpl. F. H., Bocking.
Rainbell, Pt. J., Pebmarsh.
Rule, Pt. S., Chelmsford.
Seaforth, Pt. J., Walthamstow.
Simpson, Pt. W.
Smith, Pt. G.
Smith, Pt. H.
Soer, Drmr. W.
Scrivener, Pt. W.
Searles, Pt. F., Great Leighs.
Tippins, Corpl. J. R., Mistley.
Titmus, Pt. A.
Turner, Pt. W.
White, Pt. E. S., Barking.
White, Pt. E.
Wade, Pt. G., Great Wakering.
Whiffen, Pt. J.
Wadman, Pt. G.
Wright, Pt. A.
Whybrow, Drmr. A.

GRENADIER GUARDS.

Battle, Pt. P. U., Hutton.
Button, Pt., Chelmsford.
Brewster, Pt. A., Writtle.
Footman, Pt. T. B., Leyton.
Gundry, Pt., Harwich.
Nisbet, Lance-Corpl. A. C., Southend.
Roberts, Pt. R. W., Walthamstow.

ROYAL FIELD ARTILLERY.

Bruce, Pt. B., Langdon Hills.
Bridges, Gnr. E., Barking.
Bull, A. E., Bishop Stortford.
Cooper, Gnr. G. H. W., Harwich.
Ellison, Gnr. T., Grays.
Elliston, Bombr., Colchester.
Ella, Bombr., Barking.
Joyce, Gnr. W., Great Waltham.
Pearson, Corpl. C., Saffron Walden.
Stunnell, Pt. G., Tilbury.

KING'S ROYAL RIFLES

Brook, Pt. G., Bromley.
Bond, Pt. A. E., Harwich.
Foster, Corpl. F. W., Colchester.
Hawkes, G. A., Burnham.
Spinks, Signaller F. H. W., Walthamstow.

BEDFORDSHIRE REGIMENT.

Delaney, Pt. A., Barking.
Derbyshire, Pt. A. W., Roydon.
Edlin, Pt. B. A., Woodford.
Gunn, Pt., Great Hallingbury.
Miller, Pt. F. W., Chelmsford.
Mascall, Pt. W., Sawbridgeworth.
Rayner, Pt. H., Sible Hedingham.
Rainbird, Pt. J. W., Hockerill.

OTHER UNITS.

Arda, Buckhurst Hill, 9th London Regt.
Bartrop, Sergt. W. B., Margaretting.
Brooks, Sergt. W. R. C., Mistley.
Brooke, Sergt. W., Mistley, R.E.
Brandram, Pt. W., Sawbridgeworth, 17th Lancers.
Barnden, S., Walton-on-Naze, R.E.
Cooper, Sergt. G. W., Westcliff, 16th Lancers.
Everett, Pt. S., Romford, S. Staffs Regt.
Etheridge, Pt. S., Chelmsford, Royal Engineers.
Fuller, Pt. H., Brentwood, Norfolk Regt.
Goodhart, Sergt. E., East Donyland, Dispatch Rider.
Gregory, Sergt. D. W., Tilbury, Rifle Brigade.
Gibson, Pt. W., Ilford, London Scottish.
Higgleton, Tpr. H., Chappel, Royal Horse Guards.
Holmes, Trmptr. T., Mistley, 10th Hussars.
Horsnell, C. W., Hatfield Peverel, 5th Dragoon Guards.
Ingram, Pt., Sawbridgeworth, Coldstream Guards.
Ingram, Pt. W., Brentwood, H.L.I.
Imbert, P.c., Harwich.
Kendall, Pt. C., Southend, 4th Middlesex Regt.
King, Rifleman W. C., Colchester, Rifle Brigade.
Lark, Pt., Wickford, Queen's West Surrey Regt.
Letton, Pt. T., Romford, Duke of Cornwall's L.I.
Nice, Pt. J. H., Great Maplestead, R.E.
Mantell, Pt., Brentwood, 1st Middlesex.
Martin, Lance-Corpl. V. E., Ilford, 1st Royal Berks.
Miles, Pt. W. D., Southminster, Queen's (R.W. Surrey Regt.)
Morant, Corpl. C., Upminster, Royal Fusiliers.
Parker, Lance-Corpl. J. A., Barking, 2nd Yorks Regt.
Paul, Pt. A. V., Ilford, Yorkshire Regt.
Pegram, Pt. R., Great Chishall, 15th Hussars.
Potter, Pt. A., Halstead, 3rd Rifle Brigade.
Rawlinson, Pt. A. S., Chelmsford, H.L.I.
Restell, Pt. P. J., Rainham, Royal W. Kent Regt.
Rivers, Pt. C., Southend, 2nd Border Regt.
Rutledge, Pt. H. A., 1st Norfolk Regt.
Smith, Corpl. C., Boxford, 3rd Rifle Brigade.
Stovold, Pt. M. W., Dunmow, Royal Welsh Fusiliers.
Saltmarsh, Pt. C., Chelmsford, 3rd Royal Fusiliers.
Shead, Pt. W., Bishop Stortford, S. Lancs.
Sapsford, Pt. W., High Wych, 2nd Coldstream Guards.
Smith, Lance-Corpl. H. A., Dovercourt, 2nd W. Yorks (Prince of Wales' Own).
Totman, Pt. W., Rayleigh, 12th Lancers.
Wallis, C. A., Ilford, London Scottish.
Watson, Lance-Corpl. G. J., Chelmsford, 2nd Leicesters.
Willis, Lance-Corpl. H., Ilford.
Wright, Pt. W., Ilford, 1st Norfolks.

Essex Roll of Honour
January 1915

The Chronicle had no doubt what was needed to boost the troops' morale!

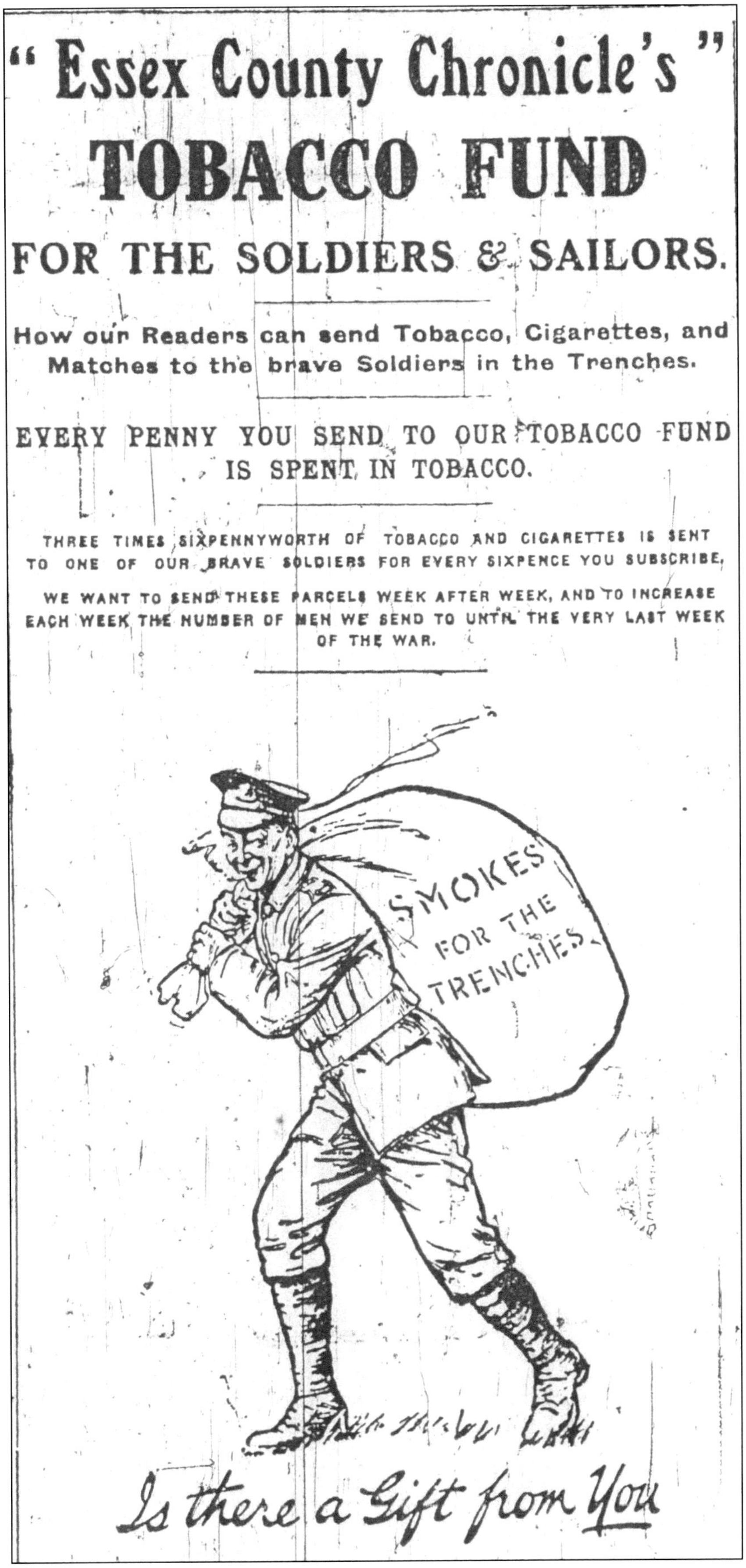

"Essex County Chronicle's"
TOBACCO FUND
FOR THE SOLDIERS & SAILORS.

How our Readers can send Tobacco, Cigarettes, and Matches to the brave Soldiers in the Trenches.

EVERY PENNY YOU SEND TO OUR TOBACCO FUND IS SPENT IN TOBACCO.

THREE TIMES SIXPENNYWORTH OF TOBACCO AND CIGARETTES IS SENT TO ONE OF OUR BRAVE SOLDIERS FOR EVERY SIXPENCE YOU SUBSCRIBE,

WE WANT TO SEND THESE PARCELS WEEK AFTER WEEK, AND TO INCREASE EACH WEEK THE NUMBER OF MEN WE SEND TO UNTIL THE VERY LAST WEEK OF THE WAR.

SMOKES FOR THE TRENCHES

Is there a Gift from You

Second Ypres, Gallipoli, Loos

In the Spring the Germans were planning their next offensive – the Battle of Second Ypres.

On 20th April Ypres was subjected to bombardment by the German heavy guns. The Cloth Hall, already severely damaged, was hit repeatedly.

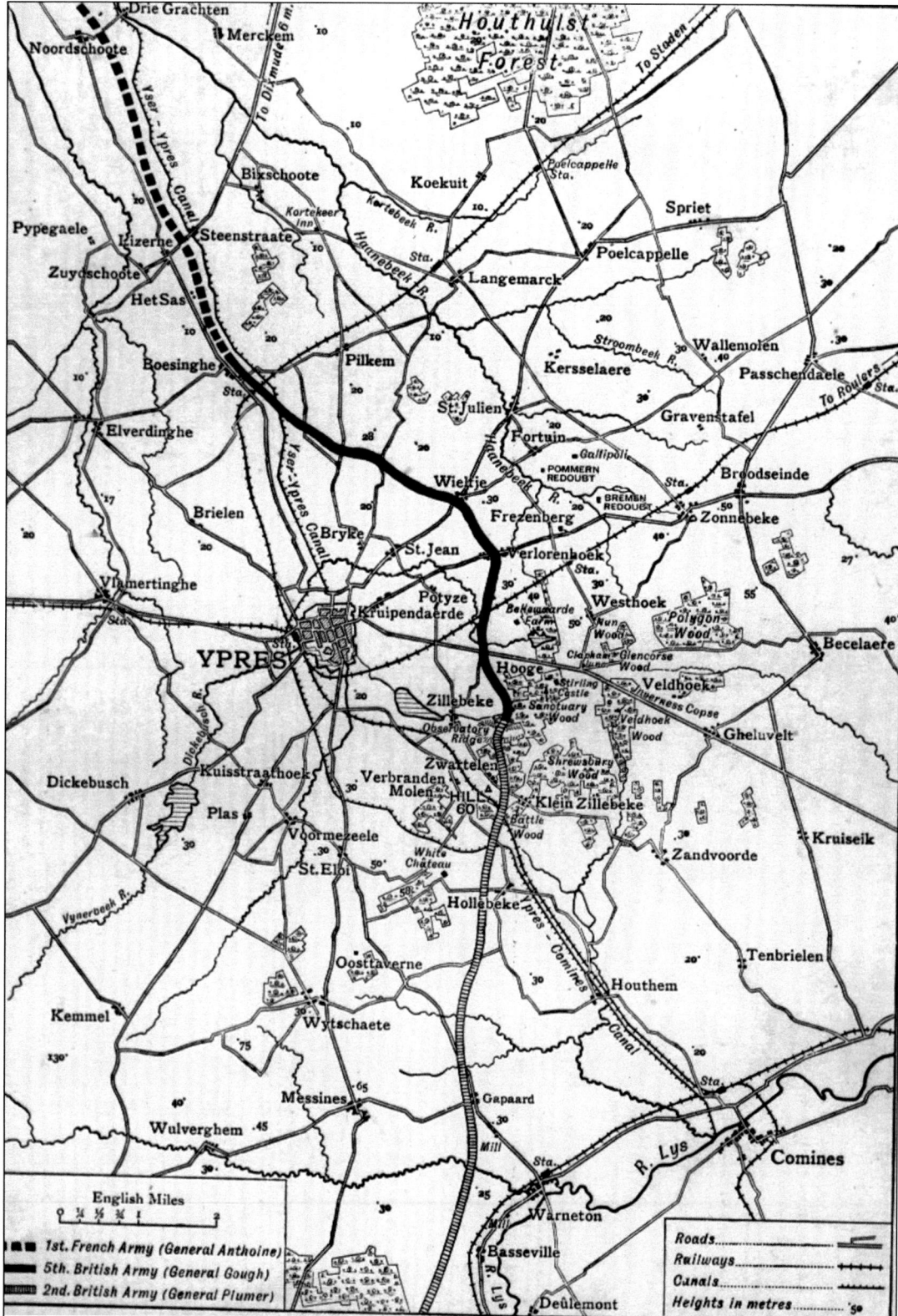

April 1915: The Battle of 2nd Ypres

The northern part of the Ypres Salient was held by French Colonial troops. On the right were Canadians and to their right, British troops. Around 5pm on the 22nd April the German shelling ceased and a strange sight was witnessed. On either side of Langemarck spurts of whitish smoke began to appear on the ground in front of the German trenches. Clouds of this smoke gathered in volume and united into one continuous low cloud bank of a greenish hue turning to yellow where it caught the rays of the sinking sun. This bank of cloud, drifting before a gentle breeze, moved slowly towards the French line. The French soldiers had been watching this cloud with some curiosity when they were suddenly seen to throw up their hands and clutch their throats. Many fell whilst their comrades ran madly to the rear in terror stricken flight.

This was the first use of poison gas on the Western Front. The Germans advanced unopposed and took possession of the trenches occupied only by those who had not fled "whose blackened faces, contorted figures, and lips fringed with the blood and foam from their bursting lungs, showed the agonies in which they had died". (Sir Arthur Conan Doyle "The British Campaign in France").

Monument to the Canadians at St Julien who took the brunt of the gas attack

By 7 pm there was no formed body of French troops east of the Yser Canal. The effect of the gas attack was to open up a five mile gap leaving the way clear to Ypres. The Canadians to the south had suffered some of the effects of the gas but not nearly as much as the North Africans. And it was the Canadians who plugged the gap at St. Julien utilising make-shift gas masks, socks and other material soaked in urine tied over the mouth and nose. All night long the Canadians held on against overwhelming numbers but slowly they were forced back.

British troops were rushed up on the 23rd April. A scratch force from different units held back a far superior force. Many of the British troops were killed in barring the way to Ypres

Second Ypres continued well into May but 23rd April was the make or break day. By the end of the Battle British casualties totalled 57,000. The perimeter of the Salient had shrunk by two miles making Ypres even more vulnerable to the German guns. But the line had held despite all the Germans had thrown at it.

The Gallipoli Campaign was an attempt to get away from the stalemate of trench warfare on the Western Front. Championed by Winston Churchill, the aim was to knock Germany's ally Turkey out of the war, the Suez Canal would no longer be threatened and pressure on Russia would be reduced. The concept had much in its favour but it required efficient planning and ruthless aggression. In the event the commanders on the spot displayed neither. Preparations for the landing were inadequate, largely relying on tourist guidebooks. The Turkish army was under-estimated and the Allied senior commanders were largely out of touch with what was happening on the beaches.

The landings on the 25th April were characterised by the strange movements of the commanders-in-chief. General Sir Ian Hamilton cut himself off from what was happening by staying in the "Queen Elizabeth" cruising well off shore. No senior commander had any clear picture of the battle and by default it was left to the junior officers to use their initiative. This they did with great bravery and heroism but lack of overall control meant that many opportunities were missed and, more culpably, many lives were lost needlessly.

Neuve Chapelle in March had been the first of the major trench battles and achieved some success albeit that the end was somewhat unsatisfactory.

May saw the Battle of Aubers Ridge but the Germans had learned a lesson from Neuve Chapelle and had constructed strong fortifications. Despite the incredible bravery of the British troops the attacks foundered on the German wire. Later in May came the Battle of Festubert and despite some successes, the heavy losses sustained caused the Battle to be called off. Then came the Battle of Loos where again some success in a few places was outweighed by the casualties involved.

Lieutenant Hermon Hodge described in the Usborne Collection
"Lieut Hodge in full war kit March 22 1915. Killed end of May. Shot in head."

Percy Jones was born in Ingatestone. Subsequently he moved to Writtle and was one of the first to enlist. Amongst the troops that were hurried forward to stem the German advance on Ypres was the 2nd Battalion the Essex Regiment. By the evening of 23rd April the line had stabilised but the Essex had sustained many casualties. Amongst these was Percy who was severely wounded and died the next day.

He is buried at Strand Military Cemetery ,Warneton

The grave of Percy Jones

Strand Military Cemetery, Warneton
(Established near Strand Trench in October 1914; 1044 burials)

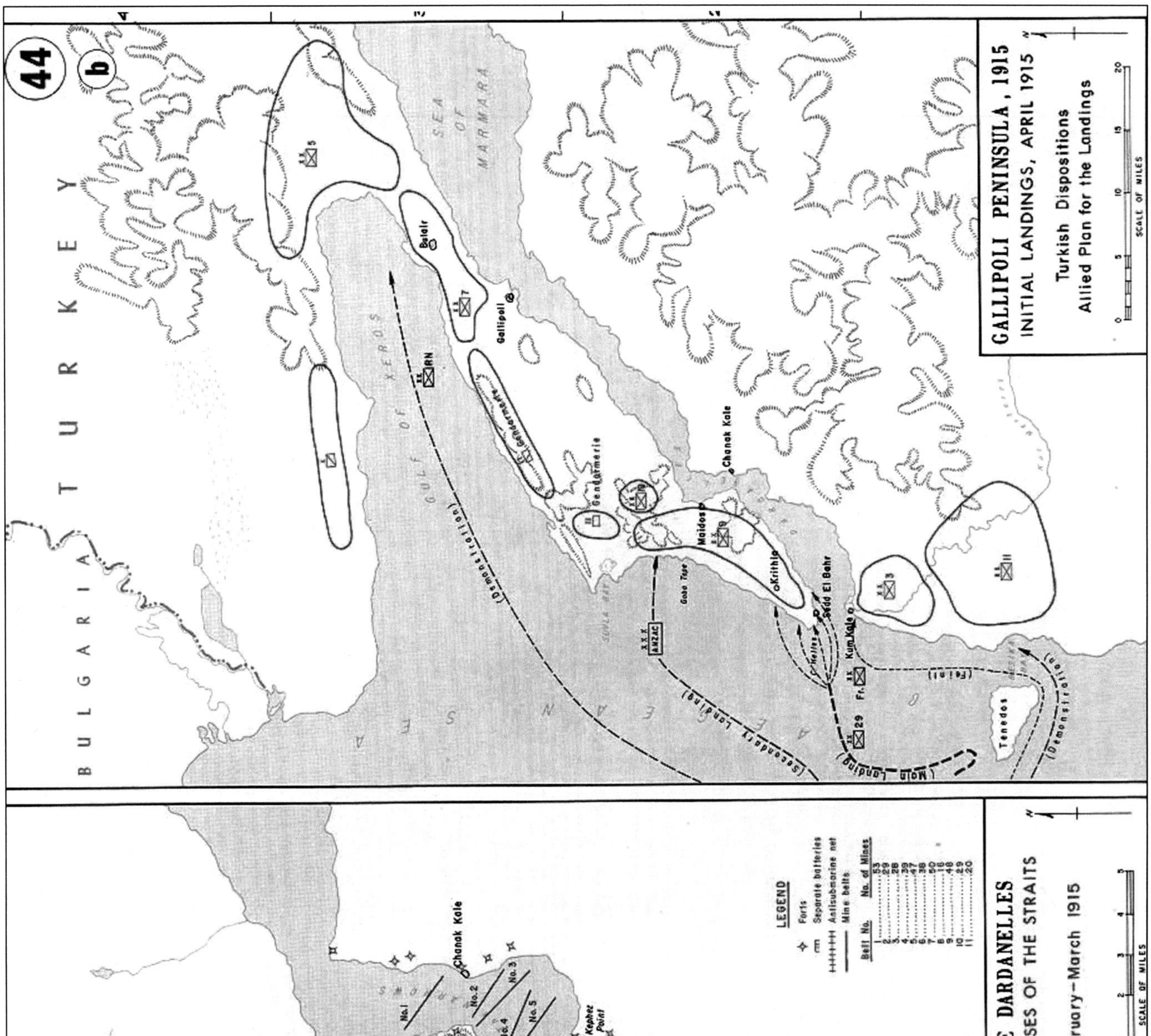

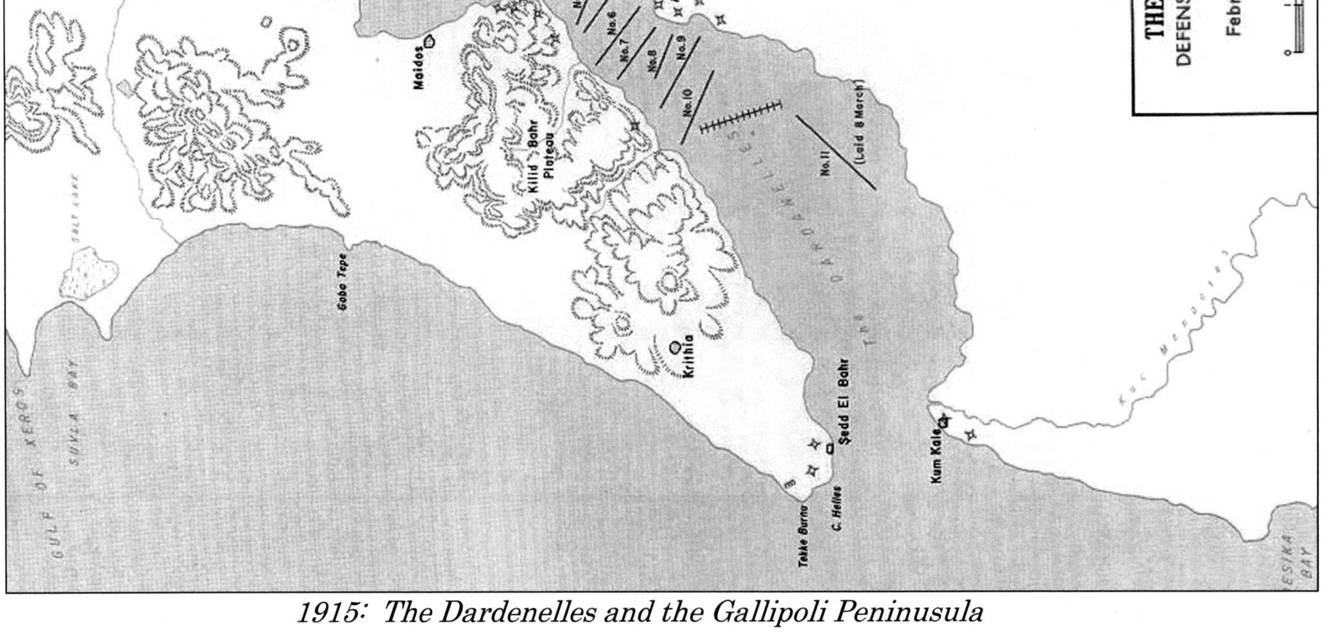

GALLIPOLI PENINSULA, 1915
INITIAL LANDINGS, APRIL 1915

Turkish Dispositions
Allied Plan for the Landings

SCALE OF MILES

THE DARDANELLES
DEFENSES OF THE STRAITS

February–March 1915

LEGEND

Forts
Separate batteries
Antisubmarine net
Mine belts

Belt No.	No. of Mines
1	53
2	29
3	28
4	39
5	47
6	36
7	30
8	50
9	40
10	29
11	20

SCALE OF MILES

1915: The Dardenelles and the Gallipoli Peninusula

James Brewster was born in Highwood and the 1901 Census shows him aged 15 living with his family at No. 13 The Causeway. Life must have been tough for them as their father James had died previously leaving his widow Ann Maria, aged 45 in 1901, who was a laundress, to bring up the family. The eldest children, Alice and Elizabeth, were domestic servants. James was an electrician's apprentice. Frederick aged just 12 was employed as a house boy and then there were the two youngest, Robert 10 and Edith 8.

James enlisted in the Essex Regiment and by 1915 was a Lance Corporal in the 1st Battalion. The Essex were to form part of the army being assembled in Egypt to attack Turkey at Gallipoli.

The Essex left Alexandria on the 14th April as part of the 29th Division. There were to be five separate landing places designated V,W,X,Y and Z Beaches and the Essex were to land on V Beach between Sedd-el-Behr and Cape Helles. To the right of Sedd-el-Behr was a small beach only some 300 yards long and ten yards wide. Here the battleship "Albion" let loose a tremendous bombardment and after an hour it was judged that the Turks were either demoralised or dead. And so the landing began.

It was vital that the largest number of troops be landed in the shortest possible time and to this end at V Beach an old collier, the "River Clyde", was to be run aground to act as a pier. At first all was quiet but as the "River Clyde" and her accompanying flotilla of small boats packed with soldiers neared the shore the Turkish machine guns opened up. To make matters worse the lighters which were to act as the bridge between the ship and the shore drifted in the current and it was the Captain himself, Commander Unwin, together with an able seaman who dived in and standing waist deep in the water dragged the lighters into position.

The men in the boats fared no better than those on the ship. They died in the boats as they stood, crowded shoulder to shoulder. When all were dead or wounded – the sailors manning the boats as well as the soldiers – the boats drifted away.

During the landing of the Allied troops in Gallipoli, the armed transport, River Clyde, was run ashore in order to protect the troops. When darkness set in, practically the entire force of 2,000 men on board was landed without a single casualty. Photograph shows the River Clyde.

This was the official information, deliberately omitting reference to the disaster in the day

On the "River Clyde" Commander Unwin had been brought onboard having collapsed through exhaustion but he was soon back in the water again struggling with the lighters. And it was to the men on the ship and the lighters that the Turks were now able to concentrate the whole of their fire. The men on the ship's gangways made perfect targets and those who did reach the lighters found themselves even more exposed to the enemy's fire. Still the attack continued even though it was hopeless. And as each fresh wave of men emerged so the Turks mowed them down until the gangways of the ship were jammed with the dead and the dying and the sea ran red with blood for fifty yards from the shore.

After an hour of this with barely 200 men having made it to the dubious safety of the beach the attack was called off.

Elsewhere the landings had mixed success, in some cases getting ashore without a single shot being fired.

The 1st Battalion, Essex Regiment land at Gallipoli; 25th April 1915
(Photograph by kind permission of the Imperial War Museum)

Later in the day bridgeheads had been established but, with no proper system of command, no effort was made to bring the troops into a position to attack where it was needed.

As the day wore on the Turkish fire slackened. They too had taken casualties from the shelling from the ships, from the machine gun on the "River Clyde" and from those men who had made it ashore and had found some sort of shelter amongst the scrub at the top of the beach. Into the night the men and supplies were delivered onto the beaches.

The Essex were fortunate in having made it ashore with relatively few casualties. They were to have landed on V Beach but wisely it was decided that a landing should be effected at W Beach. The men were loaded into cutters each commanded by young midshipmen whose skill enabled the Essex to wade ashore. W Beach was dominated by high bluffs where the Turks had located their machine guns and casualties soon mounted up. A platoon under Lt. Ward was sent forward to contact the Lancashire Fusiliers who had been first ashore but the Turkish fire caused several casualties including Lt. Ward who was killed.

The 4th Worcesters landed at 1pm and an hour later Lt. Colonel Godfrey Faussett led the Worcesters and the Essex to take two Turkish positions. They then dug in.

By the 27th April the British and French were ready to advance on Krithia. The Battle known as First Krithia commenced at 8pm on the 28th with a bombardment from "Goliath", "Euralyus" and "Queen Elizabeth". Initial success was not maintained as the Turks had the advantage of gullies perfect for defence. The losses suffered by some Battalions were appalling. In addition food, water and ammunition were running out.

At 6pm the attack was called off. Of the 14,000 Allied troops 3,000 had become casualties. The 1st Essex had numbered almost 1,000 on leaving England. They now had just 15 Officers and 659 other Ranks

The Battalion's losses for the 28th were 14 killed, 76 wounded and 33 missing. James was one of those whose body was never found and he is commemorated on the Helles Memorial.

The Helles Memorial

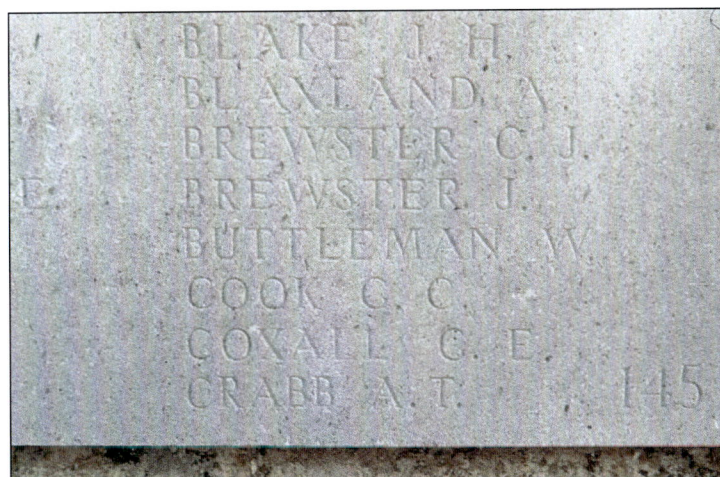

James Brewster's name on the Memorial

Another Brewster was the next Writtle man to lose his life. **William Thomas Brewster** was the brother of Arthur who had been killed at Ypres the previous November. William had enlisted at Warley and was a Driver with the Army Service Corps.

The personnel of the Army Service Corps were the unsung heroes of the British Army. They operated the transport without which the soldiers at the front line would be helpless. They supplied the Army with prodigious amounts of food, clothing, equipment, armaments and ammunition.

The Army Service Corps was responsible for supplies and transport encompassing a huge number of matters. One of their first tasks was to obtain an initial 14,000 horses. Far more were needed and the effectiveness of the Corps was demonstrated by the fact that by mid September 55000 horses had sailed with the British Expeditionary Force.

Vehicles were needed and in addition to those already owned by the Army an Order was signed on 4th August 1914 to initially requisition 900. The following were some of those required:

"12 powerful motor cars, Laundalette Daimlers or Napiers preferred. 50 moderate powered cars, Panhard or Napier taxicabs preferred, 3 vans fitted with pneumatic tyres and one motor charabanc seating 22-27 persons"

Owners were paid six shillings a day for a period of one year – evidently the ASC had the foresight to see that it would not be all over by Christmas. The Order also said that the procurement officer should try and persuade drivers to enlist.

In the event these requirements were quite inadequate. More vehicles were called in, contracts were placed in the USA for wagons and all sorts of vehicles, petrol, steam and chain driven were taken. Horses and mules were bought from around the world. To give an idea of quantities, from the outbreak of War until 1916 some 145,000 mules were purchased just from America. This alone illustrates how the war was to eventually prove to be financially crippling for Britain.

An army marches on it's stomach. Huge quantities of food had to be obtained, placed in depots, then shipped and distributed and of course cooked.

A column of lorries and horse drawn vehicles moves along the Menin Road
(photo by kind permission of the Imperial War Museum)

Of paramount importance was provision for equipping the medical services with all they needed. At the beginning of September the Wolseley Company had orders in hand for a number of 24·30 horse power 6 cylinder ambulances. On twenty four hours notice 25 of these were completed, over fifty drivers volunteered and were enlisted in the ASC, preliminaries completed and entrained to Avonmouth. From there on elements of farce crept in with the men being refused admission to the ASC depot. They were only saved from a night in the open by the Church. Eventually when ambulances and crew did set sail there was no officer or NCO assigned to accompany them so in best democratic style they solved the problem by electing two of their number to be in charge.

Perhaps given the sheer scale of events mistakes were inevitable, but on the whole it seems that the vehicles, fuel, ammunition, supplies and the whole paraphernalia of war mostly all arrived where it was required thanks to the ASC.

As a driver William would have been responsible for driving one of the thousands of lorries transporting goods to the front line. He died on Saturday 12th June aged 24. He is buried in Longueness (St Omer) Souvenir Cemetery.

Longueness (St Omer) Souvenir Cemetery

St Omer was the General Headquarters of the British Expeditionary Force. This town was a considerable hospital centre. 3013 graves are here including 23 men of the Chinese labour corps whose graves could not be exactly located and one of an airman whose grave is now lost.

Army Service Corps badges

William Brewster's grave

Robert Woodhouse J.P. lived at Longmeads, a Victorian mansion which had been built on his instruction in the 1870's. The Woodhouse family had formerly lived at The Priory. With him at Longmeads were his wife Ellen and their three daughters together with seven live in servants. One of the daughters was Dorothy. In 1901 she was aged 26 and her son was **Robert Cecil Woodhouse** then aged 7.

Earlier, Robert Woodhouse JP was exhorting Writtle men to enlist and when the War broke out his grandson did just that and enlisted in the Royal Horse Artillery (Warwickshire Battery) TF. He held the rank of Lieutenant.

The Battery was the first Territorial Regiment to go to France arriving there on the 1st November 1914 . They claim to have seen more action than any other Battery and were complimented on their splendid work by General French.

At the beginning of July 1915 the Battery was at Ledringham practising driving and gun drill. But along with the rest of the Army, they were not excused from digging, so on the 10th a party of 20 men under Lieutenant The Earl Poulett spent the day digging. More training drills took place, including practising river and canal crossings. Then more digging on the 23rd this time under Lieutentant Woodhouse. Night times were spent with parties from the Battery guarding their positions against a surprise German attack.

There then followed what must have been a pleasant interlude after the monotony of all that digging. The Battery marched to the coast on the 2nd August and, arriving at midday, spent the afternoon swimming and bathing in the sea.

Next day it was back to the permanent billets at Ledringham. During the next few days it was a return to drills and inspections and more digging.

And it is here, on the 15th August, that news was received that Lieutenant Woodhouse had been killed the previous night by a shell whilst he was commanding the 26th Trench Howitzer Battery near Hooge.

Extract from the Battalion's War Diary

Following his death on the 14th August 1915, Robert was buried in Birr Cross Roads Cemetery, Zillebeke, near Ypres

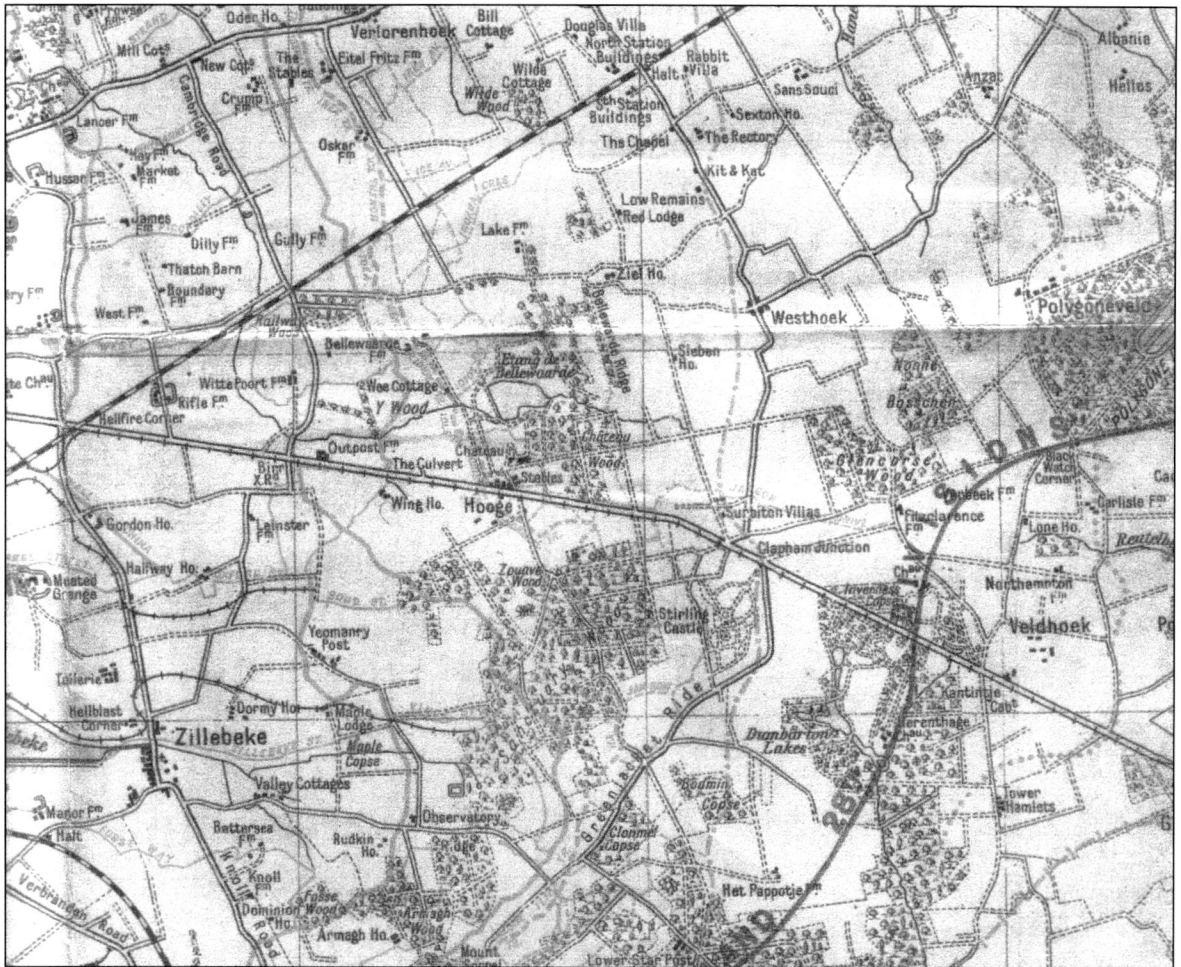

Menin Road runs left to right; Hooge in the centre; Birr crossroads to the left.

Robert's Grave

Horse Artillery – a contemporary postcard

Birr Cross Roads Cemetery
(at the Menin Road/Zillebeke Road Crossroads, 806 burials)

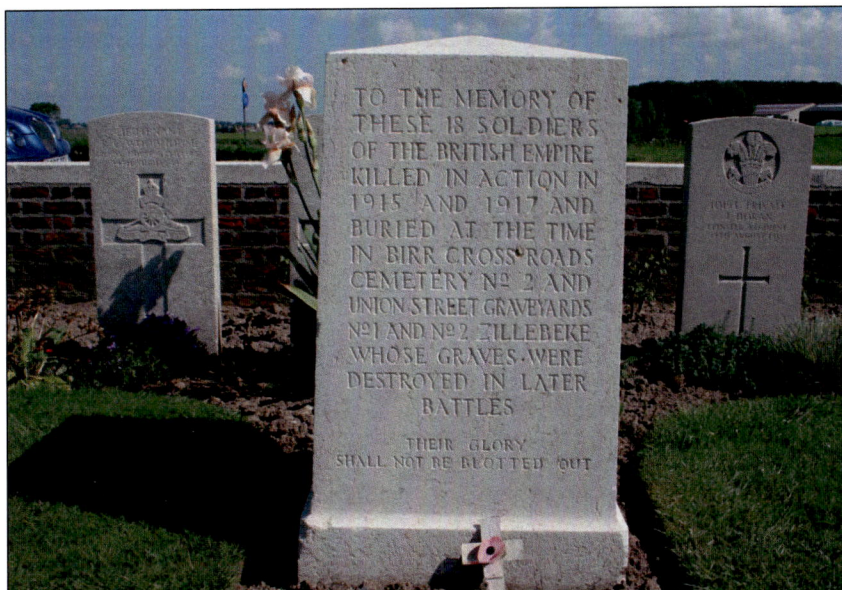

The stone to the memory of Robert (his headstone to the left) and 17 Companions

The end of 1914 had seen the professional Army drastically reduced and 1915 was just as difficult. Following Second Ypres there had been a number of separate attacks along the Front; at Neuve Chapelle, Aubers Ridge and Festubert. To a large extent untested troops of Kitchener's volunteers had been hastily thrown into battle with predictable consequences. For instance the 2nd Division had suffered some 5500 casualties at Festubert, nearly 50% of its establishment.

As a result of persuasion by the French a further attack was planned further south. The battleground chosen was around the mining village of Loos. As the British commanders agreed, this was "most unfavourable ground" but under French pressure they reluctantly agreed to the plan.

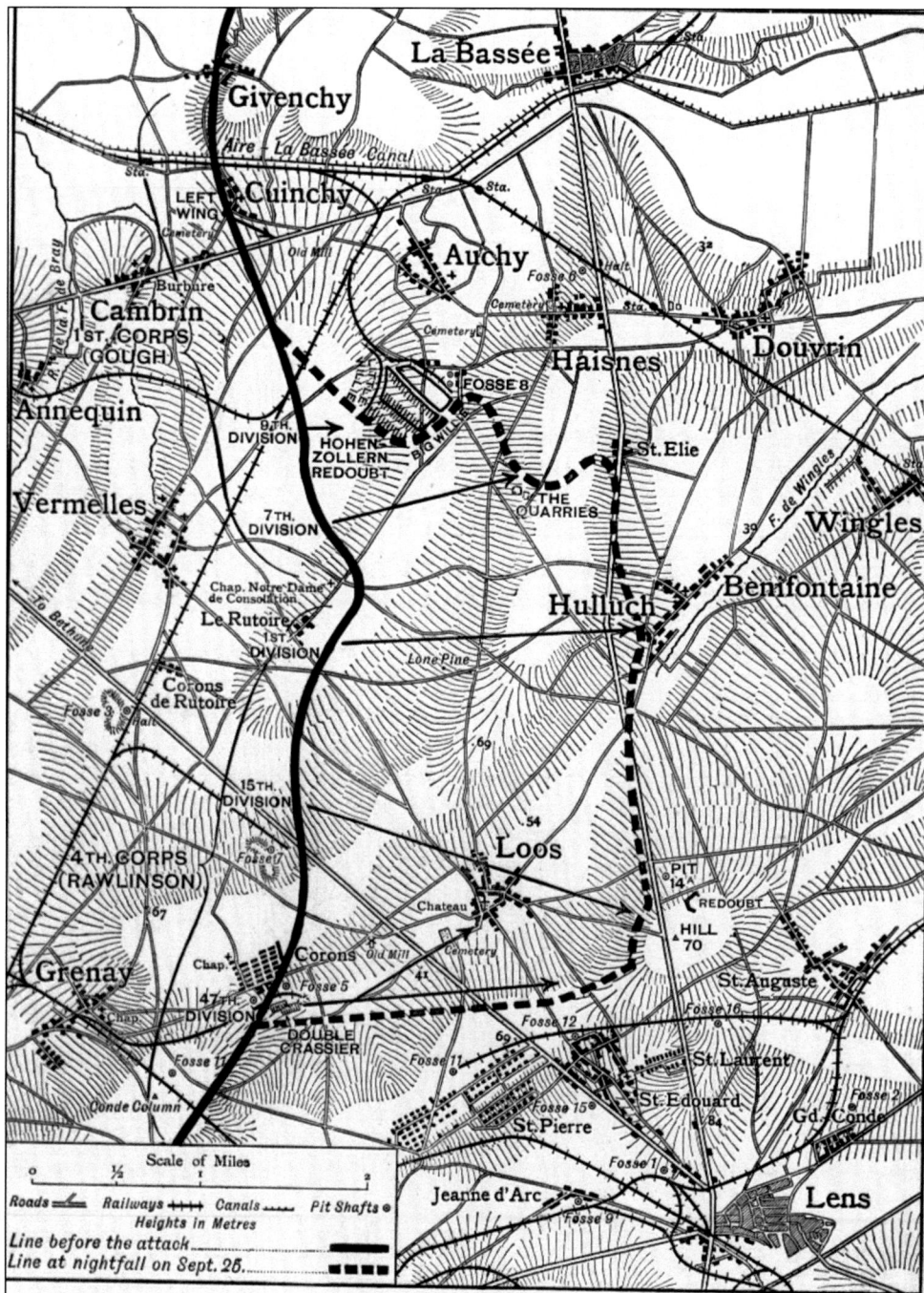

The Loos Battlefield

Over one million men were to be committed to the Battle of Loos. Of the three Corps, XI Corps comprised five Divisions. The 24th Division consisted of the 71st, 72nd and 73rd Brigades. In the 73rd were five Battalions one of which was the 7th Battalion Northamptonshire Regiment and this leads on to the next Writtle man.

Martin Vail Green was born in Writtle on 14th September 1894 and was baptised at All Saints Church on 4th November. His parents were Herbert and Emily Green. Herbert was a butcher/slaughterer and owned the butcher's shop (now the vets) on The Green. In 1906 he took over Montpelier Farm.

Martin had one elder brother, Charles, and three younger, Herbert, Thomas and Philip.

Following the outbreak of war Martin enlisted at Westminster in the 7th Battalion the Northamptonshire Regiment. The Battalion was notable for the fact that the 250 men of D Company had been raised almost instantly by Edgar Mobbs the Rugby International and Captain of Northampton Rugby club. He was as famous in his day as any sportsman today. Such was his standing that sportsmen flocked to join the 7th Northants, presenting the authorities with a problem in kitting them out. As a result many of them simply wore their own clothes and the parade ground sported straw boaters, peaked caps, bowlers and all manner of clothing. The officer who arrived to take charge, Captain Guy Paget wore the uniform of his former Regiment, the Scots Guards. And when it came to selecting men from the recruits to form a command structure a collection of coloured ribbons was found and so different colours were handed out denoting different ranks.

Other officers eventually arrived and overall command of the Battalion was assumed by Lieutenant Colonel Parkin. But the recruiting success was entirely due to Edgar Mobbs; the Battalion became known as The Mobbs Own. Perhaps Martin Green was attracted to the Battalion because of the sporting connection; maybe he himself was a rugby player.

The Battalion trained at Shoreham and Woking and then on the 1st September they embarked for France. Martin had attained the rank of Lance Serjeant.

An experiment was to be tried with the 24th Division for they were to be launched into the Battle of Loos without any previous experience in the trenches. It was hoped that by the time the Division advanced the main German resistance would have been broken. However this was not to be the case and the 7th found themselves in the thick of the fight with no clear orders. It was an experiment with men's lives which turned out to be disastrous. Moreover, an experiment that, even with the benefit of hindsight, was always doomed to failure given the chaos of the battlefield and the fact that attacks rarely kept to the planned timetable.

"Good-morning; good-morning!" the General said
When we met him last week on our way to the Line.
Now the soldiers he smiled at are most of 'em dead,
And we're cursing his staff for incompetent swine.
"He's a cheery old card" grunted Harry to Jack
As they slogged up to Arras with rifle and pack.

But he did for them both with his plan of attack.
"The General" - Siegfried Sassoon

A different battle but the sentiment is the same.
(copyright Siegfried Sassoon by kind permission of George Sassoon's Estate)

Charging through the German Trenches at Loos - September 25th 1915.
A typical contemporary picture

So it was hoped that the 24th Division would be called upon on or after the initial assault had pushed the Germans into retreat. Also in reserve was the Cavalry even though they would be useless in this terrain and against such firepower, facts which were ignored by the British commanders, Haig and French, both former cavalry officers. Furthermore the whole assault at Loos was being mounted with far fewer Divisions than required. And all this against a background of complaints about the number of failures in the shells which were needed for the preliminary bombardment.

The 7th Battalion left Torcy on the 21st September and marched for six hours to arrive at Lairdes at 2 am. They left Lairdes at 6pm to join up with the 73rd Brigade and then it was a nine hour march to L'Ecleme where they were allowed to rest for the day. On the march they carried all their equipment – around one half of body weight.

As it turned out it was necessary for Haig to order up his reserves but they were still a full day's march away. In spite of this he ordered them to the front – so in addition to their inexperience the men would now arrive exhausted. And so on the 25th September the Battalion marched to the front to occupy trenches captured by the Scottish Brigade. "As they drew near they saw what looked like washing flapping on a line. But moving closer the grim reality became plain to see – the material flapping in the breeze was the kilts of dead Highlanders whose bodies were hanging on the barbed wire."
(The late Percy Slarke quoted by David Woodall "The Mobbs Own".)

The 7th, no doubt with many of them shaken by this introduction to warfare, occupied the trenches. They were joined by the Scottish troops falling back from their more advanced positions. Then the Germans counter-attacked. The sportsmen, cobblers and miners of the Northants who had never before experienced warfare, found themselves facing elite Prussian troops. Initially checked by the Lewis gunners of the Battalion, the Prussians stormed back and a brutal and desperate hand to hand struggle ensued. Crossing from one trench to another Colonel Parkin was shot in the head and died instantly. Edgar Mobbs rallied the men time and again and with their bayonets in a frantic life or death melee the 7th managed to prevent themselves being over-run. But then they found themselves in dire danger as owing to little support on the flanks the Germans were able to infiltrate the sides and with the position rapidly becoming untenable, the 7th and the remnants of the Scottish were forced to retire.

On the morning of the 27th following a heavy artillery bombardment the Germans began a number of attacks. During the night the 91st Reserve Regiment and the Bavarian Composite Regiment had moved into No Man's Land within rushing distance of the trenches at the junction of Fosse and Slag Alleys. This attack was launched at 6 am against the 7th Northants and the 12th Royal Fusiliers, soldiers totally exhausted from the last two days and nights.

By 7.30 am the Northants, owing to heavy casualties, were driven from their front line trenches and took up a second line about 100 yards to the rear. This was lost and re-taken several times during the day. The Germans bombed their way northwards forcing the Northants back into the Corons de Pekin north of The Dump. They then took control of The Dump itself giving them domination over the plain below. South of The Dump the Royal Fusiliers were forced back making the British line untenable. The commanding Brigadier considered there was no alternative but to withdraw his exhausted troops from the area of the Corons and to abandon Fosse Trench and Dump Trench with a view to regrouping along the eastern face of the Hohenzollern Redoubt.

Trench map of 1915; Fosse and Slag Alley Trenches and The Dump 5A and C;
Hohenzollern Redoubt 4B

Upon hearing of this the General Officer Commanding, Major-General Thesiger went to assess the situation himself but upon reaching the eastern side of the Redoubt he too was killed. It was virtually impossible to emerge from cover without being mown down in a hail of shot and flying metal.

The 73rd by this time were running short of ammunition. Reinforcements brought some relief. By now the Germans were attacking from both sides of The Dump towards the the Hohenzollern Redoubt. There was much close quarter fighting but time after time German counter attacks were driven back and with the arrival of the reinforcements the German advance was halted.

The overall Commander, Lord French gave his verdict. "No men could have fought with greater gallantry under adverse circumstances." But the result for the Battalion amounted to a disaster.

The Northants' casualties for the 27th September were very heavy, some 40% of the Battalion's strength. The total came to 402 all ranks killed, wounded and missing. (Edgar Mobbs came through virtually unscathed but on the 29th July 1917, by then a Lieutenant Colonel, he was killed whilst attacking a German machine gun emplacement). The Battalion Diary reported the events of the 27th September.

The Battalion Diary was subsequently typed out and is reproduced setting out a brief account of the 27th September.

27/9/15	6 am The enemy again made another attack and advanced on our Front line trenches in mass, by 7.30am owing to heavy casualties and no relief we were driven from the front line trenches and took up a second line about 100 yards in rear; this was lost and re-taken several times during the day, fighting continuing incessantly.
11pm	The Batn. was relieved when this took place we still held the second line of trenches.
Note	Owing to continual shelling no food or water ever reached the men, thus they had no food except the iron ration, since leaving Beuvry. During Saturday night rain fell heavily, with showers on Sunday, conditions were very bad as the soil being a clay mixture made quick movement impossible.

The casualties were very heavy the total being 402 all ranks killed and wounded and missing. The commanding officer (Lt.Col. A Parkin), Capt. V.D. Shortt and Lt. L.L. Phipps were killed, Major Fisher, Capt. E. L. Mauntell, Capt. Paget, Lt. Marshall, 2/Lt. Saunders were wounded. Captain D. H. Farrow wounded slightly but remained at duty. Lt J. H. Morley 2/Lt. J.L. Urquhart wounded and missing. |

The Battalion Diary

Martin was one of those casualties. His body was never found and he is commemorated on the Loos Memorial at Dud Corner Cemetery.

Martin's name

Dud Corner Cemetery

The Loos Battlefield today

As a footnote, the 27th September is noteworthy for two other deaths. Firstly, Captain The Honourable Fergus Bowes-Lyon, son of the Earl of Strathmore and brother of Elizabeth, who was to become the wife of George VI and later Queen Elizabeth, the Queen Mother.

Secondly, Lieutenant John Kipling, only son of Rudyard Kipling, certainly then one of the world's greatest authors. Kipling who had used his influence to get his medically unfit son into the Army, spent the rest of his life in a fruitless quest for the whereabouts of his son's body.

It was Rudyard Kipling who composed the wording to be found upon the thousands of headstones marking the graves of those soldiers whose remains could not be identified - "A Soldier of the Great War Known Unto God".

Sir Daniel and Lady Gooch of Hylands House lived in considerable style. There were 17 inside staff,-maids, cooks, footmen and a butler together with outdoor staff comprising 3 chauffeurs, a coachman, a groom, an engineer and numerous outdoor staff. Entertaining was on a grand scale and in 1912 Hylands House hosted the wedding of the year. It was known as the "Aero Wedding" as the groom, Claude Grahem-Wright, arrived by aeroplane which he landed on the lawn. Unfortunately the marriage did not last and ended in divorce.

At the outbreak of War Sir Daniel was with Sir Ernest Shackleton's Imperial Trans-Antarctic Expedition. The Expedition had set off from the West India Docks in the S.Y. "Endurance" and reached its base in South Georgia by way of Buenos Aires where additional supplies had been taken on.

Thick ice around the shores of Antarctica in the Weddell Sea resulted in the postponement of the trans-continental journey to October 1915. By then the world was far too pre-occupied with the titanic struggle between the Allies and the Central Powers to take any great note of the Expedition.

The "Endurance" in West India Docks

Sir Daniel was in Buenos Aires when news came through that Great Britain was at war and he immediately proposed to the Government that Hylands House become a 100 bed hospital. Initially there were 30 beds under the control of Sister Routling with four nurses and members of the Voluntary Aid Detachment.

Sir Daniel Gooch, seated third from right in the second row back. On his right Sir Ernest Shackleton

Hylands Park itself was given over for training purposes. It saw many thousands of soldiers carry out their training there and amongst the notables who inspected the troops were King George V and Field Marshall Kitchener. The picture above was on a postcard sent on the 20th December 1915 and is believed to be taken in Hylands Park.

Lancelot Edward Daniel Gooch was Sir Daniel and Lady Gooch's elder son. He had been training as a naval cadet at Dartmouth prior to August 1914 and on the outbreak of war he was made a midshipman and assigned to HMS "Implacable". He took part in the Gallipoli landings where it was reported that twice there had been landing boats sunk under him.

On 4th October he was struck down with paralysis and died very suddenly from asphyxia caused by an inflammation of the spinal cord. He had just turned 18. His body was brought back to this country to be buried at St. Mary's Church, Widford.

The picture from the Daily Sketch shows Lord Kitchener inspecting troops in Hylands Park

St Mary's Church, Widford

Lancelot's Grave

Gallipoli: British troops on a tug on the way to landing pass HMS Implacable
(photo by kind permission of the Imperial War Museum)

HYLANDS BEREAVED.

SIR DANIEL GOOCH'S ELDER SON DIES IN THE WAR.

On Tuesday Sir Daniel and Lady Gooch received a cable message from the Dardanelles stating that their elder son, Midshipman Lancelot Edward Daniel Gooch, of H.M.S. Implacable, was very ill, and paralysed in both legs. They hastened to the Foreign Office on their way to go to him, but before they had left London a second message arrived to say that the gallant young sailor had unfortunately passed away. His parents have now started on the voyage to bring the body home for burial at Widford.

The young Midshipman reached his 18th birthday only last month. He was a handsome lad, the heir of the house, very bright and very popular, devoted to and very successful in his profession, loving also his home, and much interested in shooting. He was educated at Wexingford School, near Wokingham, and thence he went to Osborne, going from there to the Implacable, in which he was through the landing at the Dardanelles. The Implacable has been specially mentioned for her good work, and Midshipman Gooch had been complimented more than once upon the services he personally rendered. He twice had a landing boat sunk under him. Only last week a cheerful letter was received from him, stating that he was quite well, and his death occurred on Monday.

Before this sad event, Sir Daniel and Lady Gooch had two sons, the deceased and Robert Douglas Gooch, aged 10 years, who now becomes the heir. There are also two daughters.

Hylands Bereaved; Essex Chronicle 8th October 1915

OCT. 8, 1915.

"ESSEX COUNTY CHRONICLE" PHOTOGRAPHS

The Late Lord Petre.

The Late Lieut. C. C. Tower.

The Late Capt. W. M. Hughes-Hughes.

The Late Midshipman L. E. D. Gooch.

Photo. Spalding, Chelmsford.

The last death in 1915 is not recorded by the usually reliable Commonwealth War Graves Commission.

Charles William Gardener was baptised on the 29th April 1894. He was the son of Robert, a blacksmith, and Bertha. The family lived at Waterloo Road (now that part of Lodge Road between the junction with Bridge Street and up to Paradise Road). In 1901 the children also comprised Edward aged 6 and Robert aged 5.

Charlie Gardener

Writtle Archives' records show Charles as buried in All Saints Churchyard but his grave is not marked and appears to have been grassed over. As the War Graves Commission have no record of him, finding documentation about his death proved difficult. Research traced a Charles W Gardener having died in University War Hospital, Southampton aged 21 on the 9th November 1915. Death was due to acute dysentery. The death certificate not only confirms that this is indeed Charles Gardener of Writtle but also shows that he was a Driver with the Army Service Corps.

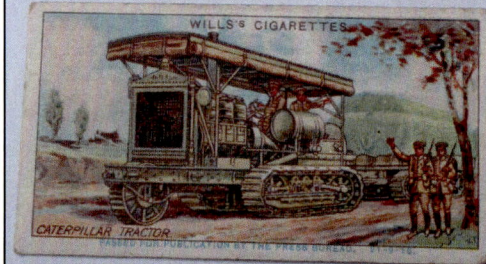

The varied types of vehicles for which drivers were needed
From Will's Cigarettes series dated 21/09/16

Christmas

Christmas would still have been celebrated albeit probably with muted enthusiasm. There were families who had lost loved ones and even more families concerned about men who were away in the Army or Navy. And on the Western Front there was no repeat of the previous year's Christmas truce.

In Writtle the Women's Thrift Club paid out its members who received in addition a bonus of 3 ½ d. (just under 2p).

The meeting of the Attwood Village Hall Club took place in Writtle Brewery because the Hall was being used by the military. The accounts showed there was £114 to be shared out.

The Rechabites were unable to obtain a suitable room for a Christmas party and instead presented 80 books to the juvenile members of the society.

Towards the end of the year the death of Mrs Inns was reported. For 40 years she had carried on the business of grocer in the village before selling to Mr T Fairhead. She had also been organist at the Congregational Church of which she was a lifelong member.

The advertisement in the Chronicle by Bolingbroke and Sons, whilst extolling the virtues of its Christmas goods, did so in a somewhat reserved fashion.

However, no such inhibitions on the part of J.R. Roberts Ltd of Stratford who took a large spread advertising all manner of toys most of which would have been well out of the price range of most families. It is noticeable that they have used a military theme wherever possible.

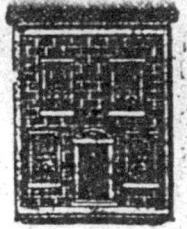

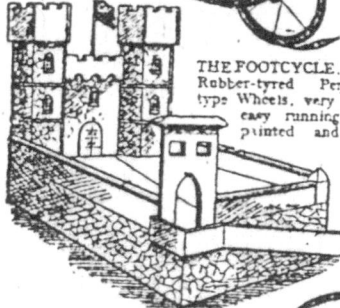

December saw the formation of the Writtle Junior Social and Athletic Club. The object being the betterment of the youth of Writtle. The aim was "to capture the youth either before or on leaving school, to control and train them in manners, give them useful instruction by means of educational courses. Introduce debates and talks on topical subjects, and provide them with seasonable games during the year".

Christmas at the Boys Home was spent with attendance at All Saints in the morning and then the rest of the day was given over to games and enjoying Christmas fare. Some of the villagers provided gifts and the Guardians provided privately a substantial toy for each boy.

Looking further afield, the Chronicle reported that, in the much diminished Football League, West Ham lost 3 -2 to Arsenal in the New Year's Eve fixture.

And the Chronicle wound up the year where it had begun - supporting the troops in a most positive and practical way!

THE ESSEX COUNTY

A Duty for those at Home

All of us know what a soldier's duty is, but do we all realise what is the duty of those not in khaki? Whether we are over age, medically unfit, or members of the weaker sex, we too have a duty, and one which is just as important in its way as the duty of the soldier or sailor who takes the King's shilling. That duty is to see that those who are fighting for us are not forgotten, and that they get whatever we can afford in the way of little luxuries. One of the few luxuries that Tommy has an opportunity of enjoying is the chance to have a good smoke. There is nothing more mistaken than the view that because a thing is serious you must be thinking about it seriously all the time. Tommy Atkins has some serious things to do and to think about, but he has some moments of semi-leisure, when anything that takes his mind off the thing he has on hand affords him the greatest enjoyment. Something to smoke fills this want admirably.

A soldier recently returned from the front was asked by a friend whether he found tobacco helped him much? His answer was that they simply could not do without it. "When a chap is badly hit," he said, "we simply shove a lighted fag into his mouth, and he does not care a rap about anything. If it was not for tobacco we would all be dead, and you may well guess a trench is not a nice sweet scented place."

So don't forget to see first of all that your friend or relative at the front has plenty to smoke, and don't forget those also who have no friends at home sufficiently in a position to be able to afford to send them anything like a regular supply. We are trying to help you. We have opened our Tobacco Fund for this purpose. We are buying cheaper than you can buy. We have arranged that all the tobacco and cigarettes you send through our Fund go duty free, and furthermore, we save you all the trouble of packing and posting. Read through the details of our scheme given here, then send us your money, as much as you can afford. We will do the rest. Every penny subscribed is spent in smokes, our efforts being entirely voluntary.

- 79 -

Trench Life

The First World War conjures up a number of images and amongst the strongest are the mud and trenches of Flanders.

By the time 1915 had ended the line of trenches stretched from the English Channel all the way to Switzerland. The mud, whilst of course not year round, was a reality for many months; mud which pervaded the soldiers' kit, mud which blocked the rifles, mud in which a man could drown.

A sea of mud with water filled shell holes
(photo by kind permission of the Imperial War Museum)

Trench warfare on a massive scale caught the British Army by surprise. The heroic vision of victorious cavalry chasing the enemy across open countryside followed by the infantry mopping up any remaining resistance was replaced by a more prosaic, and certainly dirtier, existence of living virtually underground in trenches and boltholes. Not at all the popular picture and probably something of a shock to our lads from Writtle fired up by the rhetoric they had heard at home.

In fact for some of those from Writtle digging trenches must have seemed little different from digging ditches back on the farm – albeit that in Writtle no one was shooting at you.

No doubt the soldiers felt that they spent more time digging trenches than tackling the enemy. The following is an extract from the diary of Edwin Hare of the Scots Guards for a fortnight in January

1st Jan	Digging 8.30 – 12 noon. Wet through	8th Jan	Digging Rain
3rd Jan	Digging	10th Jan	Digging Rain
4th Jan	Digging	11th Jan	Digging Rain
5th Jan	Digging	12th Jan	Digging
6th Jan	Digging Rain	13th Jan	Digging
7th Jan	Digging Rain	14th Jan	Digging Rain

If his Battalion is typical then proficiency with a spade came before skill with a rifle!

No doubt there was much grumbling about all this digging but it was essential. A trench needed constant maintenance as it rapidly deteriorated from the effects of the weather, from German shelling and from the sheer number of soldiers living in the trench. There would be a rotation of men between front line

Preserved trenches at Sanctuary Wood near Hooge show the zig-zag effect. If one part of the trench was captured the enemy would be unable to fire along its whole length and if a shell burst in one part the blast would not wipe out men in the next.

trenches, second line, reserve and then back to rest areas. Taking over a trench from another unit could also give rise to complaints about the state in which the previous occupants had left it. After all this particular trench was to be their home for the next few days.

Edwin Hare comments regularly on conditions and his words would no doubt reflect the views of any of the men.

"Very bad trenches. Overrun with rats". "1st line in bad state, bits here and there". But not all was doom and gloom. Despite being subjected to regular shelling, the digging and the route marches, the loss of friends and the desperate fighting when the line came under periodic attack, there were times when life was pretty good. Another entry, "Fairly quiet all day. Good dugout, nice fire. Tray bon!"

Both the Government and private enterprise turned their attention to ways of developing weapons suitable for trench warfare, of ways of creating adequate defence to protect the soldiers living in the trenches and of making life more bearable for them. For many, especially Officers, purchasing their own equipment from stores such as Selfridges, Army and Navy and Gamages was a way of supplementing the official issue.

But no matter how good the equipment, mud was a pernicious enemy. Mud got into the rifle mechanism and the barrel. When it rained the trenches filled with water and mixing with the mud created a glutinous muck, rotting uniforms, causing horrendous health problems and reducing living conditions to a battle for survival against the elements, let alone the enemy. Mud made moving about exhausting and shifting equipment required Herculean efforts on the part of men, machinery and animals. The problem for the Allies, invariably occupying land lower than the Germans, was that digging trenches in low lying Flanders meant digging below the water table.

A soldier named Albert (unfortunately the letter gives no clue as to his identity) writes to his sister Em "When we are in the trenches it takes all our time to try and keep a bit dry it is awful in them now it as been pouring up till today. We were up to our knees in mud and water."

The Weekly News gave an account of life at the Front by a soldier invalided home to Braintree. Lance Corporal Herbert Nash had taken part in the retreat from Mons, Battle of the Aisne and the Battles round Ypres.

"The war is simply hell let loose on earth – no other description fits it. The mud is terrible, and our men have to stand in trenches partly filled with mud and water. The ground in places is a kind of brick earth all mixed up to a 'pug' and the wet does not go away"

A mule team in trouble in the mud

In addition to the frequently flooded trenches, constant shelling tore up the landscape to create appalling conditions in which soldiers struggled to maintain any sort of military preparedness. Because it could never be forgotten that on the other side of No Mans Land the enemy was waiting to attack, either in a major operation or by trench raids. And in turn the British soldiers had to be ready at all times to defend the trench, to go over the top in a planned attack or to mount a trench raid.

Night in particular in the trenches was a dangerous time. Lance Corporal Nash again on putting up wire entanglements in front of the trenches, "We creep out at night with a crow bar and make holes in which the stakes are placed for the wire. To deaden the noise a sack is laid on top of the stake when driven in. But the German snipers soon get wind of what is happening and we feel the bullets flying around and past us. Then we have to lie down flat on the muddy ground".

Officers in a communication trench

A flooded trench - presumably at a quiet time.

Patrols would be sent out to examine the state of the wire protecting our defences or to try and form an accurate picture of the wire entanglements in front of the enemy's trenches. Trench raids had certain basic aims. The grabbing of a prisoner, preferably an officer, could yield essential intelligence about German plans. The British High Command believed such raids kept the men battle ready and in turn weakened the enemy's morale. And lastly, to kill Germans.

Encounters between the opposing forces in these circumstances would be intensely personal, brutal affairs. A frightening and desperate struggle for survival. Later raids took on the nature of small battles but for much of the time and especially in the first couple of years there were just a few men, moving as quietly as possible, with the aim of taking a prisoner or simply killing the enemy. Fighting of this nature was bloody and violent. Conventional weapons were no good in this situation with the result that soldiers took up knives, knuckledusters frequently with a sharpened spike, clubs, coshes, sharpened entrenching tools, anything which would kill or maim in such close quarters combat.

The men from Writtle were ordinary men as might be found in any town or village. To imagine ourselves in their situation is probably impossible. One can only marvel at what they underwent.

Trench scenes

CHAPTER 3 - 1916

The Year in Brief

The situation at the beginning of 1916 offered the Allies little encouragement. Despite costly offensives, large areas of France and Belgium were still in German hands. The Russians had been forced back to a line 200 miles east of Warsaw. The beginning of 1916 saw the evacuation of the Dardenelles being completed following the failure of the Gallipoli campaign. Encouraged by the success of the Central Powers, Bulgaria entered the War on their side resulting in the over-running of Serbia. In April came the surrender of the British garrison in Mesopotamia.

At sea, the two most powerful fleets the world had ever seen faced each other in the Battle of Jutland on 16th May. The result was inconclusive but a British win. Although the British sustained heavier casualties, the German fleet never ventured out again. The Battle is forever immortalised by the award of the posthumous Victoria Cross to Boy Jack Cornwell aged 16 who, despite mortal injuries, remained at his post throughout.

The British Navy did indeed rule the waves and the blockade of German ports increasingly denied the Central Powers the supplies needed to sustain their war machine. The other side of the coin however was that the losses to shipping from U boat attacks were causing equal difficulties for the Allies.

On land, the opposing armies had settled into a war of attrition bleeding both sides white. As was the case throughout the War, there was constant activity by way of trench raids and minor battles but 1916 also saw two major offensives.

The Germans planned a knock out blow against the French which lead to months of crippling losses on both sides at Verdun. A series of attacks and counter attacks from February to December. It became the bloodiest engagement in history with casualties on both sides of some one million men.

The Battle of the Somme was to a great extent dictated by the need of the French to relieve the burden on them at Verdun. Unfortunately a combination of factors – some perhaps unavoidable, or at least not easily foreseen, others down to poor judgement and execution – resulted in the blackest day in British military history. The 1st July when some 60,000 were killed, wounded, or missing; the dead numbering 20,000 for just that one day. The Battle eventually petered out in November. The advance just 7 miles; the cost some 420,000 British and Empire casualties.

And so the year began. 1915 had brought home to communities up and down the country the true cost of the War. With trepidation the Writtle families must have wondered what the New Year would bring forth.

The first Writtle death of 1916 was **Ernest John William Betts** who died on 29th February 1916 aged 24.

Ernest was the son of John and Grace Betts of Chancery Place. John was a boot repairer who had a shop in Bridge Street. The 1901 census shows Ernest as the eldest of three children having been born at Aldershot on 18th January 1892. He joined the Navy on 3rd March 1911 and served on a number of ships before joining HMS "Alcantara" on 13th April 1915 as a member of the Armourer's Crew.

Ernest Betts' Service Record

HMS Alcantara

The "Alcantara" was originally a Royal Mail Line ship. In April 1915 she joined the 10th Cruiser Squadron as an auxiliary cruiser and was responsible for patrolling between Scapa Flow and the coast of Norway. On 29th February 1916 she intercepted the German raider "Greif" disguised as a Norwegian vessel. The "Greif" was requested to stop and blanks were fired across her bow. A boat with a boarding party was lowered from the "Alcantara" at which point the "Greif" revealed her identity and opened fire on the British ship which at 1000 yards was a sitting duck. The first German salvo destroyed the "Alcantara's" steering gear, engine room, telegraph and telephone system besides causing numerous deaths. "Alcantara's" guns replied and after an intense exchange both ships were left sinking. The "Alcantara" listed to port, then completely capsized remaining afloat keel uppermost for a short time before sinking.

The "Greif" which was ablaze from stem to stern was finished off by the "Alcantara's" sister liner "Andes" aided by the cruiser "HMS Comus" and the destroyer "HMS Munster". Between them they picked up the survivors from both ships. Of the "Alcantara's" company 69 lost their lives. 80 of the 300 aboard the "Greif" perished.

Ernest's body was recovered and he is buried at Lyness Royal Naval Cemetery on Hoy, Orkney, a cemetery which contains graves from both World Wars. The Cemetery was begun in 1915 when Scapa Flow was the base of the Grand Fleet There are over 450 Great War graves including those of 14 sailors of the German Navy.

Lyness Cemetery, Orkney

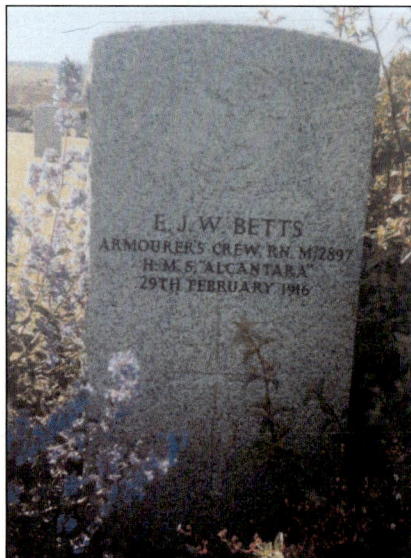

Ernest Betts' Grave

The second death of 1916 was also a Navy man – **Albert Charles Ottley** of Cooks Mill Green. He was born in Writtle and was the son of William Ottley of Causeway Cottages. He enlisted at Portsmouth and was a Stoker 1st Class on HMS "Queen Mary"

HMS Queen Mary

She had a top speed of thirty-three knots. Tonnage 27,000. Eight 13.5 inch guns, sixteen 4 inch guns. Complement nearly 1000 officers and men.

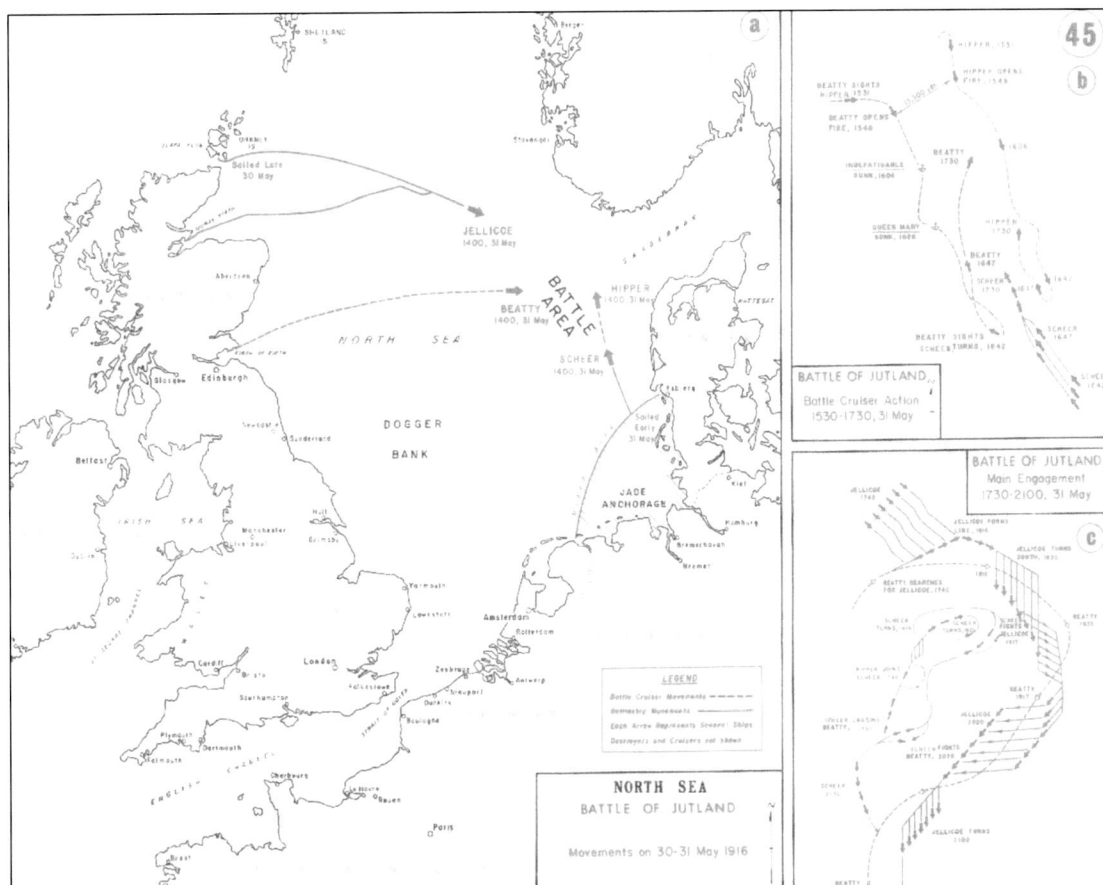

The Battle of Jutland
31st May 1916

The "Queen Mary", a battle-cruiser, was one of the heavyweights of the British Grand Fleet. The British hoped to lure the German fleet out into the North Sea to be caught by the Grand Fleet. The Germans had a similar plan. On the 31st May both fleets put to sea. The weather was fair, the sea calm and visibility only a little limited by mist. A fine day but for thousands of those who sailed it was to be their last.

Early afternoon saw the first action with the light cruisers clashing. This brought the heavy ships on to the scene some 50 miles south-west of the Skagerrak, the Channel dividing Norway from Denmark.

Problems and errors on the British side handed tactical advantage to the Germans and they were soon finding their targets. The best of the shooting by the British ships was that of the "Queen Mary" but she came under sustained fire from the "Sydlitz" and the "Derfflinger". At 4.22 pm four shells struck her forward and on Q turret and three minutes later she blew up.

Petty Officer Ernest Francis reported to his senior officer that the ship was listing heavily and the order was given to abandon ship. A crowd of seamen were at the battle cruiser's side and Francis urged them to jump but most refused saying she would remain afloat long enough to be rescued. He and a few others did jump and had swum some 150 feet when there was an almighty explosion. Francis recalled "The air seemed to be full of fragments and flying pieces". As "Queen Mary" disappeared beneath the waves a tremendous suction grabbed the men struggling in the water. Francis thought he was "Done" but found a burst of energy, grabbed some wreckage and was rescued. He was just one of eight men picked up; 1266 of their shipmates perished.

Albert being a stoker would be unlikely to have stood any chance of escape. Deep in the bowels of the ship the stokers would not have been able to ascend through the many decks before the ship sank.

Albert is commemorated on the Portsmouth Naval Memorial (Panel MR2) but is one of those whose name is not recorded on the Writtle War Memorial.

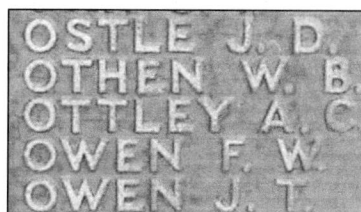

Albert Ottley's name on the Portsmouth Memorial

A huge cloud of smoke when the Queen Mary blows up
(Photograph by kind permission of the Imperial War Museum)

HMS Queen Mary commemorated on a non postal stamp

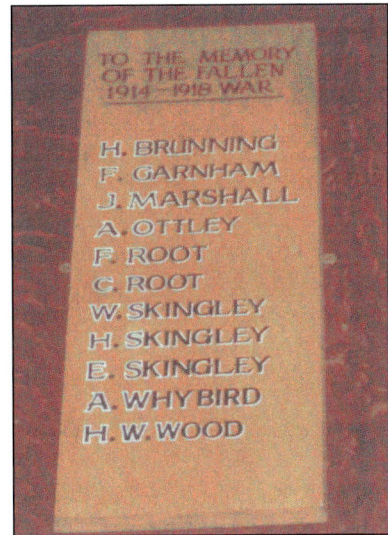

TO THE MEMORY
OF THE FALLEN
1914 – 1918 WAR

H. BRUNNING
F. GARNHAM
J. MARSHALL
A. OTTLEY
F. ROOT
C. ROOT
W. SKINGLEY
H. SKINGLEY
E. SKINGLEY
A. WHYBIRD
H. W. WOOD

Albert Ottley is commemorated on the organ loft in Highwood Church

The Portsmouth Naval Memorial

Edward Leigh Mildmay Rose is another who is not shown on the War Memorial but there is a memorial plaque to him in the Church. He was a Lieutenant in the 16th Battalion, Canadian Scottish Pioneers.

The Canadian Regiments had taken a battering at the St. Eloi Craters just south of Ypres, in March and April 1916. Tactics and techniques were worked upon and later in the year they were due to move to the Somme but first they were involved in defending the Ypres Salient. During April several incursions by the Germans were beaten off. May was quiet but the term is relative only; the Canadians suffered two thousand casualties that month.

Within the line held by the Canadian Divisions was the only remaining high point of the Ypres ridge still in Allied hands. This advantageous position extended from Hill 60, then over a knoll called Mount Sorrel and on to Hill 61 and Hill 62. Although called Hills these are misnomers – in reality they are rises where the land is just a little higher than its surroundings; nonetheless in the flat landscape of Flanders any piece of land that commanded a view over the battlefield was of supreme importance. North of the Hills the ground fell away to the Menin Road but from Hill 62 a broad spur named Observatory Ridge thrust a thousand yards due west between Armagh Wood and Sanctuary Wood. It was the high ground that the Germans wanted.

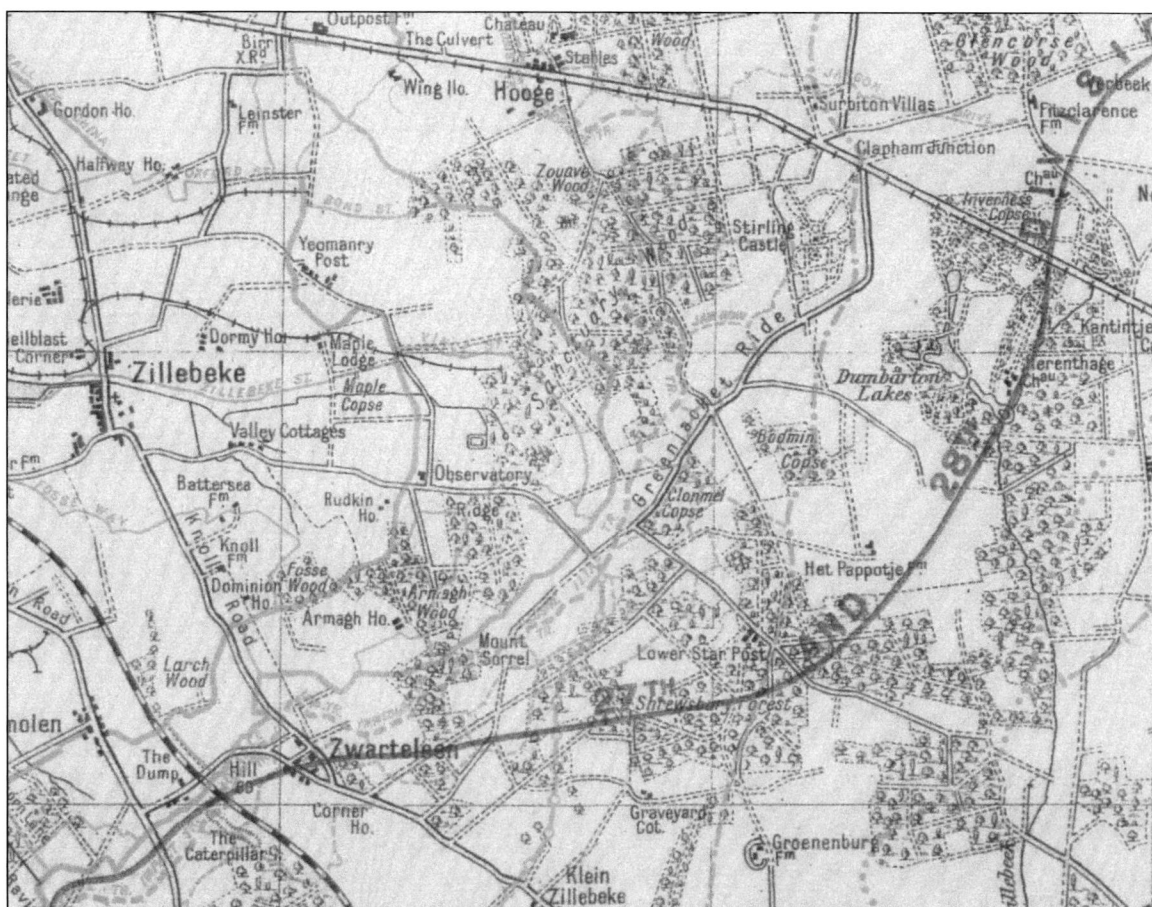

Hill 60 bottom towards left, Observatory Ridge centre,
Hill 62 to right of Sanctuary Wood centre

The Canadian Scottish Pioneers were part of Major-General Curries' 1st Division. The 1st Division had battalions spread along the front line and centred on Hill 60. Opposite them, and the Canadian 3rd Division, were the 27th and 26th Divisions of the Wurttemberg Corps.

At 6 o'clock on the morning of the 2nd June General Mercer and Brigadier-General Williams set out to reconnoitre. They had just reached the front trenches when the enemy's bombardment burst upon them. For four hours this tornado of fire swept the Canadian trenches which in many cases simply vanished and the men in them were annihilated. Neither of the Generals returned. Williams was wounded and subsequently taken prisoner, Mercer was wounded, and then, later in the morning, killed.

During the morning the enemy fire intensified. At 1pm they exploded four mines and then their infantry attacked. Wave after wave of grey coated figures stormed over the flattened trenches along Mount Sorrel and Hill 62. Where unable to defeat isolated groups defending themselves with close quarter bayonet fighting the Germans used their recently invented flame projectors. On the enemy's right however there was a determined resistance from troops who had escaped the worst of the bombardment. The machine guns of Princess Patricia's Canadian Light Infantry raked the attackers but, despite their heroic efforts, they too were over run.

The Germans then dug in. They were following orders and local commanders who, on seeing the road to Ypres wide open, could have boldly disregarded those orders did not do so. The rigidity of the command structure and the fear of making the wrong decision meant that Ypres was saved.

And so General Byng ordered his Canadians to re-take the land lost. Heavy casualties necessitated a shuffle of troops between the Divisions. Difficulties in communications meant that the attack that was launched on 3rd June lacked co-ordination and so the enemy was able to concentrate fire on individual groups and before the afternoon the right and centre had withdrawn.

It was proposed that the next attack would be preceded by a heavy bombardment but before that could take place it was the Germans who made the next move. Their target was the spur at Hooge. The spur overlooked Ypres and its possession would complete the German domination of the Salient.

At 3.05 pm on the 6th June 200 yards of the trenches were shattered by the explosion of four large mines. Two Canadian Companies were almost wiped out. Other troops moved swiftly to stem any further German advance. Hooge was however now in their hands. Despite this setback, over the next few days the Canadians were successful in re-taking Mount Sorrel, Armagh Wood, Observatory Ridge, Hill 62 and Sanctuary Wood.

Gun emplacements in Sanctuary Wood, taken by the Germans and recaptured by the Canadians

The Heroic Defence of the Canadians at Ypres

Canadian losses between the 2nd and the 14th June numbered approximately 8,000. Edward was one of those killed in the German attack on Hooge on the 6th June. He is buried in Railway Dugouts Cemetery.

Railway Dugouts Cemetery
(Begun in April 1915; contains 2,490 burials)

The Grave of Edward Rose

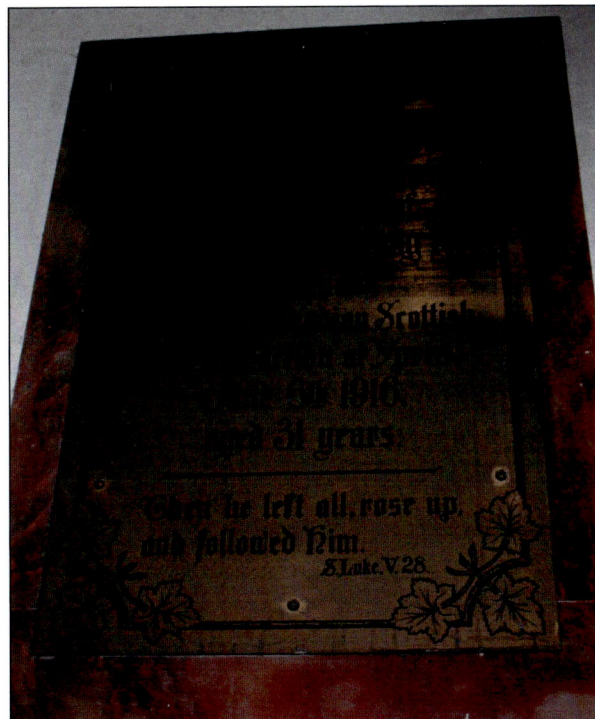

The Memorial plaque
in All Saints Church

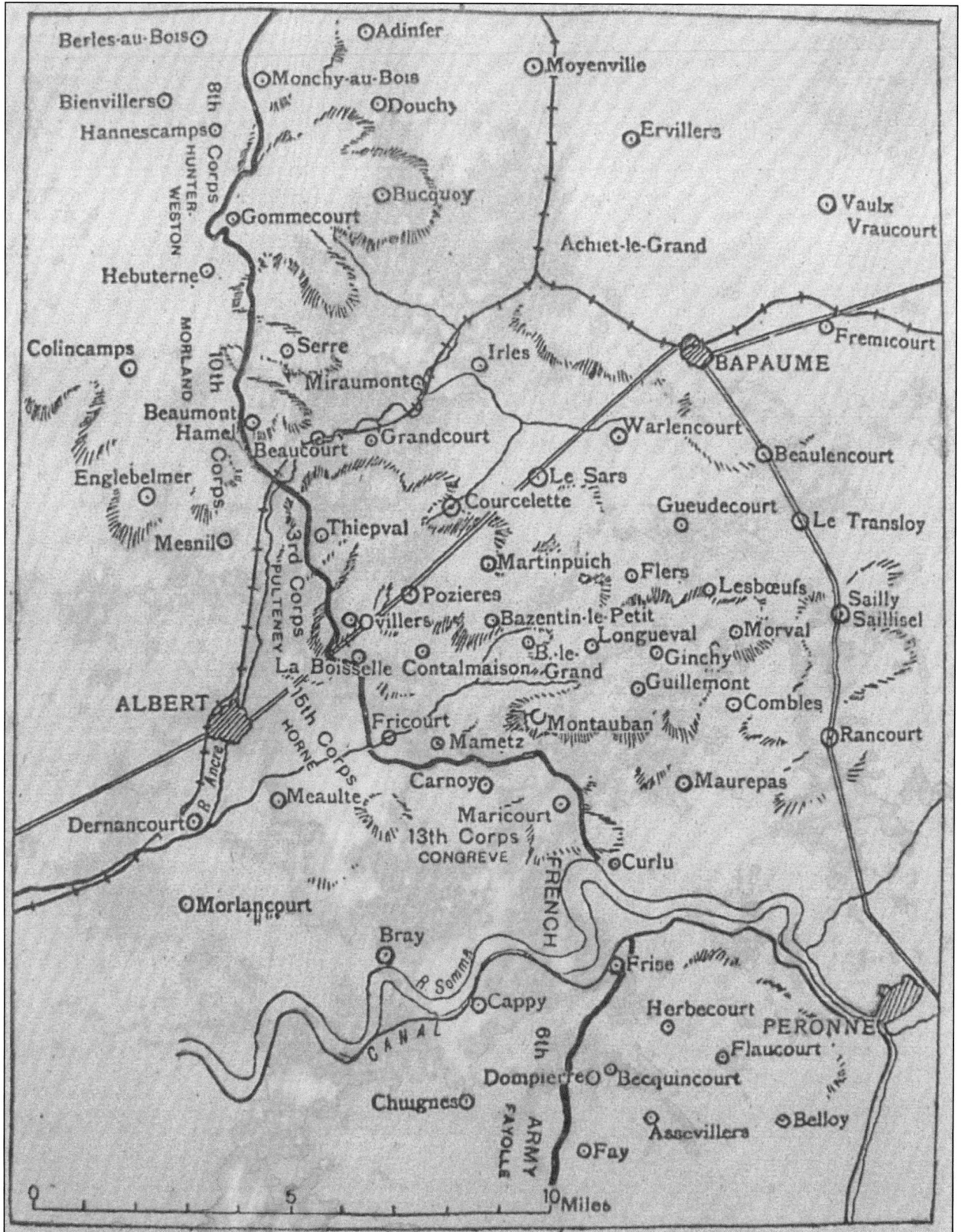

Battle of the Somme - The Front from Monchy to Fay, 1st July
showing general arrangement of the opposing armies.

The focus then moved south to the area around the River Somme. The Battle of the Somme was part of the strategy directed at the German lines of communication. But the inferno of Verdun drastically reduced the French involvement. The plan was therefore altered and would now involve a sweep by the British from their lines east of Albert with the intention of reaching Bapaume in a matter of days. The French would have a limited role to the south.

The Somme had been a relatively quiet sector, the opposing forces adopting an unofficial "live and let live" policy. From a strategic point of view the Somme was not a good choice and whatever pressure was applied by the French ought to have been resisted. The Germans had spent the last two years fortifying their lines a fact which should have been known to the British High Command or, if not actually known, should have been assumed given Teutonic thoroughness.

The Germans had indeed been busy constructing concrete fortifications and deep shelters. In addition, the topography favoured the Germans. The Somme area comprised a series of ridges and slopes – rolling countryside similar to the South Downs. The Germans occupied the ridges meaning that the British troops had to advance, laden down with equipment, up slopes largely devoid of any natural cover.

The gently rolling countryside of the Somme

The battle began on the 24th June with an Allied barrage that lasted for seven days aimed at flattening the network of German barbed wire. Unfortunately a combination of bad weather, many faulty shells and inaccurate predictions of the effects of the bombardment meant that the fortifications and the underground networks were largely unscathed.

On 1st July at 7.30 am several huge mines were exploded and immediately afterwards the troops left their trenches and headed towards the German lines confidently believing that it would be a walk over. Instead it was a disaster. The 3rd and 4th Armies consisting largely of inexperienced troops were shattered on the slopes of Thiepval and Beaumont Hamel. Losses were catastrophic and with only limited success in the south the attack was a failure.

The British casualties on the 1st July amounted to close on 60,000 of whom 20,000 were killed. Thirty two battalions lost more than 500 men out of a strength of 800. Never before had the British Army suffered losses on such a scale.

Amongst the dead were three men from Writtle; Robert Brewster, Dick Broyde and William Cresswell.

Troops ready to leave their trench on the 1st July

A roll call on the afternoon of the 1st July

Robert Arthur Brewster was born on 21st September 1891 and baptised at All Saints on 6th November. His parents were James, a labourer, and Maria. By the time of the War his father had died leaving the family to be brought up by their mother. They lived at Oxney Green. His brother James, five years older than him, had been killed the year before at Gallipoli.

Troops moving up in readiness

The final minutes

Robert was a Lance Corporal with C Company 2nd Battalion the Essex Regiment. The Regimental History of the Essex describes the First Day of the Somme with masterly understatement as "A trying day".

The Essex were part of the 12th Brigade. They were ordered to leave their trenches one and a half hours after the 11th Brigade and the plan was to leapfrog the 11th and capture Puisieux on the Grandcourt Ridge.

The 2nd Battalion left the assembly trenches at 8.36 am and immediately encountered heavy artillery fire. Their line of advance was right of Pendant Copse and in a direct line towards the church spire at Miraumont. Despite losses from shell fire small parties entered Munich Trench and the western edge of Pendant Copse but at 11am a strong German counter attack drove these small groups out of Munich Trench and by noon were back to the Quadrilateral.

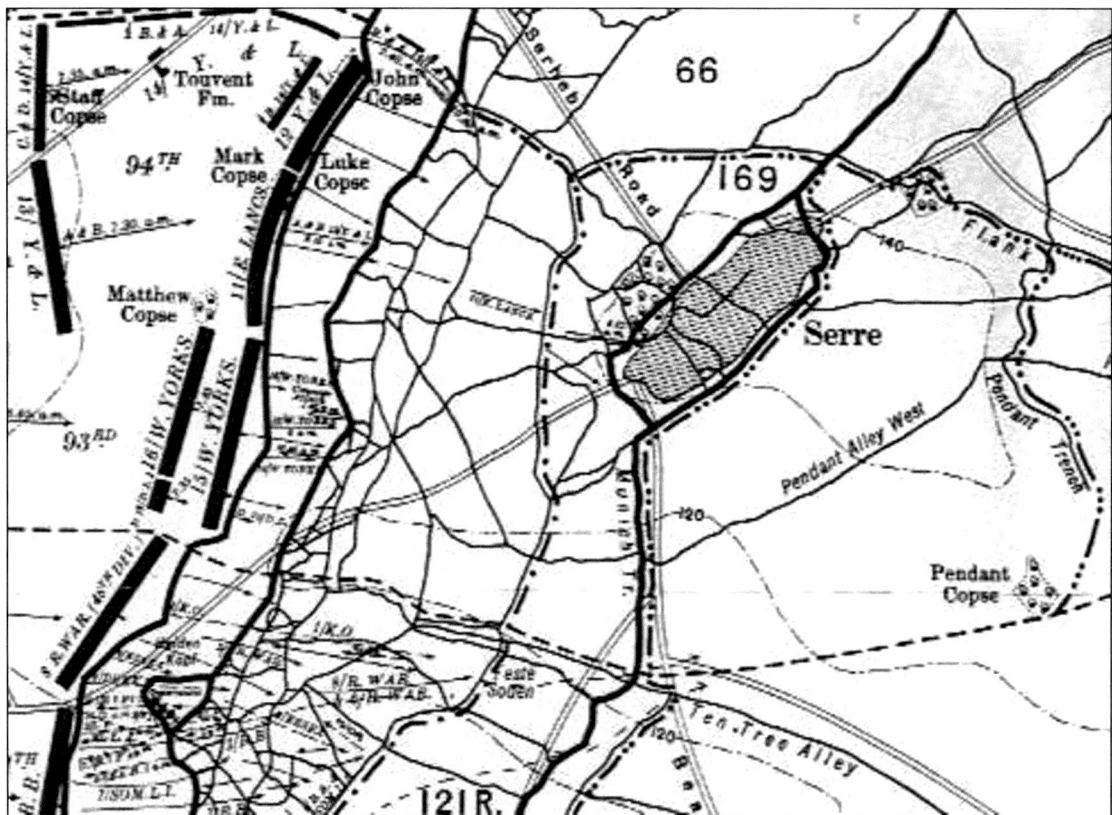

Munich Trench Centre; Pendant Copse right

The struggle to hold the Quadrilateral went on until midnight. Hand to hand fighting amongst the craters continued for hours, but by dark the Germans had regained their trench. To add to the difficulties of the Essex they were shelled by their own artillery. Short of ammunition and exhausted the Essex were relieved at midnight.

The 2nd Essex had gone into action with 24 officers and 606 Other Ranks. By the night of 1st July they were reduced to just 2 Officers and 192 Other Ranks. Robert Brewster was one of those killed, aged 26, and is buried in Serre Road No 2 Cemetery.

Dick Broyde was the son of Andrew John Broyde, a labourer, and Frances Elizabeth Broyde of St Johns Green, believed to be number 12. He was baptised on 29th September 1889 at All Saints. He too served in the 2nd Essex. Aged 29 at his death, he also is buried in Serre Road No2 Cemetery.

Serre Road No 2 Cemetery
(Begun in July 1916; contains 3365 burials)

The Grave of
Robert Brewster
"Too dearly loved to be
forgotten Mother & All"

The Grave of
Dick Broyde

The third Writtle soldier of the 2ⁿᵈ Battalion to die on the 1ˢᵗ July was Lance Corporal **William Cresswell**. His name is mis-spelt as Creswell on the Memorial.

William Cresswell was born in Writtle in 1877. The family originally came from Chalk Hill, Highwood and then moved to Chancery Place. He was a regular soldier having joined up in 1897 and served in India and South Africa. In May 1915 he was wounded but was fit again for action and ready to take part in the Battle of the Somme. On the 1ˢᵗ July he was aged 39. William has no known grave and is commemorated on Pier 10 Face D of the Thiepval Memorial.

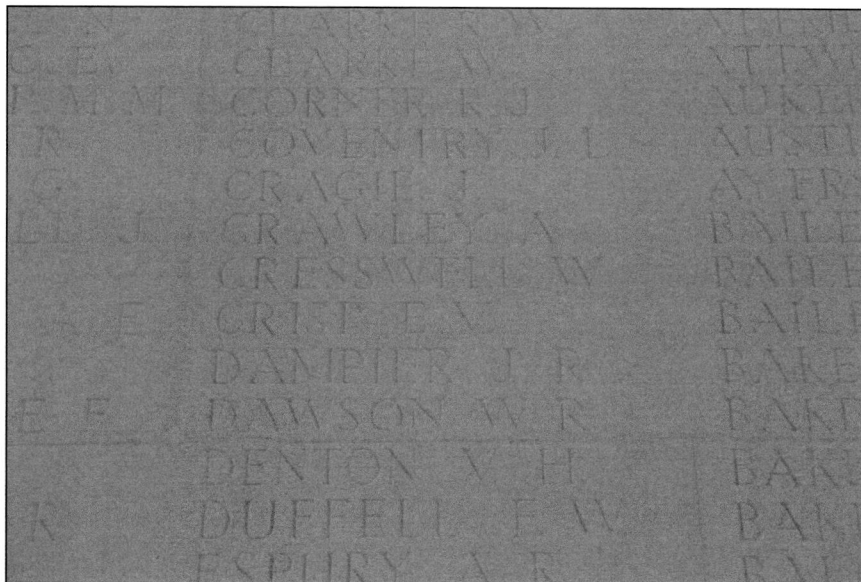

The name of William Cresswell

Mr. William Cresswell, eldest son of the late Mr. W. Cresswell, of the Rifle Brigade, and Mrs. Cresswell, of Chancery-place, Writtle, has been killed in action. Deceased was born in 1877, and after being in service to the late Judge Abdy, of High Beech Loughton, joined the Essex Regiment in 1897. He served in India, South Africa, Malta, Ireland, and France. He was the possessor of the South African Medal with four clasps for services during the Boer War. He was sent to France at the beginning of the present war, and after being in the firing line for many months was wounded and had to return home. He quickly recovered and returned to the Front, and was killed in the great offensive on July 1, after serving his country for 19 years. Great sympathy is felt with his mother and family, another member of which is serving with the Royal West Surrey Regiment at the Front.

Extract from the Weekly News 21ˢᵗ July 1916

No. Cas. 4872 Ex
(If replying, please quote above No.)

Record Office,

Station,

, 191 .

Sir,

It is my painful duty to inform you that a report has this day been received from the War Office notifying the death of

(No.) 4872. (Rank) L/C.

(Name) Wm Cresswell (Regiment) 2nd Bn

Essex which occurred ~~at~~ With the

B. E. F. France on the 1st.

of July 1916., and I am to express to you the sympathy and regret of the Army Council at your loss. The cause of death was

Killed in action.

If any articles of private property left by the deceased are found, they will be forwarded to this Office, but some time will probably elapse before their receipt, and when received they cannot be disposed of until authority is received from the War Office.

Application regarding the disposal of any such personal effects, or of any amount that may eventually be found to be due to the late soldier's estate, should be addressed to "The Secretary, War Office, London, S.W.," and marked outside "Effects."

I am,
Sir,
Your obedient Servant,
J. Walker Major
2/Lt.
For Officer in charge of Records.
9th District

Mr W. Cresswell.

War Office letter to Mr Cresswell

The Battle of the Somme did not mean that other sectors were quiet. **William Bowtell** was killed in action at Ypres on 17th July.

William was born on 4th October 1896 at Nine Ashes, Ongar. At the outbreak of war his parents William and Maria managed "The Prince of Wales" at Newney Green. (This is now "The Duck"). William was a labourer but enlisted in the 1st Battalion Grenadier Guards at Warley on the 20th November 1914. The Battalion was transferred to the 3rd Guards Brigade in August 1915 and arrived in France in October.

William Bowtell

The Battalion's War Diary records events in July 1916 in the Ypres sector. It was in trenches at Irish Farm and at the beginning of the month new trenches were dug despite a considerable amount of rain. On the 3rd one Company was so heavily bombarded that the parapet and a dug out were blown in and buried the Company Sergeant Major and nine others. Under heavy shell and machine gun fire the rest of the Company dug frantically and brought out the sergeant and three men alive but the others were dead.

By the second week they had been relieved and the various companies were engaged in training and on the 8th July a treat – a bath for the whole Battalion.

There followed a number of changes in officers. On the 11th six lucky men were selected to attend the 14th July National Fete in Paris. Then on the 15th the Battalion relieved the 1st Coldstream Guards in the trenches running from Irish Farm and north towards Forward Cottage.

Trench warfare consisted of time spent strengthening the forward parapet, making good shell damage or simply trying to make the environment reasonably fit to live in. The main threats came from shelling, sniper fire or an actual attack. Then the labouring at trench repair and the periods of almost boring sentry duty were exchanged for the desperate struggle for survival amidst the explosions, the gun fire and the bayonets.

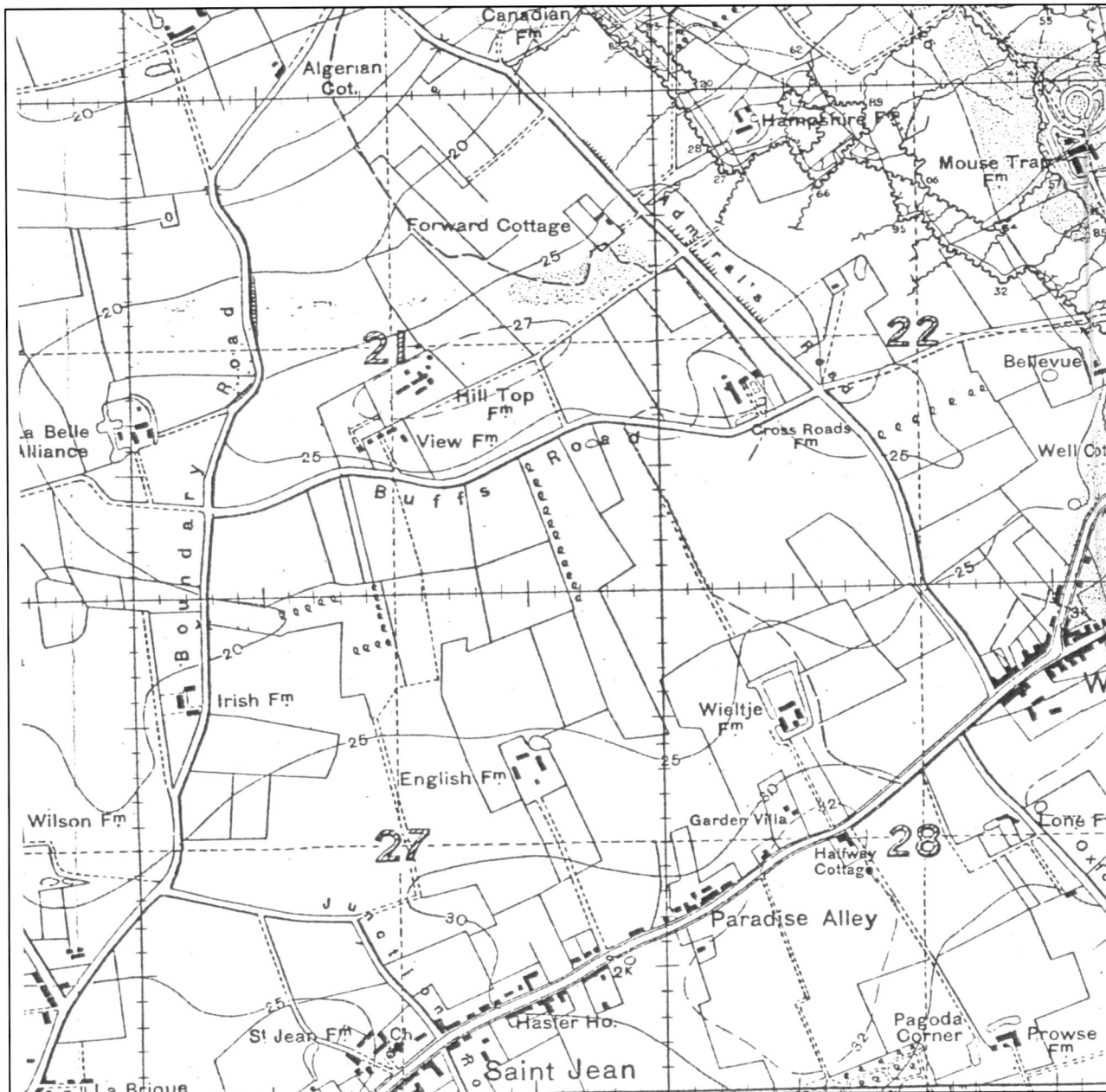

Trench Map; Irish Farm to the left with Forward Cottage to the north east

It was in the trenches that William was killed, aged just 18, by either artillery fire or rifle bullet. There is some doubt as to the actual date. The War Graves Commission have the date as 17th July whereas the Grenadier Guards records show the 16th. Probably the 16th is right because the Battalion was relieved on the 17th.

William is buried in Essex Farm Cemetery. It was here that John McCrae served as a medical officer and his poem "In Flanders Fields" became the best known of the War.

In a double tragedy for the family his father, William, also died in 1916.

An indication of the fear and loathing inspired by this sector is the comment in the Official History "on the 27th (July) it (the Battalion) left the Ypres salient without regret." Unemotional but very telling.

Essex Farm Cemetery
This was a dressing station; contains 1181 burials

The grave of William Bowtell

On the Somme the British troops pushed slowly forward throughout the summer but at enormous cost against determined German resistance. "A whole Empire walking very slowly, dying in front and pushing forward behind. And another Empire walked backwards a few inches a day, leaving the dead like a million bloody rugs"

(F Scott Fitzgerald – "Tender is the Night")

Every position was bitterly contested – Beaumont, Thiepval, Pozieres, Serre and countless other villages, ridges, woods, each of which pushed men to the limits of endurance.

Delville Wood is largely associated with the South Africans who held their positions despite overwhelming odds. But as part of the 53rd Brigade the 10th Battalion of the Essex Regiment was also involved there in the most stubborn wood fighting in military history.

Delville Wood - ammunition limbers
(Photo by kind permission of the Imperial War Museum)

Amongst the men of the 10th Essex was **Christopher John Osborne.** Christopher was one of the children of John and Sarah Ann. John was a bricklayer and the family lived in Oxney Green Road although by 1920 they had moved to 3 Clifton Villas, St Johns Green. Christopher was their eldest child.

The 10th Essex were engaged in the fighting in Delville Wood from the 17th July. On the 18th following a heavy artillery barrage and an onslaught by the Germans they were forced back to Buchanan Street. Fierce fighting took place amongst the tangled undergrowth and ruined trees throughout the 19th July. Early in the morning of the 20th the Essex were in the line from the junction of King Street and South Street to the eastern end of Princes Street. Despite all the Germans threw at them, the line held but at a cost.

Delville Wood
King Street to the right running between
Princes Street and South Street

Casualties of the Essex for the three days were 4 officers killed and 19 wounded; other ranks 75 killed, 38 missing and 402 wounded. Christopher was killed on the 20th July aged 22; his body was not recovered and he is commemorated on the Thiepval Memorial.

The name of Christopher Osborne

The blasted tree stumps of Delville Wood

The only tree to have survived

Thiepval Memorial

William H Garwood was born in Writtle in early 1873 the son of Robert and Elizabeth of Back Road. In 1901 he was aged 29 and living in Walthamstow with his wife Sarah and young family.

William enlisted in the 12th Battalion Royal Fusiliers (City of London Regiment). The 12th Battalion was deployed on the Western Front from the late Summer of 1915 through to the Spring of 1918. The Battalion was formed at Hounslow and went to France on 1st September 1915 under the command of Colonel C J Stanton. He was called to Headquarters during the Battle of Loos and command passed to Lieut. Colonel Garnons-Williams who, unfortunately, was mortally wounded on the very same day.

The 12th had an exceedingly tough time at Loos. Next year at the Somme the Battalion was originally in reserve. On the 1st September it was ordered up to that part of the front lying to the north of Delville Wood. On the way up a two hour delay occurred in Caterpillar Valley owing to a very heavy gas barrage and the guides going astray. Many of the men were very sick from the effects of the gas and it was only at 3.30 am that the Battalion arrived in Carlton Trench between Delville Wood and High Wood.

No. 3 Company was sent to reinforce the 3rd Rifle Brigade. On the 2nd September No1 company was sent to assist the 2nd Leinsters in the bombing post in Worcester Trench. The Germans attacked this post in strength but were repulsed albeit at the expense of several casualties.

Early in the evening the remainder of the Battalion took over the section of line from the Rifle Brigade and on the following day, the 3rd September co-operated in the general attack which swept over Guillemont into Ginchy. At midday the whole line advanced. The sector between High Wood and Delville Wood was strongly defended by the Germans but from Orchard Trench the Lewis guns of the Fusiliers did considerable damage. Ginchy was seized but intense counter attacks meant that the village was re-taken by the Germans. On the 9th September however the British troops finally pushed the enemy back.

On the 3rd September the 12th Fusiliers suffered 58 casualties, 10 killed. William, aged 43, was one of those killed but his body was never recovered and he is commemorated on the Thiepval Memorial.

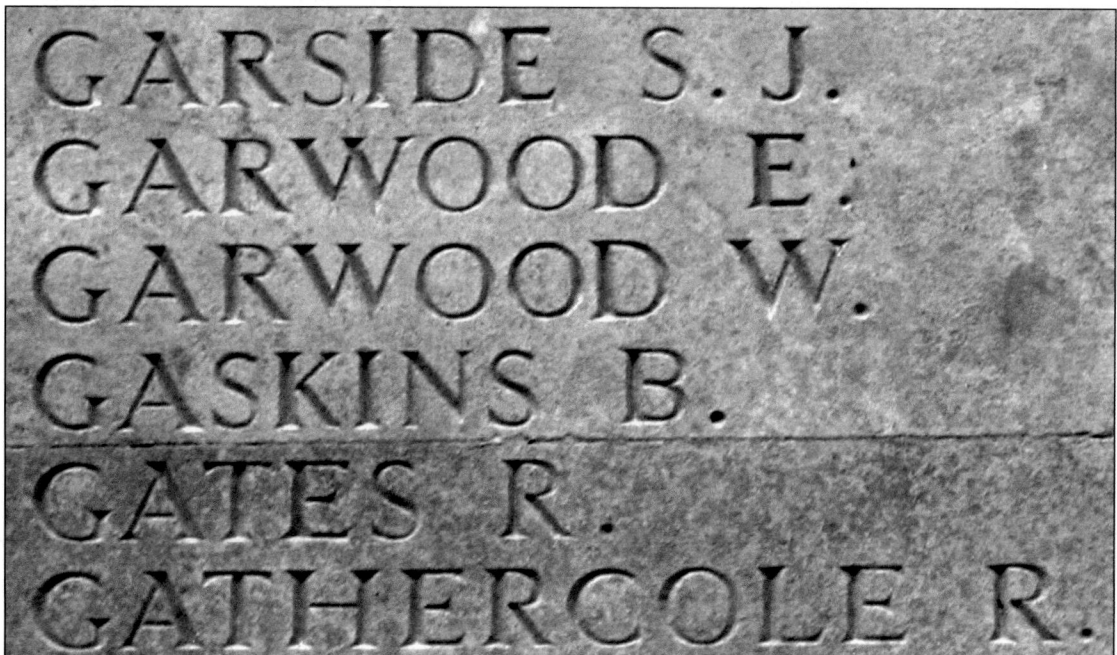

William's name on the Memorial

The most notable difference between the Great War and previous wars was the fact that earlier wars had been fought by professional soldiers. Now we see men flocking to join up and from all levels of society. This is illustrated by the next Writtle man – **The Reverend Geoffrey Seldon Arnold-Wallinger**.

He was the son of Maud and Robert Nasmyth Arnold-Wallinger of Kitts Croft. Robert Arnold-Wallinger was the local GP. Geoffrey was baptised at All Saints on the 10th July 1889. He obtained a B.A. and subsequently an M.A. at Trinity College, was ordained in 1915 and then joined the Inns of Court.

Inns of Court Officer Training Corps Badge

Geoffrey enlisted on the 7th January 1916 in the Inns of Court Officer Training Corps. The Inns of Court Regiment, under various designations, can trace its history back to Elizabethan times. From then until 1859 the four Inns of Court in times of national crisis raised bodies of men for the defence of the country. These were disbanded when peace again prevailed. The continuous history of the Regiment dates from 1859. Two detachments took part in the Boer War.

However it was during the Great War that the Regiment carried out one of the most important roles in its history, training and commissioning no less than 11,000 officers

Geoffrey went to Berkhamstead for training where he served in the 6th and 2nd Companies. Illness struck him and he died aged 27 in the Military Hospital at Aylesbury on the 24th September 1916.

A CADET IN ORDERS.

The death has occurred at the Military Hospital at Aylesbury of the Rev. Geoffrey Seldon Arnold-Wallinger, a lance-corporal in the Inns of Court O.T.C. He was the elder son of Mr. and Mrs. Robert Nasmyth Arnold-Wallinger, of Kitts Croft, Writtle, Essex, and was 27 years of age. An M.A. of Trinity College, Cambridge, he was ordained last year by the Bishop of St. Albans, and when he joined the Inns of Court he was an assistant master at St. George's School, Harpenden.

"The Times" of 26th September 1916

He is buried in Writtle Churchyard although the grave is not marked by the usual War Graves Commission headstone but by a family stone.

The grave of Geoffrey Arnold-Wallinger
in All Saints Churchyard (2006)

The Grave (2008)

All Saints Churchyard

The Somme continued to claim lives, one of whom was **Percy Edward Everard.**

Percy was born on the 16ᵗʰ September 1897 and was baptised at All Saints on the 21ˢᵗ November. The 1901 Census shows the family as Joseph, a brewer's labourer, and his wife Margaret together with Percy then aged 3, and his elder sisters Gertrude and Daisy and brother Leonard together with the baby of the family Sidney then aged 1. The family lived at 4 Front Road, Oxney Green.

Percy had enlisted in the Queen's (Royal West Surrey Regiment) and was a Private in the 7ᵗʰ Battalion.

The Official History of the Regiment shows that the 7ᵗʰ Battalion, as part of II Corps, was assigned the task of capturing the ridge running from Courcelette to the formidable German stronghold of the Schwaben Redoubt.

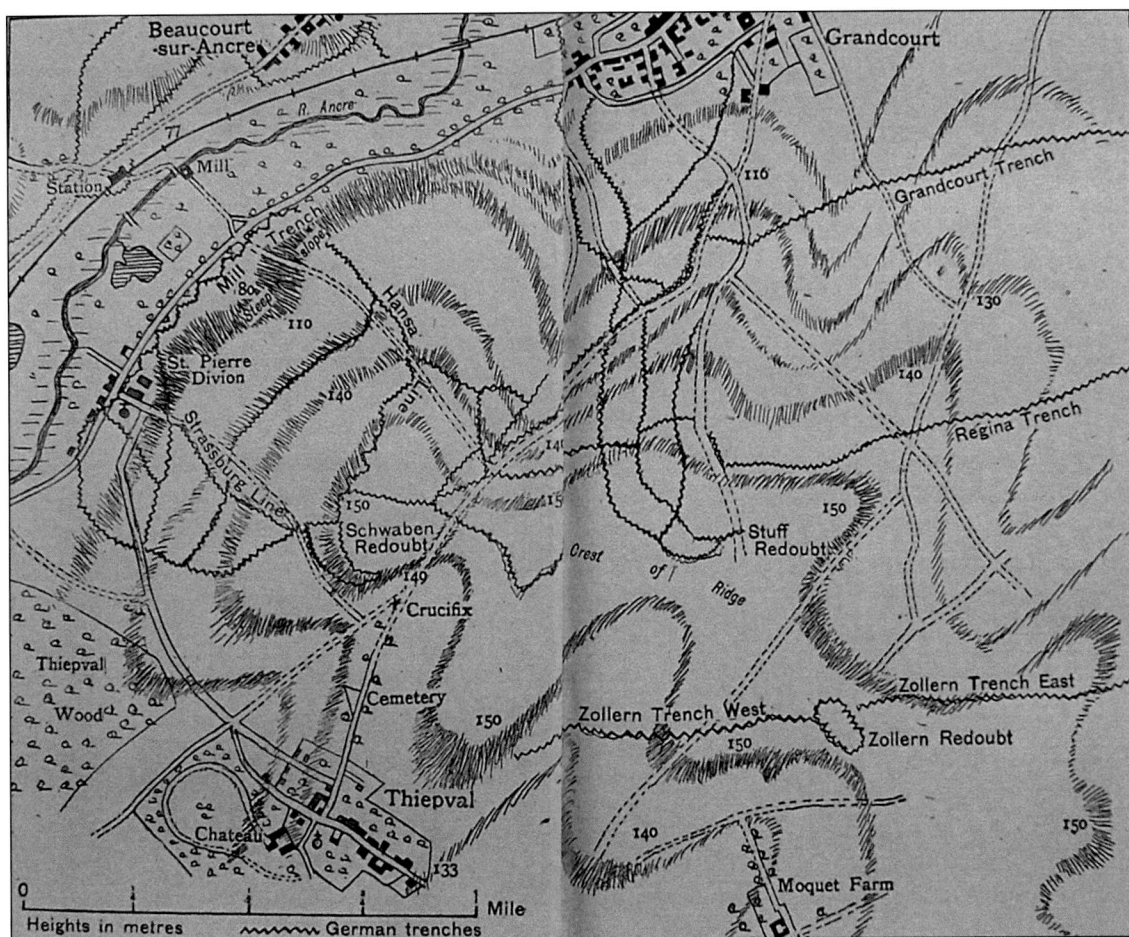

The Thiepval Ridge

After three days of preliminary bombardment the attack was launched on the 27ᵗʰ September. The 7ᵗʰ Queens with the 8ᵗʰ Suffolks were directed to attack the Schwaben Redoubt.

The Battalion left Blighty Alley at 10.15 on the morning of the 28ᵗʰ but on leaving the cover of Authuille found itself in full view of an enemy observation balloon. So on forming up around noon the Battalion found itself under fairly heavy shrapnel, machine gun and rifle fire. Pushing forward they took Bulgar Trench at about 1pm but now they came under heavy fire from the south face of the Schwaben Redoubt causing casualties. The next trench – Market Trench – proved even more difficult. It was cleared by Captain Walter leading D Company in bombing along the trench. Meanwhile Captain Longbourne of C Company moving between shell holes with a bag of bombs was able to knock out two enemy machine guns. Sergeant Pinter led a bombing party up the west face of the Redoubt and although pushed back was able to set up a strong point.

As night fell the line was consolidated although it was not until 5th October that the Schwaben Redoubt was captured.

Percy, then aged 19, was killed in the fighting on the 28th and is buried in Connaught Cemetery.

10, Dover Place, Clifton, Bristol. Native of Disley, Stockport. XII. C. 8.

EVERARD, Private, PERCY EDWARD, L/11300. 7th Bn. The Queen's (Royal West Surrey Regt.). Killed in action 28th September 1916. Age 19. Son of Joseph and Margaret Everard, of 4, Front Rd., Oxney Green, Writtle, Chelmsford. X. C. 7.

FAIRBROTHER, Private, S. 16919. 11th Bn. Royal Inniskilling Fusiliers. Killed in action 1st July 1916.

Percy Everard's entry in the Cemetery Book

Connaught Cemetery

Percy Everard's grave

Whilst many soldiers were killed during the Somme offensive, far greater numbers were wounded. Some were patched up to return to the fray. The more seriously wounded were treated in hospitals in France or returned to Britain. **Frank Jones** was one of these.

Frank is shown in the 1901 Census as one of the five children of Julia Jones, housekeeper to William Hutley of Bridge Street.

He was a Gunner with the Royal Garrison Artillery but, having been brought back to England, unfortunately he died from his wounds on 29th September 1916. He is buried in Hampstead Cemetery.

Frank Jones' grave

Hampstead Cemetery

On the first day of the Battle of the Somme Dick Broyde had been killed. As the Battle raged on throughout the Autumn it claimed the life of his brother, **Sam**. He too was in the Essex Regiment - a Private in B Company of the 1st Battalion.

At the beginning of October the 1st Essex was resting in Poperinghe to the rear of Ypres. On the 7th the Battalion was on the move to the Somme and by the 11th it was part of the 88th Brigade. The Brigade's objectives were to take the first line of the German trenches, known as the Green Line and then to proceed a further 400 yards to take the next line (the Brown Line). These lines were in front of the strong point in the ruins of the village of Gueudecourt. Originally the Essex were to the rear in support but during the night the 2nd Hants took over and the Essex moved up to the front to the left of the Newfoundlanders.

Rain had fallen incessantly for many days and conditions were deplorable, the 12th Division had mounted several attacks in the past few days all of which had failed with heavy casualties. The ground was a quagmire. The pack horses had to be unloaded as they were simply sinking in the mud, and on two occasions men were found drowned in mud holes.

An officer wading through a trench at Gueudecourt
(Photograph by kind permission of the Imperial War Museum)

The ground approaching Gueudecourt, 2008. The flatness of the landscape giving no cover.

Such were the conditions in which the men would go forward and on the 12th October at zero hour, 2.05pm, W and X Companies of the 1st Essex left their trenches and despite heavy shell and machine gun fire they took the German first line. Reinforced by half of Z Company they then mopped up killing some 300 Germans and then attained their objective, the right flank of Bayonet trench. The intensity of the fire brought against them forced a halt and a phased retirement saw them back in the original German first line which, despite counter attacks, they held until relieved at nightfall.

Casualties for the Brigade for the day were about 600 men. Sam was one of these and like so many he has no known grave and is commemorated on the Thiepval Memorial.

Sam Broyde's name on the Thiepval Memorial

Arthur Edward Whybird was born in Writtle and, although he lived in Writtle at the time of the War, he is not named on the Memorial.

He enlisted in the 11th Battalion of the Essex Regiment at Warley and by 1916 was a Lance Corporal.

At the end of September the 11th Battalion returned to Meaulte from the front line. As they marched back "every man possessed of some German souvenir – a hat or a cape – and wearing it. A clatter of hooves – an indignant voice – the Colonel's 'Is this a _____ Boche Battalion?" (The Essex Regiment- Burrows).

In early October the Battalion received 6 Officers and 50 Other Ranks and on the 8th it was off to the trenches at Gueudecourt. It was a difficult journey there and when they relieved the Somersets the men were told it was a "poisonous spot". 2 ½ days later they were relieved having suffered 47 casualties.

The Battalion was back in the thick of it again on the 13th October ready for the attack on the Le Transloy trench system. Zero hour was set for 5.35 am next morning but it soon became apparent that things were not going too well. The Durham Light Infantry on the right had been unable to achieve their objective owing to the heavy German machine gun fire with the result that the Essex found themselves sharing Mild Trench with the Germans. The two sides were bombing each other and exchanging rifle fire but then came a strong surge by the Germans forcing the Essex out of Mild Trench. As night fell parties went out scouring the ground for wounded.

The morning of the 15th the attack was to be resumed. Unfortunately the German artillery opened up before the Battalion moved off and in the confusion the attack started late thus losing the cover of the barrage.

Lieut. J Ackman reported that when they moved off they were a good way behind the barrage. He reached a road with a few men and could not understand where the others were. A machine gun nearby was firing close to them and so he and his group rose up, and rushed the gun. His fellow officer went down, he was hit in the mouth and then his left leg collapsed under him and he fell into a shell hole. Things quietened down a bit and rather than be pinned down in the open he and the remaining men with him made a break for a nearby trench to reinforce those there. Lieut Ackman then lost consciousness.

Casualties were severe - 9 officers and 164 other ranks. Amongst those killed was Arthur Whybird. His body was not recovered and he is commemorated on the Thiepval Memorial.

Arthur's name on the Memorial

Arthur is also commemorated on the organ loft in Highwood Church. His fellow church member Albert Ottley who died on the 31st May 1916 is also named there.

The Somme offensive continued until mid November when it came to an end, both sides totally exhausted. The final stages saw the troops struggling through sleet and snow, in many cases in waist deep mud and water, and finding all too often the German barbed wire and their defences intact.

Some in the High Command wanted to continue but common sense prevailed as it was clear that with the weather turning the whole battlefield into a sea of mud that the troops could go no further in such appalling conditions.

And so five months later the battle ground to a halt. The high ground around Bapaume which it had been confidently predicted would be taken in a matter of days was never reached. Casualties on the British and French side about 620,000; German losses at least that number. In view of the failure to reach Bapaume the Battle achieved little but on the other hand the Germans had been forced on the defensive and had been unable to take back the ground lost. The significance of this was that whatever the German High Command had thought previously it must now have been obvious that they could not actually win the War. The tragedy for the Allies was that all that they had gained at such a cost was lost when the Germans swept through in their Spring offensive of 1918.

In the slough of the Somme

The Somme Battlefield
The solid red line showing the Front on 1st July 1916
The large broken red line showing the Front on 19th November 1916

Writtle News for 1916

It is a curious feature of the village news in the local press that in all the reports of parish meetings, social and fund raising events and deaths of parishioners there is rarely anything about the men who are in the battlefields. The news remains firmly rooted in Writtle.

And so the Chronicle and the Weekly News give us a snapshot of village events making the news in 1916.

Deaths reported in January were those of Harry Widocks and Mrs Kennell. Mr Widocks was a Parish Councillor who died, aged 49, from heart disease. Mrs Kennell, of Meadowside, Lordship Road was 81 and for thirty six years had been landlady of the Rose and Crown Hotel.

On the 16th March a motor car driven by William Wallace junior in turning the Town-end corner had to pass some military huts. At the same time a governess cart in which Mrs Shanks of Great Moor Hall, Newney Green and two of her children were riding came from Oxney Green and the wheel of the cart struck the car. Forty yards on the wheel of the cart collapsed (why did she not stop?) and the occupants thrown out but fortunately nobody was injured.

The Weekly News of the 24th March carried a report of a more curious accident. Charles Brewster of Waterloo Place got on a Chelmsford bound omnibus near the Cock and Bell and went upstairs. As the bus drove along Bridge Street it collided with a tumbrel parked at the roadside (parked vehicles, Bridge Street, collisions – all very familiar and showing there is nothing new). Charles, still standing as he made his way along the open top, was thrown to the side and struck his head on a water pipe of a house.

He was knocked out of the bus, turned a complete somersault, hit the ground and then got up and walked home, bruised but otherwise none the worse for his spectacular fall.

Next week came a more serious accident involving Mrs Robert Gardiner of Waterloo Cottages. Her husband was a soldier then stationed at the School of Gunnery at Shoeburyness. A cow which had been purchased at Chelmsford Market for Jubilee Farm, Newney Green, and which (for reasons unexplained) was on The Green was chased by some boys. At the bridge Mrs Gardiner was tossed by the cow and badly injured. Dr Arnold-Wallinger and the District Nurse, Nurse Newton, treated her and she was then removed to the Chelmsford Hospital.

Accidents continued to dominate Writtle news and the 21st April Weekly News carried an account of the death of Frederick Newman, a labourer aged 50, who was employed by Mr Edwin White, threshing machine proprietor of Margaretting. The threshing machine was being taken from Rolleston's Farm to Reed's Farm. The men stopped at the Chequers Inn.(They said only for 5 minutes-a case of being economical with the truth perhaps) When the machine was re-started Frederick tried to jump on the binder while it was moving, missed his footing and fell. The near side wheel struck his head. P C Swain rendered first aid and P S Smith went for Dr. Arnold-Wallinger. Frederick was taken by car to the Chelmsford Hospital where he died.

Subsequently an inquest was held with a jury returning a verdict of accidental death.

On Good Friday a three hour service was held at All Saints. On Easter Sunday a children's service was held in the afternoon and an appeal for new laid eggs for soldiers and sailors in hospital resulted in about 200 being contributed.

On the 1st April a meeting of the Parish Council took place with Mr A.P. Lindsell, Mr W. Easter, Mr A.R. Hunt, Mr H. Pamplin, Mr H. Preston and Mr J. Little present. A resolution proposed by Mr Hunt and seconded by Mr Easter was passed which regretted the damage caused to the Green by the Military and begged those stationed at Writtle to give consideration to the preservation of the Green as a beauty spot and general recreation ground and asked that arrangements be made to remedy the damage.

The usual round of events was duly recorded. At the annual Parish meeting Mr A P Lindsell was re-elected chairman. A rummage sale took place in the Boys' Schoolroom in aid of the Writtle and Wickford Nursing Association. An abundance of goods had been donated by parishioners and the total proceeds amounted to £35.

FATAL THRESHING TACKLE ACCIDENT.

Mr. Coroner Lewis held an inquest at the Chelmsford Hospital on the 20th inst. relative to the death of Frederick Newman, aged 45, a labourer, formerly of Colchester, employed by Mr. E. White, threshing machine owner, Margaretting.

George Curtis, a machine minder, said Monday was the first day on which he had worked with deceased. In the afternoon of that day the threshing machine, engine, barnworks, binder, and chaff-cutter pulled up at the Chequers Inn at Oxney Green, Writtle. When it was re-started deceased ran out of the inn and tried to get on the near side of the binder. He missed his hold and fell sideways on his face between the two wheels of the binder. Witness jumped off the chaff-cutter and whistled to the driver, and he stopped at once. Witness went back to the deceased, picked him up, and carried him to the bank. They had stopped at the Chequers for about five minutes, and as the men did not come out the machine went on.

William Whybrow, engine-driver, of Margaretting, who was in charge of the engine on the day in question, said he called the men out, and when he started he saw deceased standing in the doorway. He did not see the man get on to the machinery, but just after the machine started he heard a call and stopped at once. Deceased had only begun to work with him that day, but had been employed by Mr. White since November.

P.C. Swan, of Writtle, deposed to removing deceased to the Chelmsford Hospital; and Dr. Alford said death was due to the injuries which included a fracture of the skull and scalp wounds.

The Jury returned a verdict of Accidental death.

Amongst the many stalls was one selling items each priced at one penny (about ½ p in current money). A Social and Sale was held at the Attwood Village Hall to raise funds to renovate the Church Iron Room. A Gymkhana was held at Green Park; the prizes (naturally) pipes, tins of tobacco, cigars and cigarettes.

In May the local press carried a Notice to all inhabitants of the Borough of Chelmsford forewarning everyone that circulars were to be distributed giving instructions on what to do in the event of invasion.

NEWS. FRIDAY. MAY 5. 1916.

DEFENCE OF THE REALM

To the Inhabitants of the Borough of Chelmsford.

IMPORTANT NOTICE.

A CIRCULAR containing PRECAUTIONARY INSTRUCTIONS to be OBSERVED by the INHABITANTS of CHELMSFORD in case of INVASION has been prepared by the BOROUGH EMERGENCY COMMITTEE and approved by the Military Representative for the District. A COPY of this CIRCULAR will be LEFT at EACH HOUSE in the BOROUGH and ALL PERSONS are REQUESTED to CAREFULLY READ the same and MAKE THEMSELVES FULLY ACQUAINTED with THE DIRECTIONS THEREIN CONTAINED.

THESE INSTRUCTIONS ARE ENTIRELY OF A PRECAUTIONARY NATURE AND THERE IS NO NEED FOR UNDUE ALARM.

FURTHER COPIES OF THE CIRCULAR CAN BE OBTAINED upon application to me, the undersigned, at my OFFICE, 16, NEW LONDON ROAD, CHELMSFORD.

GEORGE MELVIN,

Town Clerk.

Municipal Offices, Chelmsford.
3rd May, 1916.

And what events concerning Writtle were reported in the local press whilst the Battle of the Somme was raging across the Channel.

14th July   The annual outing of the employees of Russells Brewery to Southend.

21st July   The Bishop of Chelmsford ordered prayers throughout the Diocese for fine weather in the face of a strong body of opinion that the abnormal quantity of rain and lack of sunshine were due to the terrific gunfire.

4th August   The Regent Theatre was due to open next Monday

CHELMSFORD'S NEW REGENT THEATRE.

OPENING ON MONDAY NEXT.

The new Regent Theatre on the Cross Keys site in Moulsham-street is practically completed, and will be opened on Monday next with a very attractive programme, full particulars as to which appear in another column. Mr. F. Burdett Ward, of Wisbech, is the architect, and no pains or expense have been spared in building a thoroughly up-to-date, comfortable, and well-arranged theatre, due regard having been paid to official requirements.

The seating accommodation is excellently planned, a clear view of the stage being obtainable from all quarters. In the balcony are four boxes which will seat 16 persons; the stalls and balcony seats provide for 354; and on the ground floor 712, comprising 1,082 seats in all. The auditorium is 81ft. by 70ft. on the ground floor; there is an extra large crush hall or foyer, with ante-room; while the balcony has a similar ante and spacious landing. The stage measures 46ft. by 24ft. It is fully equipped with an asbestos and iron-framed safety curtain, which will always be down during the exhibition of pictures. Limelight stages, flies; and grid are provided, and the scenery is all treated with non-flammable liquid, in addition to which there is a fire-hydrant with box, scenery hook, and firemen's appliances. Artistes' dressing-rooms for both sexes, with separate accommodation, are provided, and on either side of the stage are exits leading to the open-air. On the ground floor the exits are arranged at wide distances, affording a ready means of egress from all parts. The two emergency staircases are in reinforced concrete and iron. In this respect nothing has been left undone to safeguard patrons in case of fire. The entire building has brick enclosing walls and is partly steel-framed from the foundations.

4th August   The children from All Saints Sunday School were treated to an afternoon in the grounds of The House. They marched there headed by the band of the 2/7th Scots and enjoyed a tea, amusements and sports with prizes presented by Miss B Hilliard.

11th August   The death of Fred Parlett who built Stoke House. He was a leading authority on ducks and poultry.

28th August   Joseph Jopson of Highwood was fined five shillings for being drunk and disorderly in Writtle.

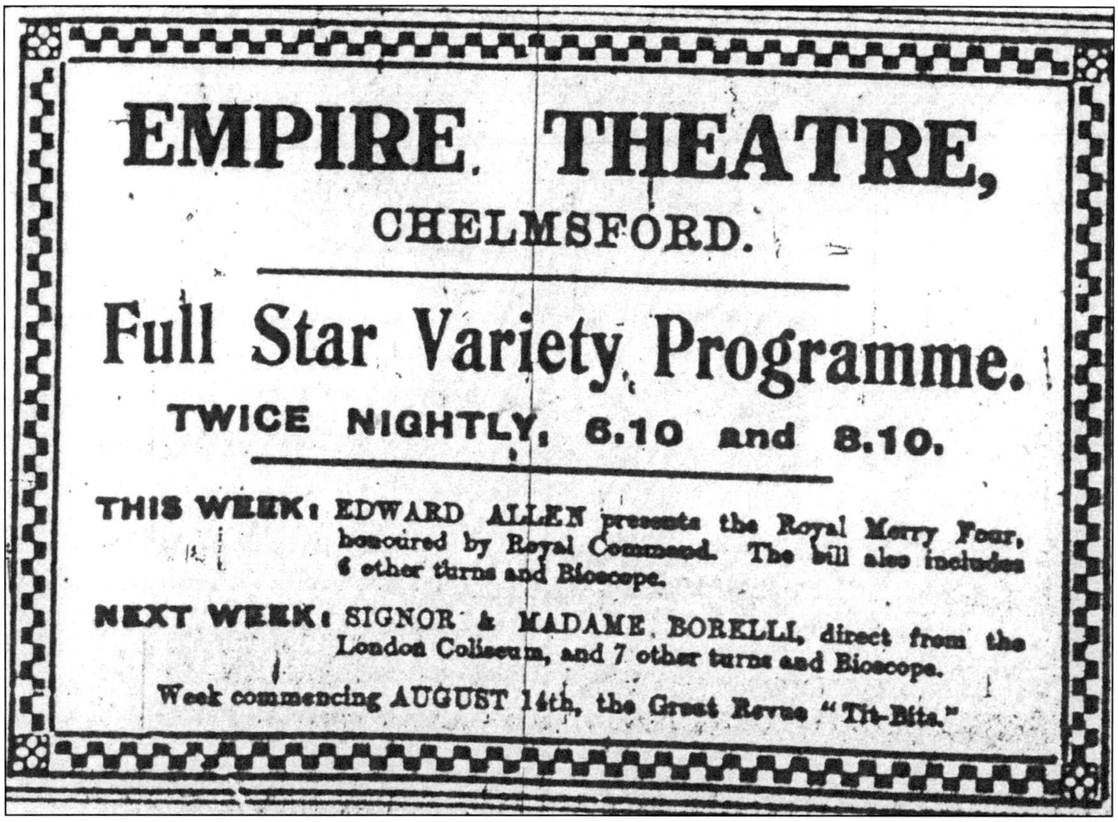

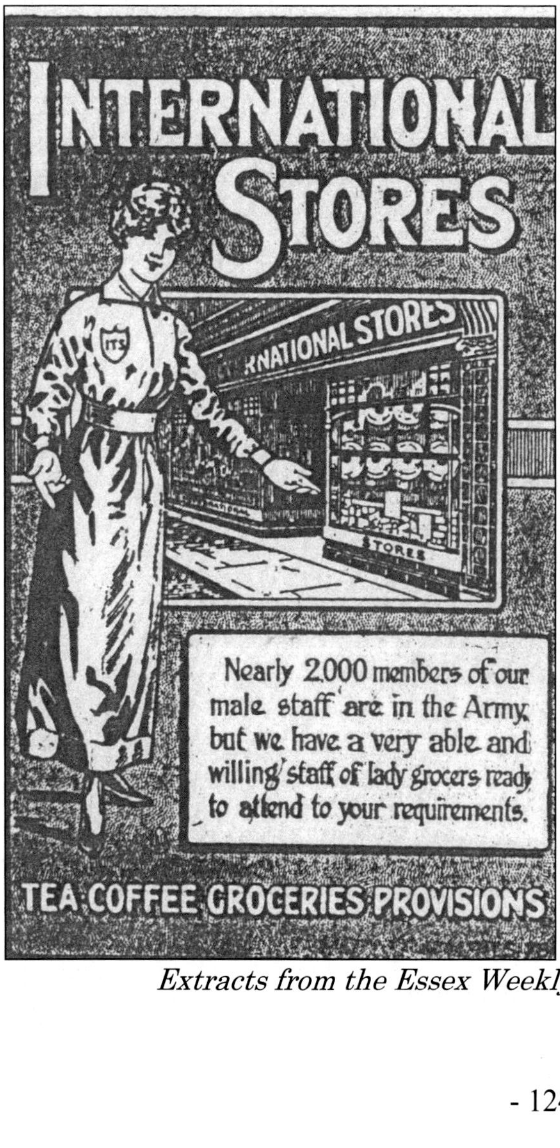

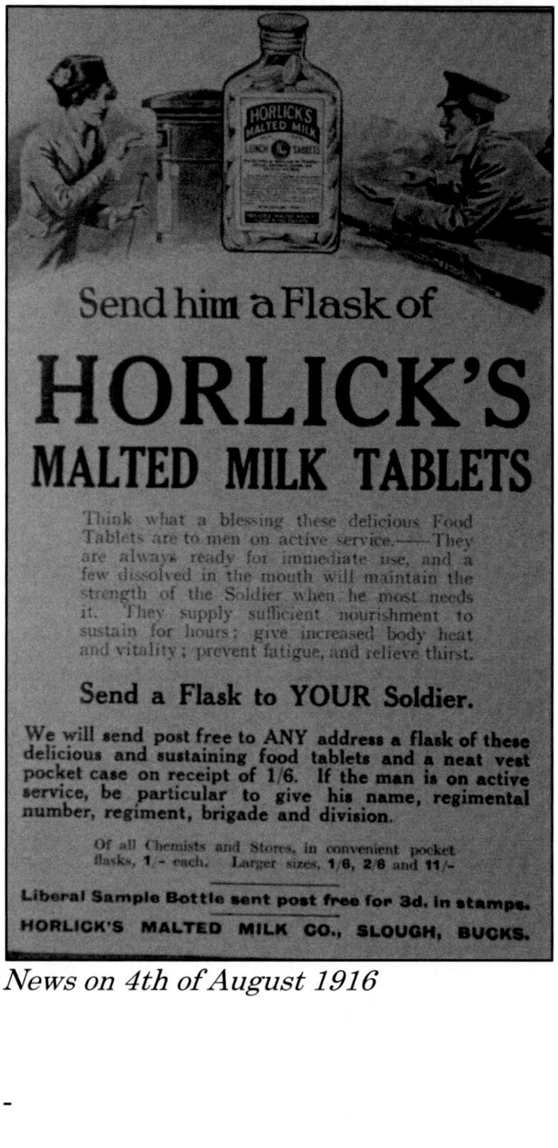

Extracts from the Essex Weekly News on 4th of August 1916

15th September	The Regent Theatre was showing "Battle of the Somme" a Government approved film.

24th September	Harvest Festival celebrated at All Saints. At the Children's Service contributions of fruit and eggs were received for the wounded.
29th September	The death of Mr Charles Lawson, aged 80 of Bush House, the Writtle representative on the Board of Guardians. Through him the Board purchased the property for the Boys Home. He was a member of both the Rural District Council and the Parish Council.
29th September	Messrs Alfred Darby acting as agents for Reverend Rust owner of a cottage in The Causeway applied for an ejectment order for non-payment of rent by the Tenant Frederick Gibson. Frederick was a soldier serving in France. The Court, on hearing of this, refused the application.
29th September	The theft of a bicycle worth £2 from Harry Woodyard. The offender, Lewis Burgin, was sentenced to one month's hard labour.
13th October	The Writtle detachment of special constables had a dinner at the Cock and Bell followed by a smoking concert.

Cock and Bell 1916

| 20th October | William and Mrs S Emery of Oxney Green celebrated their Golden Wedding |
| 27th October | Eight boys were invested into the Writtle Scout Troop. Badges were presented by Miss M Usborne. A display of drill exercises and signalling was given. The evening had been arranged to commemorate the Scout hero John Travers Cornwell. A subscription was raised towards his memorial |

WRITTLE.

BOY SCOUTS.—On Wednesday, at the head-quarters of the Writtle troop of R. P. Boy Scouts the investiture of eight boys into the ranks of the scouts and the presentation of badges took place. The badges, which were presented by Miss M. Usborne, included first-class, cooks, first-aid, gardeners, handyman's, second-class, tenderfoot, and service stars. A display of staff drill, physical exercises, and signalling by the boys was much appreciated. The boys were sworn in by District Scout-master F. W. Edwards, assisted by Instructor H. Martin, who is serving with the R.F.A. Before presenting the badges Miss Usborne complimented the boys on the way in which they had carried out the various exercises. The evening had been arranged for the com-memoration of the scout hero, John Travers Cornwell, and the subscription of the boys towards the scout's memorial taken during the evening amounted to 6s., various other sums being promised.

27th October   The funeral took place of Miss Blanche Rumsey

DEATH OF MISS B. A. RUMSEY. The funeral of Miss Blanche Alice Rumsey, youngest daughter of Mr. and Mrs. George Rumsey, of the Rose and Crown, Writtle, who passed away after twelve months' suffering, aged 22 years, took place in All Saints' Churchyard on the 18th inst., the Rev. F. S. Grover, vicar, officiating. The chief mourners were Mr. G. Rumsey, father; Sapper G. T. Rumsey, brother; the Misses Sarah, Frances, and Bertha Rumsey, sisters; Mr. and Mrs. H. Rumsey, uncle and aunt; Mr. T. Rumsey, uncle; Mrs. S. and L. Howland, aunts; Miss Lewis, Mrs. Wilson, Mrs. Williams, and Mrs. Johnson, cousins; Mr. W. Wallace, Mrs. Groom, and Mr. and Mrs. O. Fitch. Two brothers on service in France were unable to attend. Floral tributes were received from the father and mother and sisters, Mr. and Mrs. H. Rumsey, Mrs. J. Rumsey, Mrs. S. Howland, Mrs. L. Howland, Miss Lewis, Miss Williams, Mrs. Wilson, Mrs. Johnson, Mrs. Groom, Mr. and Mrs. A. Fitch, Mr. and Mrs. Beeson, Mr. and Mrs. Wallace and family, Mr. and Mrs. A. Wallace, Mrs. Spearman and family, Mrs. Brazier, Mr. and Mrs. T. Wallace, Mr. and Mrs. Lodge and Mabel, Mr. and Mrs. Watkinson, Mr. and Mrs. and Miss Dennison, Mrs. Page and family, Miss Florrie Frith, Mrs. Widocks and family, Mrs. Dunbar Cubbitt, Mr. W. J. White and Mr. and Mrs. F. Butty, Mr. and Miss Kennell, Mr. and Mrs. H. Pigg, and the Writtle Loan Society.

Death of Mrs Blanche Rumsey; The two brothers on service in France incuded
James who survived the actual War but died in 1919

3rd November   The funeral of Thomas Hockley of St Johns Green. For
                                      many years he was the coachman to Mr T Usbourne

And throughout the year more and more men were needed

?, John Dot, Charles Everard, Edward Cardnell
Those in civilian clothes are wearing lapel badges to denote they are in the forces.

Footnote

As a footnote to the story of the Battle of the Somme Lyn Macdonald's "Somme" concludes with an account which typifies the courage and endurance of the troops who took part in the Battle.

The Allies called a halt in mid November still some four miles short of Bapaume. Roll calls were taken and typical of these was the roll call for the 16th Highland Light Infantry- the Glasgow Boys Brigade Battalion. Of their 21 officers, only 8 returned and out of 650 other ranks, 390 had been killed or were missing.

However a message was received that 90 of them were not missing but had been trapped by a German counter attack and were now marooned in Frankfurt Trench behind enemy lines. This had also come to the attention of the Germans who, anticipating they would surrender, were much surprised to find that this small bunch of British troops far from surrendering was determined to fight on. And this they did from the Tuesday repulsing every attack from the Germans who surrounded them. British attempts to break through to rescue them all failed.

By Thursday 50 of their number lay wounded and on Friday another German attack depleted the able bodied still further. In the night some of the wounded died. On Saturday the Germans offered them the opportunity to surrender. They were given an hour to reply but after taking a vote decided not to respond.

On Sunday, desperately short of ammunition, out of food and medical supplies and reduced to drinking polluted water from shell holes, the men prepared for the final assault. The Germans attacked simultaneously from all sides overwhelming the fifteen able bodied men defending the trench. Of the original ninety, thirty badly wounded men were left alive.

These were the men who made up the British Army from whichever part of the country they came from. And how many other desperate fights to the finish took place with no survivors to record the unsung courage of the men who in a previous life were clerks, labourers, shopkeepers, professionals, farm workers. Ordinary men performing extraordinary deeds far above and beyond what was ever expected of them.

CHAPTER 4 - 1917

The Year in a Word

A year of false dawns, some successes but also setbacks. A year when poor judgement by the British High Command caused many setbacks but equally the weather, our allies, a change in German tactics and political squabbles all played their part.

The War had become very much a fight between just Britain and Germany and, for both, a fight to the finish. Lloyd George, now Prime Minister, and Ludendorff, German Commander answerable only to the Kaiser, both promised a knock out blow; victory. Everything in both countries was subordinated to the war effort.

Lloyd George had no faith in the British Commander in Chief, Haig, and indeed little faith in any of the generals. In turn the generals distrusted the politicians. Haig enjoyed the protection of King George V and was virtually unsackable. Neither Lloyd George nor Haig trusted our allies who to some extent were now bit players in the Anglo-German dual.

Notwithstanding all of this, it was the French General Nivelle whose plans were to have a major bearing on the conduct of the War in 1917. He got his way because Lloyd George saw this as a means of undermining Haig and so the strategy for the year evolved more from the mutual detestation of all parties than through military concerns.

To cap it all, Nivelle's plans envisaged the Germans doing nothing. The Germans however did not stick to the French script and effected a strategic withdrawal to the Hindenburg Line, straightening their line and falling back to immensely strong fortifications. Nivelle was undismayed and, despite the fact that everyone disagreed with him they all disagreed with each other more, so his plans were adopted and the year brought some successes but equally some failures and as always the usual harvest of death.

1917 saw America enter the War – albeit that their troops would not be in a position to make any meaningful contribution until mid 1918 – and Russia leave – thus freeing up great numbers of German troops who were switched to the Western Front. Mutinies broke out in the demoralised French Army and thereafter it appeared that French strategy was to wait for the Americans next year. The Italians collapsed at Caporetto. And so the Allied endeavour on the Western Front largely fell to the British.

Adding to the sense that Britain and her Empire were on their own was the loss of any optimism; the exuberant enthusiasm of the early days had long since gone. What was left was a grim determination to see things through to the bitter end. The mood of the year was encapsulated in one word – Passchendaele.

Passchendaele, or the Battle of Third Ypres as the whole campaign is known, began in July and ended in November. Before that had been the Battle of Arras in April and May. For once the attack proved successful. Vimy Ridge was captured by the Canadians. But then the old story was repeated. The offensive went on too long. The Germans brought up reserves and once more the line settled down. The cost - about 85,000 British casualties, 75,000 Germans.

Stretcher Bearers at Passchendaele, 14ᵗʰ November 1917
(Photograph by kind permission of the Imperial War Museum)

In Germany, the Allied blockade was biting hard, leading to the Germans adopting a policy of unrestricted submarine warfare. They had also changed tactics by a strategic withdrawal to the Hindenburg Line. The Germans' hope was for a decisive victory or at least a victory which would be enough to lead to a negotiated peace before the Americans arrived in any effective strength.

For many men of Essex there was a change of scenery; they exchanged wet and muddy Flanders for the heat and dust of Palestine. Here there was steady progress by the Allies against the Turks.

Third Ypres continued into November despite nightmarish conditions in which men drowned in liquid mud. And then finally Cambrai where tanks were used in a successful manner but the early achievements could not be followed up largely due to a lack of men following the months of attrition at Ypres.

The New Year was only a few days old when the next man from Writtle died.

Edward George Harvey was born in Colchester in 1892. He married Britannia Webb at Chelmsford on 20th October 1914. They had two children Patrick Charles, born 11th October 1915 and Edward born 19th November 1916. The family lived at Little Oxney Green.

Prior to the birth of his second son Edward had enlisted on 20th November 1915. He was a Gunner in the Royal Garrison Artillery, 216th Siege Battery.

Edward Harvey's Attestation

Edward arrived in France on 22nd December 1916 but shortly afterwards was wounded. He was treated at 60th Field Ambulance but died on the 10th January and is buried in Grave X1.E.9 in the Guards Cemetery at Lesboeufs, Somme.

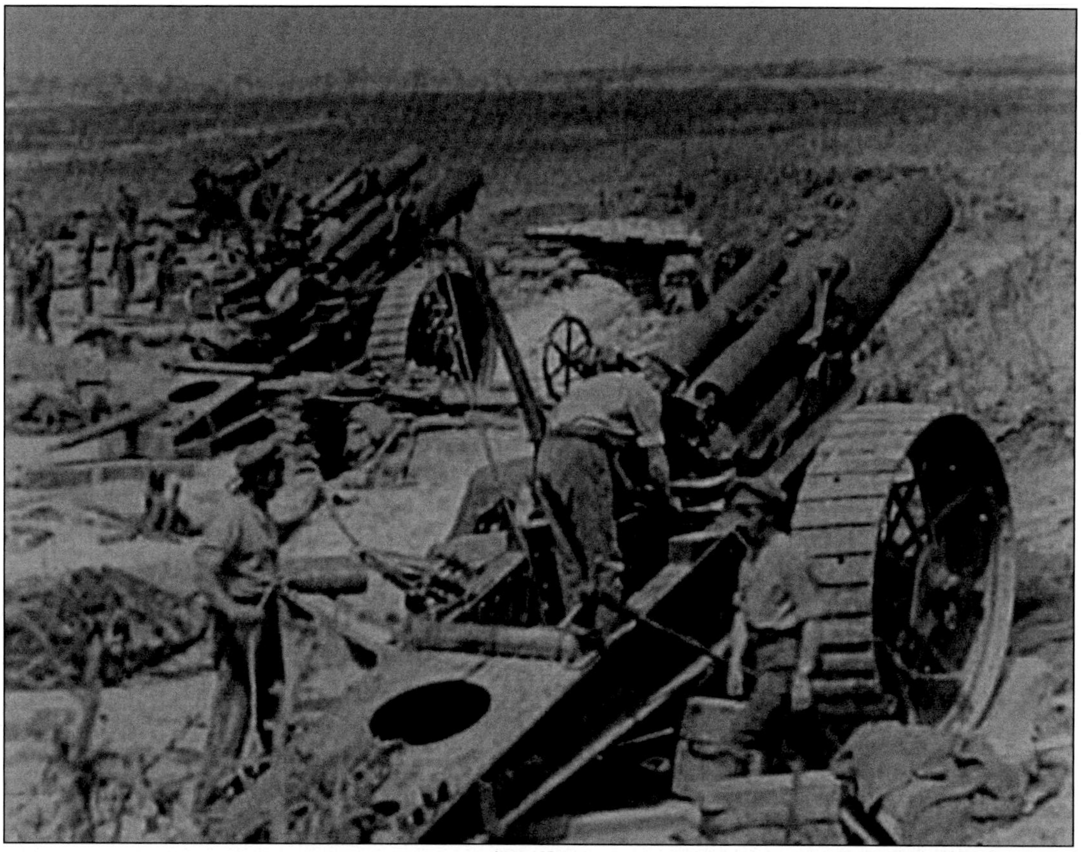

Artillery

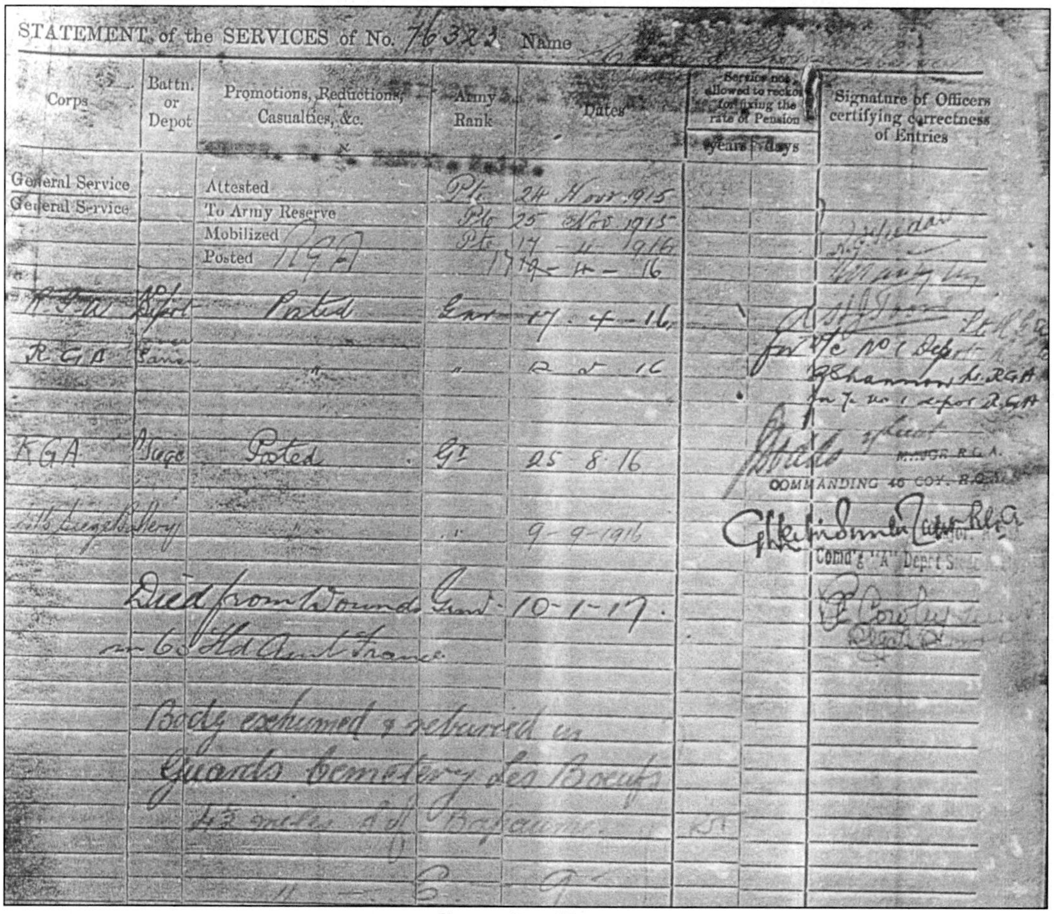

Casualty Form

The Guards Cemetery Lesboeufs
(contains 3045 burials)

Edward's Grave

John William Little was the eldest child of William and Emma Little. William was an omnibus proprietor. The family lived at 21 (or possibly 2) Sunnyside Oxney Green.

"Sunnyside", Victoria Road, Oxney Green

He was a groom but joined the Navy on 18th October 1912 and was a Stoker 1st Class. His death aged 25 was particularly tragic as it occurred as a result of a collision between two of our own vessels. He was on board the submarine E36 which was lost with all hands on the 19th January.

E Class Submarine

At 7.30 am on the 19th January E36, under the command of Lieutenant McGregor-Robertson, and E43, commanded by Lieutenant Poland, left Harwich Harbour for two patrol areas off Terschelling. E36 was on the port beam but by 3pm had dropped behind. A strong sea carried away the bridge screen of E43 and she slowed and altered course to enable a new one to be fitted. This meant that E36 overtook her and when E43 picked up speed again suddenly she saw the other submarine just 50 yards off. Despite putting the helm hard-a-starboard and putting her full astern E43 struck E 36 ten feet from the stern, rode right over her and saw her vanish.

Despite a search nothing more was ever seen of E36. John, along with his crew mates, is commemorated on the Portsmouth Naval Memorial. Submariners also have a Memorial along the Embankment.

John Little's Record

Submariners' Memorial on the Embankment

An E Class submarine as modelled in china
(China models of military items were extremely popular; they came in all shapes
and sizes and varied in their accuracy)

A Panel on the Portsmouth Memorial

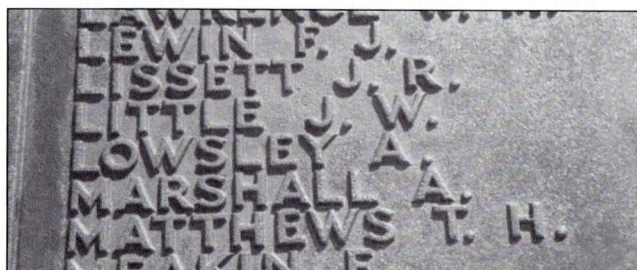

John's name on the Portsmouth Memorial

The next month saw the death of another seaman – **Amos Harry Gentry**. He was the son of Maria Gentry of Oxney Green. His father, Walter William Gentry had died aged 28 in 1894.

Amos was a merchant seaman and in 1917 was Second Cook on the S.S."Vedamore". She was a Johnston Line ship of 6330 tons built in 1896. She had been defensively armed but had no opportunity to defend herself being torpedoed without warning by the submarine U85 on the 7th February some 20 miles west of Fastnet.

Out of the crew of 63 seamen only 39 managed to get away in the boats. The weather was bitterly cold and by the time they were picked up ten hours later 2 of their number had died of exposure. Amos, then aged 21, was one of the 24 who did not manage to get away. Although not named on the Writtle War Memorial, he is commemorated on the Tower Hill Memorial in London. The inscription over the top of the Memorial reads "1914 – 1918 To the glory of God and to the honour of twelve thousand of the Merchant Navy and Fishing Fleets who have no grave but the sea"

Tower Hill Memorial

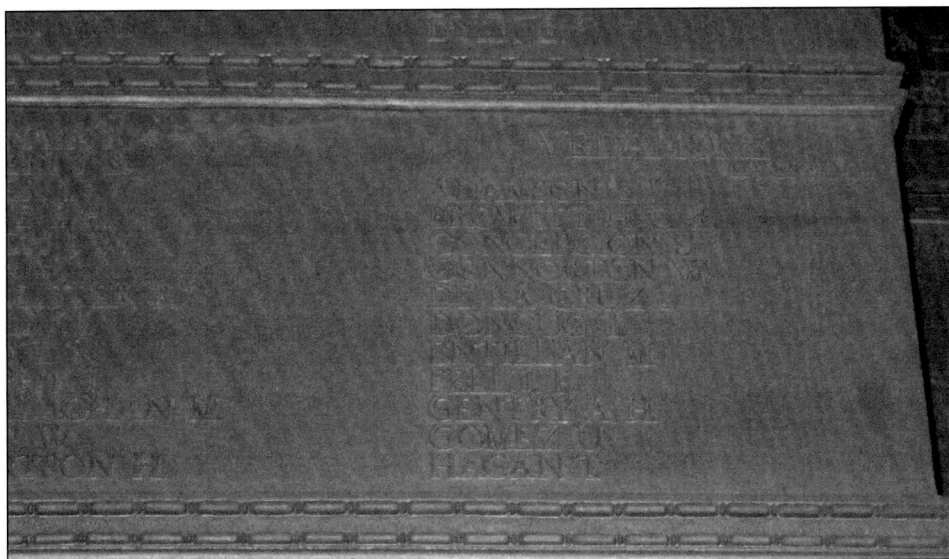

The panel containing Amos Gentry's name

Without the Army Service Corps the Army could not function. Much of the Army's fuel needs initially centred around fodder for its enormous number of horses. But it became obvious - to some at least – that the longed for breakthrough by the cavalry was never going to happen. This was a mechanised war and vehicles needed fuel.

Henry George Hart was one of those responsible for the delivery of petrol. He was a Private in the Army Service Corps, Auxiliary Petrol Company. The Auxiliary Petrol Company had various companies operating in the Western Front all with their own insignia. For instance the 3rd Company had white letters ET on a black background, the 4th a black five pointed star in a red circle on black square, the 5th a white dove on black background. The insignia painted on the lorries created some individuality. The most common lorry was the Albion petrol tanker.

Abbeville Communal Cemetery Extension
(Three hospitals were situated in Abbeville; when Abbeville Military Cemetery
was filled this extension was used; contains 1,755 burials)

Henry was the son of George and Lucy Hart and the 1901 Census shows them living in Lawford Lane. The house must have been crowded because in addition to George and Lucy there were children, Frederick 21, George 16, Henry 14, and Horris 10, and then Elizabeth described as a mother's helper, mother-in-law Caroline Sewell and finally the lodger, James Styler. Subsequently the family moved to Deadmans Lane (now St Johns Road).

Henry got married and he and his wife Emita lived at Oxney Green Road.

During the course of his war service he was wounded and subsequently died on Thursday 8th February aged 30. He is buried in Abbeville Communal Cemetery Extension.

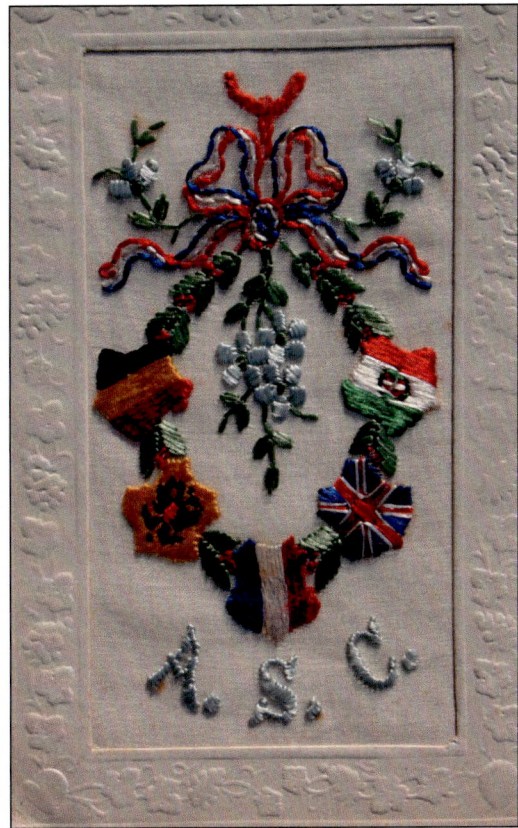

Postcards were at the height of their popularity · Silk cards provided a lucrative cottage industry for the French and were eagerly snapped up by the soldiers to send home. The bottom two are Army Service Corps cards, the top two show typical messages.

Operations in Palestine 1917

Henry Jeayes, Frederick Malyon and Harry Perrin all died on the same day, 26th March 1917. They were in the 1st/5th Essex Regiment. Joseph Young of the 6th Battalion died the day after. All were soldiers of the Essex Regiment who found themselves in Palestine.

Following the failure at Gallipoli the campaign against the Turks had switched to pushing against the southern part of their Empire. The support of the Arabs was enlisted. They sought independence from the Turks and the creation of their own nation states. How that was achieved and the mistakes that were made have repercussions today. However in 1917 the only consideration was to keep the disaffected Arabs as allies.

The 5th and 6th Battalions of the Essex Regiment were part of the 161st Brigade marching from Egypt into Palestine with the aim of attacking Gaza. During February they marched along roads of varying quality. They bivouacked amongst the fig trees of el Arish where all ranks were inoculated against cholera.

In March came the final steps of their journey crossing the frontier into Palestine. A cheer went up as they left the sandy desert and entered into an area of green herbage with the pungent aroma of sage. An officer recorded that few of them failed to be inspired on crossing to the Promised Land. Their first impression was of a green and fertile country with villages surrounded by orange groves. Unfortunately closer sight revealed the villages for the most part to be squalid affairs and in spite of the greenery the way was hot and dusty. And yet there remained a certain glamour and from the ridge of In Seirat they could see the famous city of Gaza.

"Gaza" is one of the honours which the Essex Regiment is permitted to bear upon its Colours for its part in the War. It was won by the 4th, 5th 6th and 7th Battalions constituting the 161st Brigade of the 54th (East Anglian) Division.

The overall plan for 1917 had been to ensure the defence of Egypt. With Egypt secure, the next objective was to defeat the Turks in Southern Palestine and occupy Jerusalem. To do that it was first necessary to take Gaza. This meant not only defeating the enemy but also overcoming the terrain and the lack of water.

The Essex, as part of the 161st Brigade, entered Palestine on the 25th March and halted at In Seirat at 7.30 in the morning. The 1st/5th under the command of Lieut. Colonel Gibbons was on outpost duty but subsequently was withdrawn to rest in readiness for the fighting which was envisaged for the next day. The Officers looked at the defences of Gaza City which was surrounded by entrenched positions.

Next day the troops were up early and by 10 am had reached the south side of El Burjabye Ridge. They were about to make tea when they were on the move again following the sandy bed of the Nukhabir until Mansura Ridge was seen a thousand yards away. In intense heat the Battalion advanced and it was here they suffered their first casualties from enemy shellfire. Captain Willmott of A Company was wounded and Lieut. Chester killed. In addition, several of the mules carrying the Lewis guns were killed by shrapnel so that the guns and ammunition had to be carried by hand.

Their objective was the hill known as Green Hill but the Turks were in a strong defensive position with their machine gunners having a mile and a half of plain ahead of them with little in the way of obstructions to impede the traversing of the guns. For reasons unknown, artillery support, which might have enabled Green Hill to be taken sooner and at less cost in casualties , was not forthcoming.

The 1/4th and 1/5th Essex were entrusted with the attack. The 1/5th had C and D Companies in the first three lines with A and B Companies as the fourth line. The enemy machine guns opened up with about a mile to go but at a fast pace, almost a run, the lines pressed on. Many were hit by machine gun fire and it was at this stage that Lieut. Colonel Gibbons was wounded.

An eye witness report:
"The Battalions did not rest at any time during the attack. When the hostile machine gun fire opened, both the 1/4th and 1/5th Essex quickly broke up from artillery formation into extended order, the forward movement being unchecked during this process. The attack was then pressed home. Although the casualties were heavy, it is the general opinion that they must have been heavier still but for the swift and determined advance of the Brigade through what was nothing less than a hurricane of machine gun fire".

An onlooker with the Signal Company also described the attack:
"Our headquarters were in a gully just below a large flat plain across which the Essex advanced under a terrific machine gun and rifle fire. They started in company columns, which rapidly split up into small groups, which, in turn, spread out until they were in long single lines advancing across the plain towards Green Hill, which was their objective. As they neared the Hill they fixed bayonets and charged, taking the Hill in just under an hour from the commencement of the attack, but, unfortunately, they suffered rather heavily from machine guns. The enemy had a clean sweep over the plain and the hideous tat-tat seemed almost incessant. Of all the horrible sounds of war, I think the devilish tat-tat of a Maxim is the most fear inspiring".

When the men neared the Turkish wire they found the protection of a slight rise. Lt. Colonel Gibbons having been wounded earlier in the attack, Captain Colvin lead the men in the final assault. The barbed wire proved a great trouble, men being caught in it and killed whilst extricating themselves. It was during this stage of the attack that Colonel Jameson, Commanding Officer of the 1st/4th Essex was mortally wounded.

The centre of the objective of the 1/5th Essex was a small stone hut. Three platoons of B and D Companies were halted with considerable casualties within

50 yards due to the machine gun fire. Captain Finn of No 5 Platoon B Company gave an account of this part of the attack.

> "I straightened out the line, but many more men were hit as the bullets continued to fall about us like hail. Windsor (2nd Lieut) called out to me that he was hit, so did Gilmore (2nd Lieut) who was some way off. Not only did he give this information, but he shouted out the details; this despite the fact that he dared not to move for fear of being hit again and that the engagement was continuing vigorously. A few minutes later Womersley (signalling officer), who was near to me on the left, got up and said that he was going to try and get in telephonic communication with the gunners to see if they could fire on to the stone hut. This was very desirable, as in part of the line we had no artillery support during the operation. Womersley, I heard afterwards, only got a little way before being hit twice. Those of us who were not wounded kept up a brisk fire".

Then they heard cheering as A and C Companies together with the remnants of the 1/4th and men of the 1/6th attacked and captured the defences. This was a notable feat for in addition to the wire entanglements the Turks had dug pits and filled them with barbed wire. Elsewhere along the line the Essex with bayonets fixed and with the impetus of the fresh troops from the 1/6th seized the Turkish trenches at about 5.50 pm. Those Turks remaining were bayoneted where they stood whilst others were shot down as they ran down the communication trenches.

As night fell the whole of the defensive position and the south eastern side of Gaza was in the hands of the British troops. They dug in and then did what they could for the numerous wounded but unfortunately there were no facilities to remove them for medical treatment as the advance had outstripped the Medical Corps. The evacuation of the wounded on the night of the 26th/27th proved a difficult task and some of them lay out on the ground all night. The heavy casualties of 26th March were mainly caused by three well protected Turkish machine guns. The total casualties of the 1st/5th Battalion on that day amounted to 341 including 9 of their officers killed.

And this leads on to the three Writtle men.

Henry Lawrence Jeayes was a Lance Serjeant in the 1st/5th Battalion. Originally rejected by the Public Schools Brigade because of defective eyesight he then enlisted in the Essex Regiment. He was the son of Isaac Herbert and Eva Mary Jeayes of Sunnyside, The Green.

Henry's death is mentioned in the Official History. He was then aged 26. He is buried in Gaza War Cemetery. The report of his death was carried in the Chronicle on the 27th April. Henry is also commemorated on the Old Merchant Taylors School Memorial.

Frederick Charles Malyon was a Private in A Company of the 1st/5th. He was born on 20th November 1894 and was baptised at All Saints on the 23rd December. He was the eldest child of Walter, a labourer, and Mary Ann who lived at St Johns Green.

He too is buried in Gaza War Cemetery.

The grave of Henry Jeayes

The grave of Frederick Malyon

Gaza War Cemetery

Henry Frederick Perrin – known as Harry – was a Private in the 5th Battalion. He was born on the 10th May 1897 and baptised at All Saints on the 18th July. He was one of the six children of Henry, a labourer and Annie Hannah Perrin of Oxney Green. Harry was 19 when he died. His body was not recovered and he is commemorated on the Jerusalem Memorial.

Henry Perrin

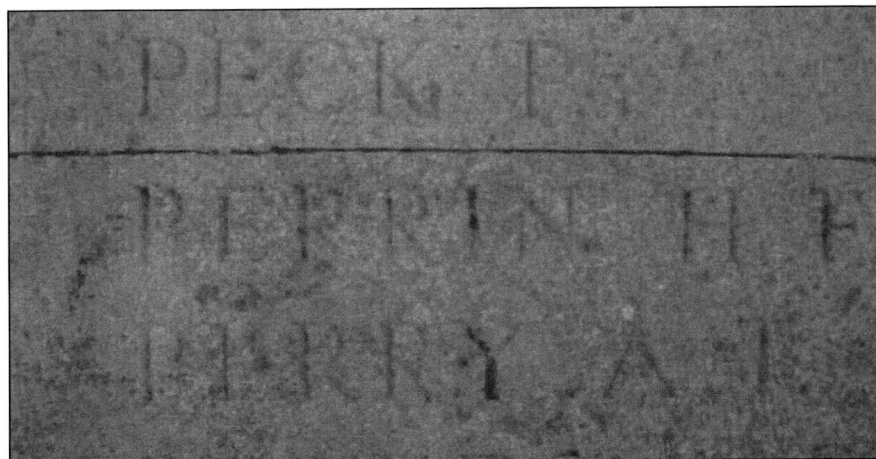

The name of Henry Perrin

It is perhaps unfortunate to say the least that the hard won position was given up two days later. In the face of a build up of Turkish troops, British Headquarters – despite what would appear to be opposition from commanders on the ground – felt that there was no option but to pull back to where they had started from.

Joseph Young, a Private in the 6th Battalion was involved in the attack on the 26th and the subsequent withdrawal on the 27th. Joseph was the son of Joseph and Elizabeth Young of Writtle Wick Cottages, Chignal Road - then part of Writtle Parish.

The 6th Battalion was part of the 161st Brigade of the 54th (East Anglian) Division. On the 26th March at 9.40am the Battalion moved closer to the firing line. Marching behind the 1/5th Essex they reached Mansura without loss. At 4.30pm the 6th went forward. By night fall C and B Companies were in a trench at Green Hill. Then it was learnt that the troop were to be withdrawn.

Three companies of the 6th were rearguard and were the last to quit the Hill at 2.25 am on the 27th. As they marched back they picked up wounded men and arms and at 5.15 am the Battalion was back to its starting point, tired and hungry. At 7 am the men having cleaned their rifles and filled their water bottles were awaiting tea when orders came to move forward to reoccupy the position that had only just been evacuated during the night.

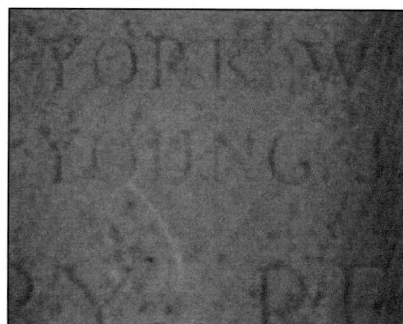

Joseph's name on the Memorial

The 6th held the forward slopes and later that morning the enemy launched an attack in strength. To avoid being cut off the advanced troops fell back by stages. From three sides the Turks attacked getting to within thirty yards of the parapet. Next day the weary Battalion was moved back to Headquarters. Casualties had been heavy over the two days. Of 27 officers, 7 had been killed and 11 wounded. On the 27th March, 5 of the officers were killed, and 209 other ranks killed and missing, mainly incurred when the Battalion disengaged from the encircling forces of the enemy.

Joseph, then aged 21, was one of those missing and he is commemorated on the Jerusalem Memorial.

Jerusalem Memorial

Back on the Western Front, April was again a cause for mourning in Writtle with three more deaths.

The Battle of Arras was forced upon the British by Nivelle. By a powerful blow at Arras the Germans would be drawn away from the French push on the Aisne. For once the British had plentiful ammunition and the troops were fresh, sheltered from the German shelling by the underground town in the caves and tunnels beneath Arras. The attack began on Easter Monday, 9th April, amidst sleet and snow squalls. In many places, notably Vimy Ridge, success was achieved. This would have been a good time to stop but the less than impressive progress of the French made it necessary to prolong the British offensive. And so, by May the troops were depleted and exhausted. By mid May the British had suffered 159,000 casualties in 39 days.

Leonard George Moss was born on 31st May 1894 and baptised at All Saints on the 29th July. The 1901 Census shows that he was the youngest of the four children of Frederick and Elizabeth Moss. His sisters were Emma, Margaret and Florence. Frederick was a carpenter/builder and they lived at Oxney Green. By the time of the First World War they had moved to Sycamore House in Writtle.

Leonard's Medical History

Leonard enlisted on the 25th November 1915 and the Attestation shows that he was then employed as a clerk with the London County and Westminster Bank and was living at 14 Musgrove Road, New Cross. He was admitted to the prestigious Honourable Artillery Company on the 2nd February 1916. Initially with B Company of the 3rd Battalion, he transferred to the 2nd Battalion and arrived in France on the 1st October 1916.

In March 1917 preparations were under way for the Battle of Arras. Preliminary work was required and in mid-March the 2nd Battalion was ordered to send patrols into Bucquoy. Colonel Ward objected most strongly because of the obvious strength of the enemy but to no avail. Men from A and B Companies went forward with the predictable result that they came under heavy fire and of course lost heavily. On the evening of March 16th the Battalion again attacked Bucquoy and by the 18th the enemy had retired. A great amount of repair had to be undertaken and to add to the men's discomfort the weather turned bitterly cold. Storms of sleet and snow succeeded each other day after day.

The Battalion relieved the Border Regiment on the 30th March and took over the line which ran midway between Mory and Ecoust St Mein. Shortly before dusk on the 31st the Battalion's advanced posts were subjected to heavy shelling and then a large force of Germans forced the H.A.C. out. So on the 1st April an attempt was made to recapture these strongholds. Zero hour was fixed at 2 am. A Company attacked under cover of a barrage. That attack failed as did another attack by C Company, the enemy machine guns proving an insuperable obstacle.

In these attacks 2 officers and 28 of the 2nd H.A.C. were killed. The positions were eventually captured on the 2nd April, taken back in a counter attack by the Germans two weeks later and then recaptured in September.

Leonard was one of those killed on the 1st April and is buried in the Honourable Artillery Company Cemetery at Ecoust St. Mein, which lies between Arras, Cambrai and Bapaume. This Cemetery was begun after the battle when the H.A.C. men who fell on the 31st March and 1st April were buried in what is now Plot 1 Row A.

THE TIMES, SATURDAY, MAY 5, 1917

KILLED.
55026 W. (Ston
Gnr. W. (Nan
lverley, 55891
rby); Cutler,
19 Gnr. C. (Sa
2842 Gnr. J.
S.E.); Jones, !
I. C. (St. Marg
85 Gnr. A. (W
mpton); Nutt
225 Gnr. A.

... Yearsley, 90437 Gnr. F. (Goldenhill).
H.A.C.—Amor, 7299 F. P. (Brixton, S.W.); Beaumont, 9279 H. A. (Wanstead, N.E.); Britton, 9013 B. H. (Walthamstow, N.E.); Brooks, 4895 W. C. (Catford, S.E.); Buck, 9022 W. B. (Walsall); Clemishaw, 7482 W. (Leeds); Clubb, 6996 R. E. (East Ham, E.); Cooke, 9281 E. R. (Tilehurst); Davidson, 5401 Cpl. W. H. (Manchester); Doughty, 9517 C. L. (Watford); Hutchinson, 6508 L.-Cpl. S. F. (Carshalton); Knight, 5282 L.-Cpl. E. J. (Clapham, S.W.); Lawrance, 4281 H. E. (Thornton Heath); Livett, 5537 L.-Cpl. A. E. (King's Somborne); Masham, 9469 F. H. (Wallington); Moss, 6900 L. G. (Writtle); Phillips, 3154 Sgt. P. C. (Holloway, N.); Pilcher, 9158 F. G. (Walmer); Rainer, 6531 W. W. (Norwood, S.E.); Smethurst, 7288 C. V. (Finsbury-circus, E.C.); Sworder, 9098 J. L. (Ipswich); Taylor, 5115 A. G. (Putney, S.W.); Trinder, 5789 H. C. (Maida Vale, W.); Walton, 9472 W. G. (Runcorn); West, 5120 E. A. (Camberwell, S.E.); Wilson, 9245 C. J. (Leyton, N.E.); Yealley, 7567 J. K. S. (Colyton).

Extract from The Times of 5th May 1917

On the 3rd August the War Office authorised the release of Leonard's personal property to his father. The rather meagre number of personal possessions comprised a pipe, flash lamp, air pillow, razor strop, pair of mittens, a French book and a scarf.

Ecoust St Mein Cemetery
(Contains 1,845 burials)

The Grave of Leonard Moss'
"Gone but not forgotten"

Leonard is buried in the same grave as his comrade in the Hon. Artillery Company, Private F.H. Masham

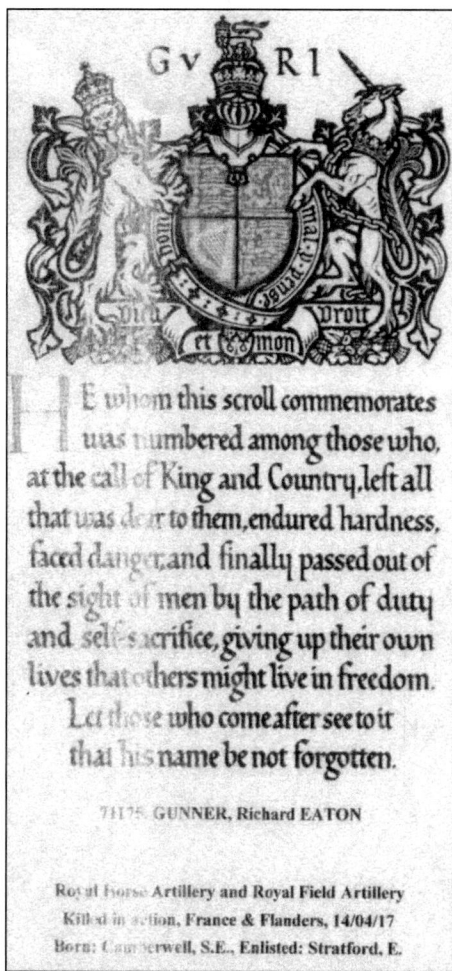

Richard's Commemorative Scroll

Richard Eaton is named on the Memorial but tracing which Richard Eaton proved difficult as no family details whatsoever were shown. Of the Eatons listed it was possible to reduce these down to three likely names and then by process of elimination arrive at the man believed to be our Richard Eaton. This indicates that he was born in Camberwell. He enlisted in Stratford and was a Gunner in the 122nd Battery Royal Field Artillery/Royal Horse Artillery.

Richard died during the Battle of Arras on the 14th April 1917 and is buried in Athies Communal Cemetery Extension, Pas de Calais. Athies had been captured on the 9th April and the Cemetery Extension was begun immediately after the capture and used for subsequent casualties.

Although nothing is known of Richard's family, a copy of the commemorative scroll has been traced.

Athies Communal Cemetery Extension
(Contains 310 burials)

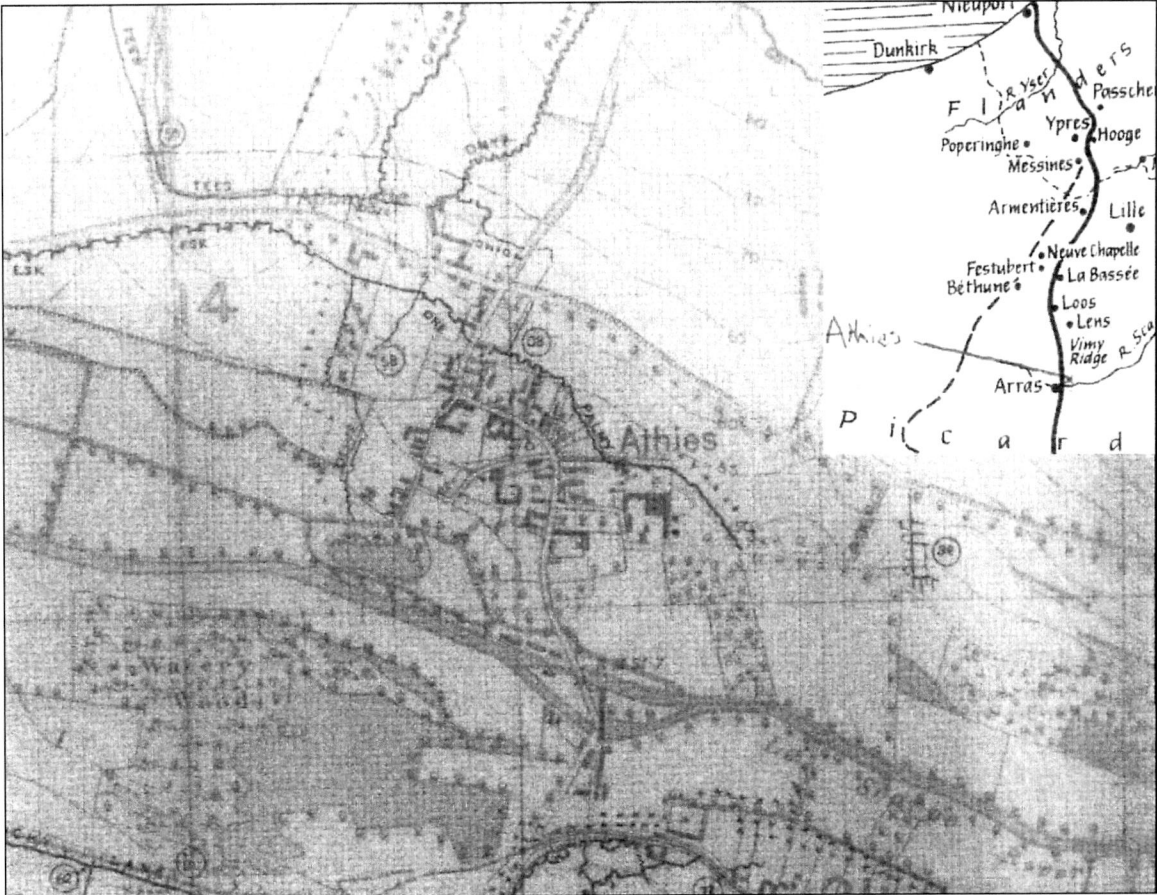
Trench Map of Athies and area

April 1917 Athies; a field gun crew move the gun to a new position
(photograph by kind permission of the Imperial War Museum)

The Cross of Sacrifice,
Athies Communal Cemetery

Richard Eaton's Grave

April 1917; Artillery Ammunition and supply limbers pass through the ruins of Athies
(photograph by kind permission of the Imperial War Museum)

Another artilleryman was **Alfred James Usborne**. He was Acting Major in the 50th Brigade, Royal Horse Artillery and Royal Field Artillery.

Alfred was born on the 13th June 1889 although the records show that he was not baptised at All Saints until 28th July 1897. His parents were Thomas and Frances Alice Usborne. Thomas' life is described with some detail in The Events in Writtle 1915.

Alfred joined the Royal Horse and Field Artillery as a 2nd Lieutenant on the 29th July 1908. He served in India between November 1908 and December 1912. The War saw him promoted to Captain and then as Acting Major.

The War Diary for April shows the 50th Brigade in almost constant action in the Fampoux/Arras area. Alfred was in command of D Battery. The Artillery laid on creeping barrages ahead of troop advances, bombarded enemy positions, engaged in specialist tasks such as wire cutting and shelled the opposing artillery. Of course their opposite numbers on the German side engaged in much the same activities.

British infantry around a ditched tank on the Fampoux Road April 1917
(photograph by kind permission of the Imperial War Museum)

On the 11th April at dawn the Artillery moved forward to positions behind Fampoux and opened fire at 10 am. The troops' target was Roeux and a creeping barrage was laid on. The attack failed and in the ensuing counter fire from the enemy Alfred was slightly wounded but remained on duty. The Diary records that heavy snow fell in the evening.

The collection of warehouses, chimney stacks and other buildings making up the Chemical Works at Roeux had been fortified by the Germans. The Works was connected by tunnels to a big concrete blockhouse hidden amongst the outbuildings of a nearby chateau. It was one of the strongest defensive positions in the Arras sector.

As April progressed they were engaged more or less constantly laying down covering fire for the troops. However they were frequently under fire themselves from German artillery and their casualties increased.

On the 27th April orders were received for a fresh attack on Rouex for the next day. The attack commenced at 4.25 am. The rate of fire for the 18 pounders was 3 rounds per gun per minute and then six minutes before the infantry was to assault the rate was increased to 4 rounds per minute. Again the assault failed and the line was left in practically the same position as before. The batteries were heavily shelled by the enemy.

On the morning of the 29th the batteries were again heavily shelled, D battery suffered ten casualties. B and D were to move to fresh positions and the Colonel carried out a reconnoitre in the region of the Point du Jour. But then the enemy started to shell very heavily again during the afternoon. D Battery took the brunt of this with three officers killed by one shell – Lieut. Jacobson, Lieut. Turner and Major Usborne.

Alfred is buried in St Catherine British Cemetery near Arras. There is a plaque in All Saints Church commemorating the Usborne sons showing Alfred's name

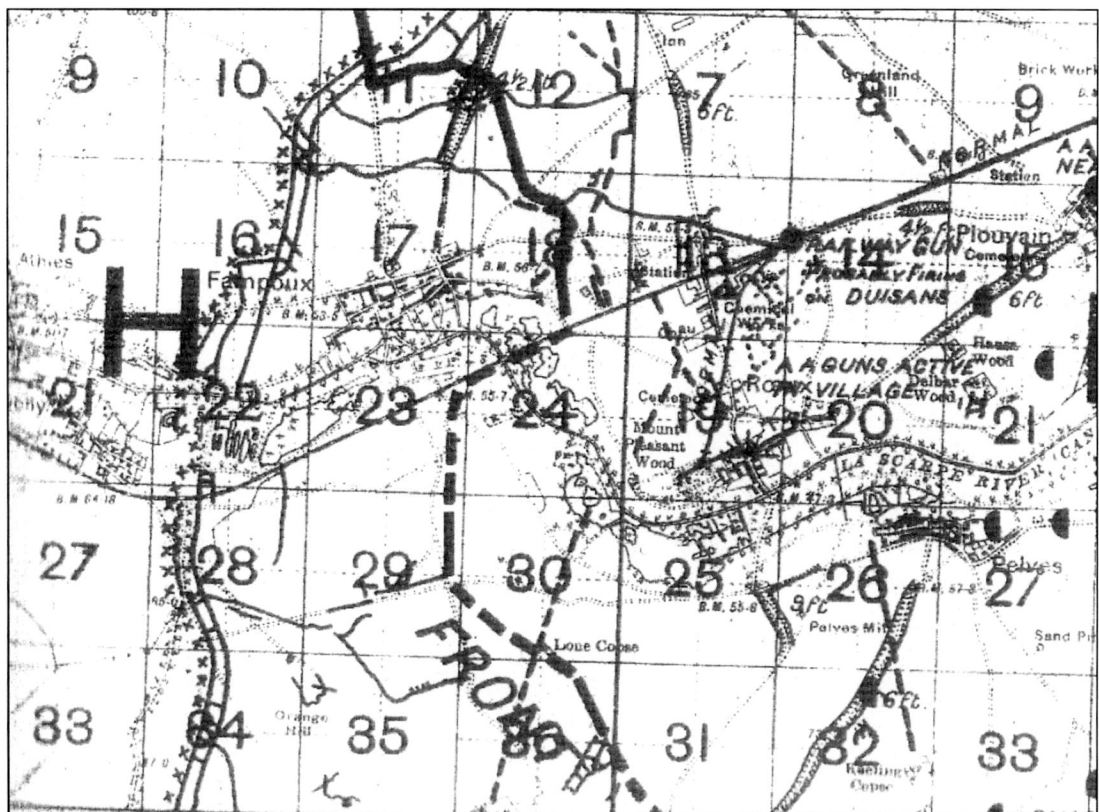

Fampaux to the left; the Chemical Works centre. The map comments on German gun emplacements. The Chemical Works was finally taken on the 11th May. These villages lie a few miles to the east of Arras

Bringing up an 18-Pounder

The Male Usborne Family
Left to right: Alfred James; John; Robert Arthur; Edward Francis; Henry
Lawrence; Thomas Masters; Thomas (father)

The Female Usborne Family
Left to right: Frances Alice (mother), Margaret Anne; Mary Elizabeth (Collier),
Winifred Maud (Scofield), Mabel Elexina, Edith Hardcastle (known as Enid)

St Catherine British Cemetery, Arras
(348 burials)

The grave of Alfred James Usborne

ALSO OF THEIR SONS,
ROBERT ARTHUR,
BORN FEB: 23ʳᵈ 1875: DIED JAN: 21ˢᵗ 1909.
ALFRED JAMES,
BORN JUNE 13ᵗʰ 1880: KILLED IN ACTION APR: 29ᵗʰ 1917.
JOHN,
BORN SEPTEMBER 7ᵗʰ 1878: DIED SEPTEMBER 18ᵗʰ 1934.
THOMAS MASTERS,
BORN DEC:11ᵗʰ 1800 : DIED FEB: 1ˢᵗ 1952
HENRY LAWRENCE,
BORN SEP: 2ⁿᵈ 1800 : DIED AUG: 21ˢᵗ 1954
EDWARD FRANCIS
BORN MAR 30ᵗʰ 1873 DIED APR: 8ᵗʰ 1961.

The Usborne plaque in Writtle Church

John Poole enlisted in the Buffs, The East Kent Regiment

Les Buffs chargeant les troupes alliées pendant l'assaut du Château des Flandres à Radinghem.

D'après "The Sphere"   par C. Clark.

The Buffs in action at Radinghem – a contemporary postcard

John's family lived in St Johns Green in what must have been crowded conditions. The head of the family was John Poole Senior described in the 1901 Census as an agricultural labourer; he was also Church Sexton.

His wife was Esther although there is some confusion as to her name and she may have been called Elizabeth. The rest of the household comprised:-

Edward	24
Alfred	20
John	17
Henry	15
Frederick	14
Septimus	12
Octavius	10
Emily	8
Ruth	6
Alfreda	3
Barbara	10 months

And finally a grandchild, William aged 6

Possibly there was another child who had either left home or died earlier, the clue being in the names of Septimus and Octavius.

In 1917 the 4th Battalion The Buffs was amongst the troops heading for the Balkans as part of the British Salonika Force. The involvement of British troops at Salonika came about because of the alliances formed in the War. Britain had to take account of the views of her partners, especially France.

Having beaten off two invasions by Austro-Hungarian forces in 1914, the small Serbian Army was exhausted. It had been hoped to persuade Bulgaria to join the Allies and thus prop up the Serbs but better offers from Germany saw Bulgaria join the Central Powers. And so an Anglo-French force to confront the Bulgarians was required. The Austro-Hungarian navy dominated the Adriatic which left the only deep water port that of Salonika in neutral Greece. Negotiations were still ongoing when the Anglo-French troops landed.

Reinforcements came by troopship from Marseilles following a train journey through France. Most transport was in cattletrucks, cramped and with only the most basic of facilities. Marseilles must have seemed wonderful by comparison. Once out of the rest camps the soldiers could relax, explore the city, drink cheap wine and for many of the young men, enjoy the company of women, the cheap and the not so cheap.

The delights of Marseilles all too soon had to be left behind on a troopship bound for Salonika. Troopships varied. Some, the converted passenger liners, offered good if crowded accommodation. Others were appalling especially when shared with the horses.

Troops embarking for Salonika

Despite the overcrowding, the biggest worry was the threat of submarines. The Allies might control much of the surface of the Mediterranean but German and Austrian U-boats scored regular successes throughout the war.

On the 3rd May the troops left Marseilles on board the Cunard liner "Transylvania". The liner had become a troopship two years earlier. She was designed to carry 1379 pasengers but when she left Marseilles she carried 200 officers and 2800 other ranks in addition to her crew. As she crossed the Gulf of Genoa on the 4th May the German submarine U63 torpedoed her some 2 ½ miles south of Cape Vado. Hit on the port side in the engine compartment the "Transylvania's" Captain made a course for the shore. Another ship, the "Matsu" closed with her to take off men but then a second torpedo struck the "Transylvania" and she sank soon after.

414 lives were lost. The bodies recovered at Savona were buried in a special plot in the town cemetery. Others were buried elsewhere in Italy, France and Monaco. John's body was never recovered and within the town cemetery is the Savona Memorial which commemorates the 275 men whose bodies were never recovered or who have no known grave.

SS Transylvania

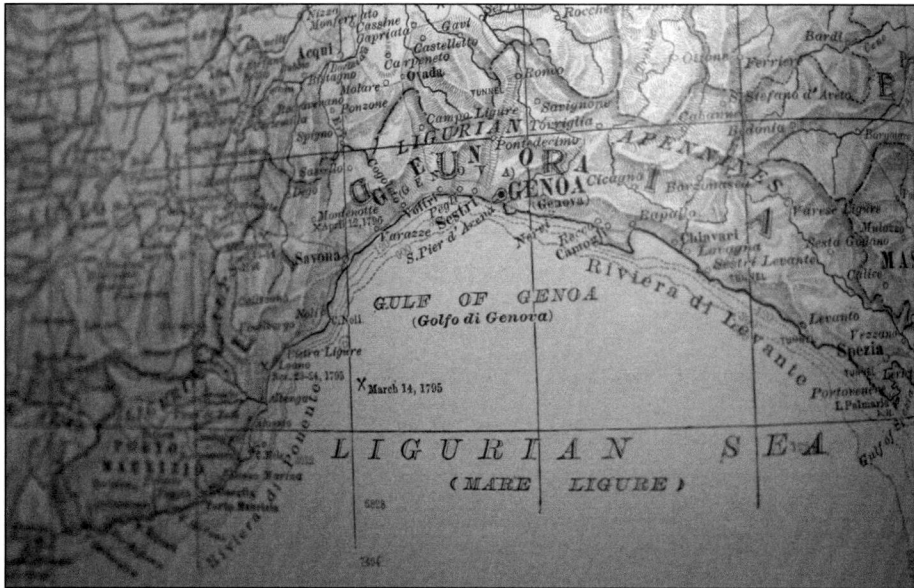

Gulf of Genoa

Savona Town Cemetery
Savona Memorial

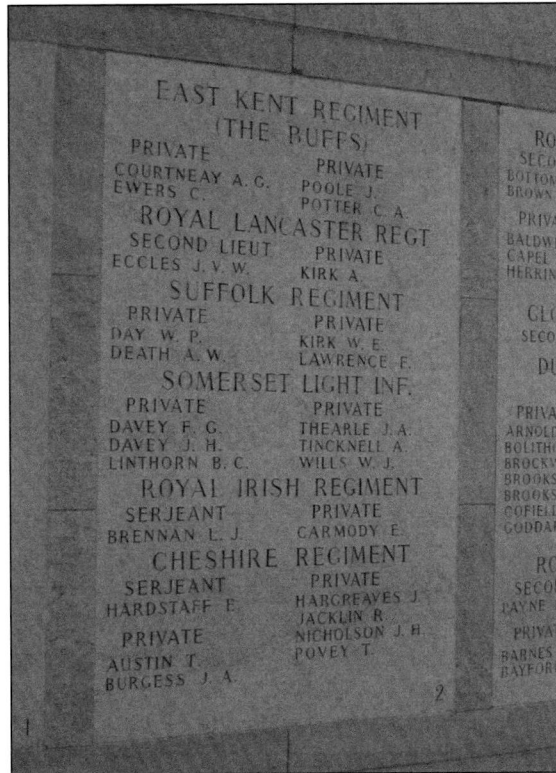

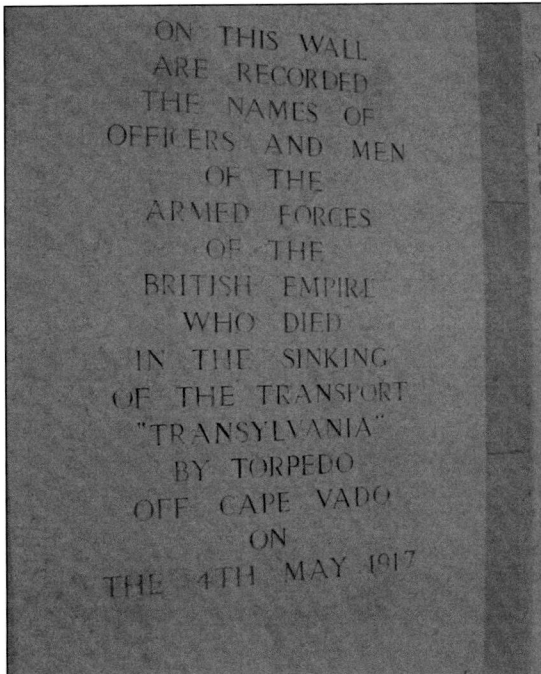

Savona Cemetery and Memorial; showing the name of John Poole.

Photographs courtesy of Roberto Giannotti and Ivonne De Luca, of the Savona Mayor's office

Ernest Sharp appears to have been the only child of Arthur and Sarah Sharp. The 1901 Census shows just them and 3 year old Ernest living at Town End, Lordship Road - until the 1960s Town End was a row of eight cottages and a shop where Prestons Garage is now situated.

TOWN END COTTAGES 1920's

Town End 1920; Town End Cottages are on the left behind the telegraph pole

Approximately the same view 2008

Ernest joined the Middlesex Regiment, 13th Battalion. The Middlesex were attached to X Corps of the 73rd Brigade 24th Division. The 24th Division had a true baptism of fire being involved in major battles from the latter part of 1915 and through 1916. 1917 found the 24th Division at Ypres.

The 13th Battalion's War Diary for June shows them practising for the next big assault. Their training ground was in the Bois de Beauvoorde just north of Steenvoorde. On the 5th they moved to a camp where they had to sleep in the open as there were no tents or huts there.

The Battle of Messines was to gain possession of the Messines – Wytschaete Ridge from where the Germans overlooked the British lines. The task of the 24th Division was to attack along a front of about 9 miles from St Yves north of Ploegsteert Wood to Mount (a misnomer) Sorrel. The final objective was to be the Oosttaverne Line.

This shows the beginning of Ongar Rd. The area on the right was known as Town End. c.1907

The cottages behind the cart and those behind the sign post are the Town End Cottages

Approximately the same view 2008

The major factor was to be the explosion of 19 deep mines. Tunnellers had been at work on these mines for many months. 8000 yards of mine galleries had been driven and over one million pounds of explosives used as charges.

At zero hour 3.07 am on the 7th June the mines erupted, the whole ground lifting into the air in a volcano of flame and smoke and debris. Added to this was a barrage of shell fire and it was little surprise that when the British advanced they found the few German survivors in the shattered earth too dazed to offer any resistance.

Earlier 13th Battalion had moved up to the Assembly Area, the trenches between Swan Chateau and Chateau Cigare. By 2am they has reached the assembly trenches; later they moved into Ecluse Trench and Old French Trench and then to the jumping off trench.

At 3.10 pm the Battalion went over the top with their objective the Green Line, a line extending from Ravine Wood via Olive Trench to the Hollebeke Road. Ravine Wood was taken but they had difficulties in capturing the left half of Olive Trench.

But at Ravine Wood the Battalion captured 120 Germans, guns and other equipment.

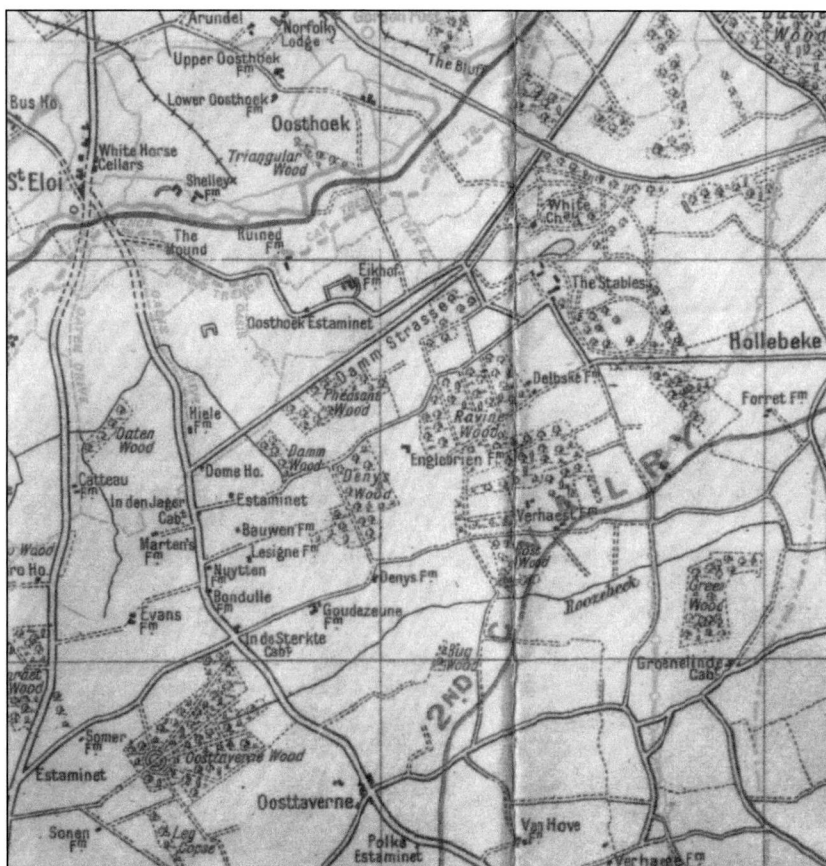

Ravine Wood in the centre

The 8th June started quietly but patrols found part of Olive Trench was still held by the enemy. Then artillery fire opened up with both sides engaged in heavy shelling in the evening. Next day a strong effort was to be made to take Olive Trench. The Battalion Diary reads as follows:-

"Strong patrols pushed up Olive Trench at dusk Trench found strongly held and could not be captured without artillery preparation. 2nd Lt. Makeham wounded and missing in this operation. Other casualties about 5. Direct hit on Battn HQ (a converted German dug out). No harm done."

The Battalion was due to be relieved on the 11th June and so the 10th was a day in which the Battalion would not have to engage the enemy, rather it would have spent the day in a tidying up operation. Unfortunately they were not to be given any rest. The Battalion Diary reads:-

"June 10th. Steady shelling at intervals. Heavy burst of fire of all calibres at 10 pm".

Aged 19, Ernest was killed that day. His body was not recovered and he is commemorated on the Menin Gate.

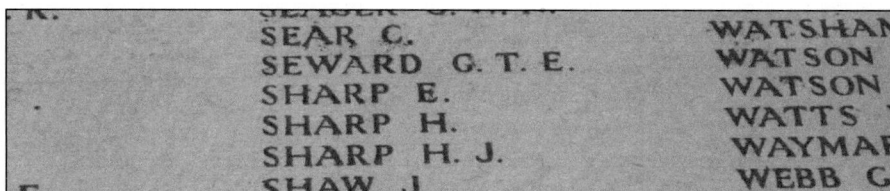

Ernest's name on the Menin Gate

The race to the sea in late 1914 ended in that part of Belgium bordering the Channel, as in the rest of the Front, in a stalemate position. The Germans had been thwarted by the King of the Belgians' order to open all the sluice gates thus flooding all the low lying ground.

The northernmost section of the Western Front was largely held by the French and Belgians but there was also a strong British contingent.

Basil Harold White was the son of Edwin and Harriet White. Edwin was a market gardener owning the Lawford Nursery. Basil had been born when they lived at Takeley.

In 1917 the Northamptonshire Regiment – in which Basil had enlisted – was part of the British Force. XV Corps relieved the French in the sector from St. Georges (now Sint Joris) to the sea. They saw particularly fierce fighting at Nieuport (now Nieuupoort) in July.

Postcards showing the ruins of Nieuport

The first postcard was sent in 1924 with the message "We have been in Nieuport today and seen the battlefield. The Belgians are rebuilding very quickly. We are enjoying the trip very much". It concludes with a message familiar to holiday makers wherever and whenever - "Please water plants".

"The Times" of 12th July carried reports of the fighting and the gains made by the Germans. The report refers to the German attack the day before, the 11th, and describes a preliminary 24 hour intense bombardment.

Basil, a private in the 1st Battalion was lost during that bombardment on the 10th. The Essex Chronicle reported some nine months later, on 19th April 1918, "Mr & Mrs E T White of Lawford Nurseries Writtle having previously been notified that their son Pte. B H White Northants Regt. was missing on 10th July 1917 the Army Council now inform them that it is concluded that his death took place on that date (or since)".

Basil, then aged 28 is commemorated on the Nieuport Memorial, Nieupoort, West Vlaanderen. The Memorial was designed by W B Binnie with sculpture by C S Jagger and bears the names of 548 men who died and have no known grave.

The Nieuport Memorial

Basil White's name on the Memorial

SET-BACK ON THE COAST.

YSER POSITIONS LOST.

CAPTURE OF HALICZ.

BRITISH RAID ON CONSTANTINOPLE.

The War : 3rd Year : 343rd Day.

British troops have lost positions on the Belgian coast. The Germans, at the close of 24 hours' bombardment, in which our defences were levelled, won the ground we held to the east of the Yser mouth on a front of 1,400 yards. The sector was isolated by the destruction of the bridges across the river. Farther south, opposite Lombartzyde, the enemy was driven back to his own lines after getting into our advanced positions. The enemy claims 1,250 prisoners.

Our advanced posts east of Monchy, on the Arras front, were very slightly pressed back in places yesterday morning.

Halicz has fallen to General Korniloff's victorious troops, who are sweeping forward on a 20-mile front in Southern Galicia with their right wing on the Dniester. In their three days' offensive

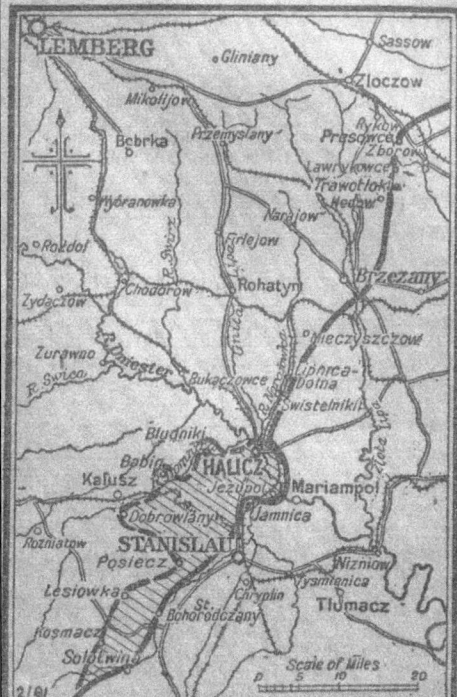

AN ENEMY SUCCESS.

ATTACK ON A 1,400-YARD FRONT.

1,250 PRISONERS CLAIMED.

The following telegraphic dispatches were received yesterday from General Headquarters in France :—

11.32 A.M.—After a very intense bombardment lasting for 24 hours the enemy made a determined attack on our positions on the Nieuport front yesterday evening at 7.45 p.m.

Owing to the concentrated and heavy nature of the enemy's artillery fire the defences in the Dunes sector near the coast were levelled and this sector was isolated by the destruction of the bridges across the River Yser.

The enemy succeeded in penetrating our posi-

tions here on a front of 1,400 yards and to a depth of 600 yards, thus reaching the right bank of the River Yser near the sea.

Farther south, opposite Lombartzyde, after gaining temporarily some of our advanced positions, the enemy was driven back to his own lines by a counter-attack.

10.12 P.M.—The extreme intensity of the enemy's artillery fire on the Nieuport front has now diminished. Our artillery continues to be active.

The enemy attacked our advanced posts east of Monchy-les-Preux [east-south-east of Arras] this morning on a front of about 800 yards and succeeded in pressing some of them back very slightly.

An attempt by the enemy to rush one of our posts north-west of Lens early this morning was driven off. One wounded prisoner remained in our hands.

Bad weather yesterday prevented aerial activity on either side until the evening. During the night we bombed two enemy aerodromes, all our machines returning safely.

Belgian report, July 11 :—

During the night the Germans continued to bombard Furnes.

To-day there were the usual artillery actions on the whole of the front, notably at Ramscapelle, Dixmude, and Het Sas.

THE ENEMY ACCOUNT.

German official report, July 11 :—

Front of Crown Prince Rupprecht.—On the Dunes sector of the Marine Corps detach-

The Times of 12 July 1917

The Home Front

And what of the Home Front as the country contemplated the onset of the fourth year of the War. On the same day – 12th July – that The Times reported the action at Nieuport there were a number of news features which have a somewhat familiar ring today.

Cigarettes were in the news but in 1917 the reason was a Board of Trade Order fixing maximum tobacco prices, the effect of which was to reduce the price of a packet of 10 of the most popular brands from 5d. to 4½d (about 2½p to 2p)

And drugs were in use then albeit perhaps not to a great extent. Two Chinese found in possession of opium were fined £50 and £5 with the alternative of 81 and 26 days imprisonment respectively.

The Balkans, the scene in recent years of bloody conflict with claims of ethnic cleansing by the Serbs, were, in 1917, the location for precisely the opposite; claims that our allies the Serbs, were being systematically exterminated.

And alcohol was a problem then as now although probably not on the same scale. Today it is anti-social behaviour; then it was reported that the successful prosecution of the War was being hampered by the excessive consumption of intoxicating liquor.

Northern Ireland now has a governing body with Sinn Fein playing a major part. In 1917 the Nationalist Party was stunned by the size of the Sinn Fein majority in the East Clare election.

Controversy raged over the conduct of the war in Mesopotamia, (now the country of Iraq). Mesopotamia had been invaded because of its oil. The Times reported that on the eve of the Mesopotamia debate in Parliament the Government had decided to hold an inquiry into the conduct of all persons concerned, both soldiers and civilians.

What could be more topical in the light of the current campaign against so-called "gas guzzling" cars than this exchange in the House of Commons. Mr MacVeagh asked the Government Minister, Mr Macpherson, if he had noticed at the Liverpool by-election a number of high-power motor-cars were being used. The Minister replied to laughter that "he had used the bus" Another MP complained that the Secretary to the Air Board was driving around London in a high-powered car to which the Minister gave equally short shrift "I do not see why he should not".

War or no War, the Summer sales were in full force. The Daily Mirror advertisements generally concentrated on food and drink but perhaps the Magneto belt should have been available to the soldiers given its wonderful properties!

In Writtle, to show that locally as well as nationally matters in the news now were news in 1917, the Chronicle carried a story of the dedication of the bells at All Saints. Two bells had been re·cast and the other five re·tuned. New fittings had been provided.

Chronicle 19th April 1917:
Writtle Bells Dedicated

In August the Hylands Park Fete was advertised, admission sixpence. A bit different from the price for today's event; it would certainly have been quieter and back then it was for good causes.

And for final proof that there's nothing new there is this advertisement in the Weekly News

J. Brittain Pash
Advertisement

At the Parish Council meeting on the 28th March the clerk was instructed to write to the Matron of the Hospital that the Council, whilst not wishing to restrict the recreation of the wounded soldiers, did not think that the square at the bottom of the village where all the traffic converged was a suitable place to play football and if continued might lead to serious injury or damage to property · the Village Green was quite free to the men.

This early postcard shows that part of St Johns Green nearest to the Cock and Bell junction which was known as St John's Square

Scouting in recent years has made an impact on Writtle with the Jamboree. The 1st Writtle Troop was busy growing food in 1917

Other Writtle news centred strongly on the war effort. Typical of these are stories carried in February. A social meeting with music and dancing was held by the Girls Club with 25 wounded soldiers at the Malthouse. At the Village Hall a meeting approved the formation of a War Savings Association for Writtle.

On the 17th August the Chronicle carried an account of air raids on Essex and Kent – a fore runner of things to come some two decades on.

FRIDAY, AUGUST 17, 1917.

AIR RAIDS ON ESSEX & KENT.

TRAGIC SCENES AT SOUTHEND.

BOMB FATALITIES NOW 32; INJURED 50

BRITISH AIRMEN'S FINE FIGHT WITH THE RAIDERS

TWO HUN MACHINES BROUGHT DOWN.

CHELMSFORD GENTLEMAN'S GRAPHIC STORY

As Christmas approached the Chronicle carried advertisements from well known Chelmsford names. Bolingbroke & Sons announced that because of the continuance of War their Departments would be filled with "useful and necessary articles".

The Chronicle urged its readers to buy War Bonds, a poster campaign re-inforced the message

PUT STRENGTH IN THE FINAL BLOW BUY WAR BONDS

George Jones served with the Royal Marine Artillery on board H.M.S. Vanguard.

George was the son of William and Julia Jones of Bridge Street and the brother of Frank Jones who died on the 29th September 1916. The War Graves Commission show Frank's mother, Julia as being housekeeper to William Hutley of Bridge Street.

George was born in April 1892 and joined the Royal Marine Artillery on the 15th January 1913 when he was 20. He gave his trade as a general labourer. On the 3rd March 1914 he joined H.M.S. "Duke of Edinburgh" and shortly afterwards, on 31st March, transferred to H.M.S. "Vanguard". His rank was that of Gunner.

"Vanguard" was laid down in 1908 as the last of the three St Vincent Class Dreadnoughts and was the ninth Royal Navy ship to bear the name. She came through Jutland unscathed and on the 9th July was at anchor in Scapa Flow.

At 11.20pm a great explosion occurred, "Vanguard" had blown up. She sank quickly taking over 800 of her crew down with her. The explosion had taken place in one of the magazines serving the amidships turrets P and Q. A definitive cause of the explosion has never been found. Sabotage was suspected but the more likely cause was unstable cordite.

George was aged 25. He is commemorated on the Portsmouth Memorial.

HMS Vanguard

HMS Vanguard in Scapa Flow

An unknown crewman of HMS Vanguard

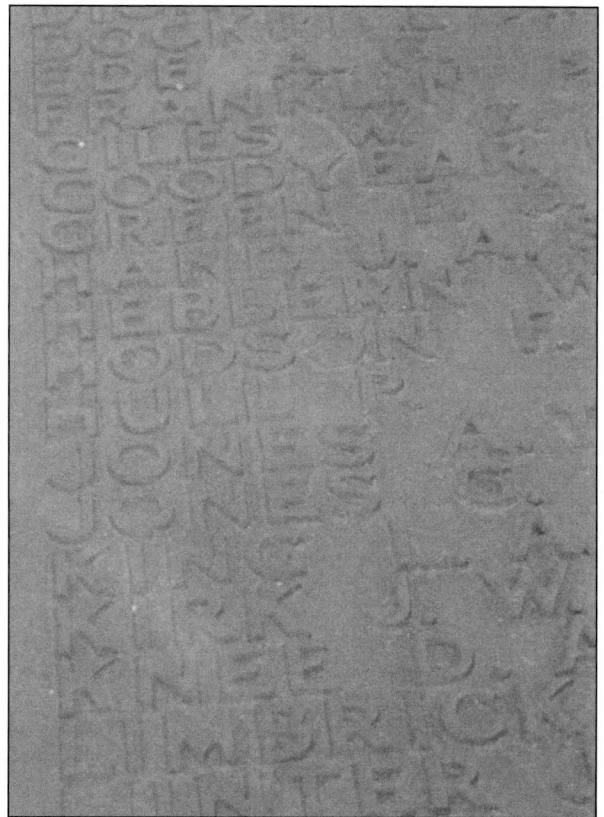

George's name on the Portsmouth Memorial

Little is known about the next Writtle man, **Charles Wilkinson.** The War Graves Commission shows C. Wilkinson as Private number 25210 in the 2nd (Garrison) Battalion, Essex Regiment who died on Monday, 16th July 1917. It is believed that he lived at St Johns Green, possibly Maypole House.

The 2nd Garrison Brigade was formed in 1915 from drafts of officers and men unfit for active service on account of age, infirmity or wounds. The 2nd was sent to the Mhow area of India in 1916.

Sending British troops to Mesopotamia (now Iraq) was done for a number of reasons but the oil factor was fundamental. But then the campaign grew with the temptation to advance beyond securing oilfields to the capture of Baghdad. The Indian Expeditionary Force was dispatched and camp was set up in Basra. The appeal of Basra was limited. Filthy, no sanitation or water supply, roads slime tracks of muddy rubbish.

A Contemporary postcard of Basra

Following disaster at Kut, recovery took time but a new offensive began in February 1917. Kut eventually fell but there was still hard campaigning ahead with a number of engagements planned but the summer heat broiled away the possibility of more extensive operations. Troops suffered severely with some men dying from heat exhaustion.

Charles is buried in Grave IV.B.1 in Basra War Cemetery

Basra War Cemetery

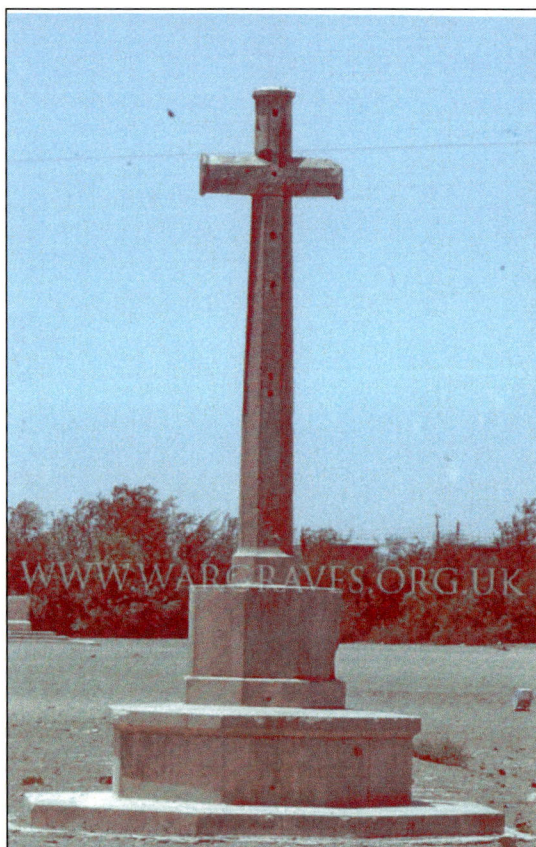
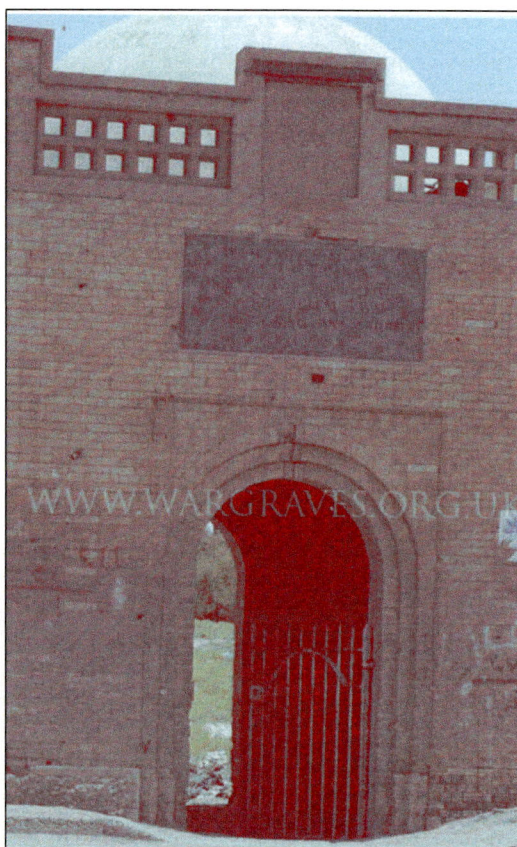

Basra War Cemetery. Photographs taken in 2006 showing damage to the headstones. The Cross of Sacrifice remains intact, although minus the sword, as does the stone bearing "Their Name Liveth for Evermore" inscription, albeit somewhat battered.

Bertie Gowers was born in Writtle on 29th May 1891 and was baptised at All Saints on the 2nd August. The 1901 Census shows his parents as Joseph, a brewery labourer, and Sarah and their children comprising Henry, 19 an agricultural labourer, Emily, 17 a domestic servant, Alfred, 15 a bricklayer's labourer and lastly Bertie aged 9. They lived at Bridge Street. Sarah died in 1908 aged 56 and her husband died in 1917.

By the time of the War Bertie was married. His wife was Phyllis Mary Gowers and they lived at 27 Angel Street, Hadleigh, Suffolk.

Bertie enlisted in the Essex Regiment but then transferred to the 9th Battalion Yorkshire Regiment. During July 1917 the 9th Battalion started in reserve at Dickebush, south west of Ypres, and over the next few days moved around the area.

On the 16th July A Company was in Canada Trench, B Company in Rudkin House, C Company in Metropolitan Left and D Company in Hedge St. Tunnels.

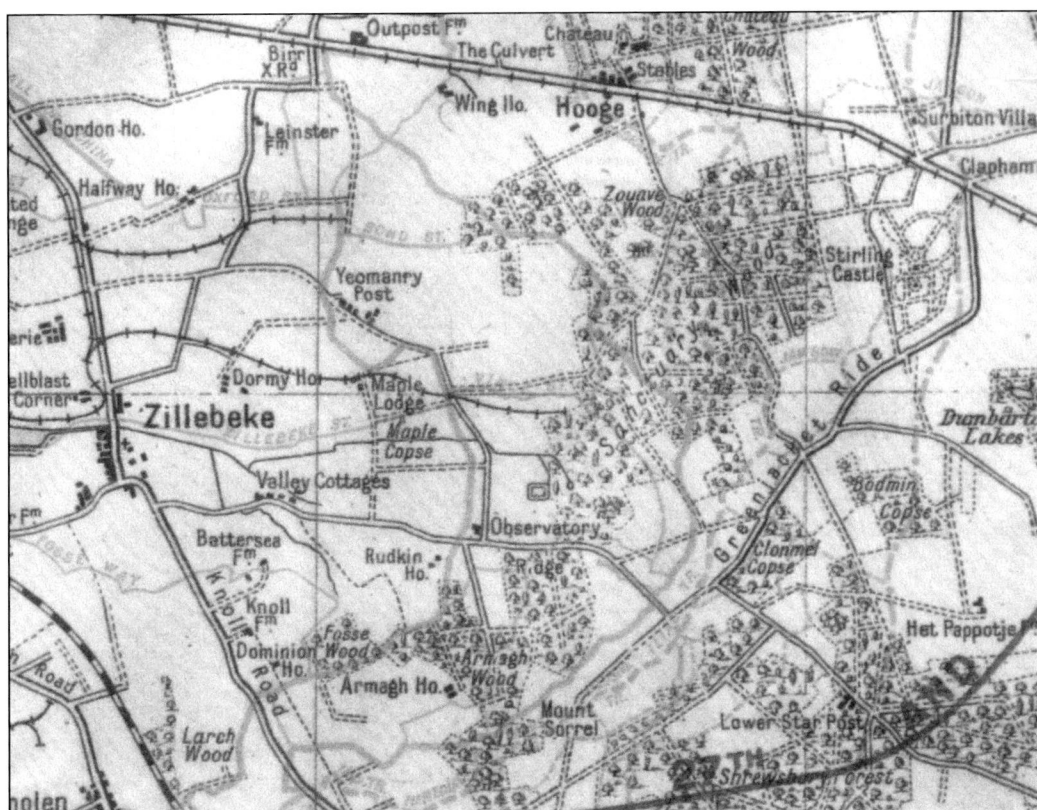

Trench Map showing Rudkin House

It is at this point that matters become confused. The War Diary for the Battalion does not record any deaths on the 17th July whereas the Commission's records clearly indicate Bertie did die on that date. The War Diary does show that the Battalion suffered four wounded on the 15th and possibly Bertie was one of those and died two days later and for various reasons the death was not recorded.

Bertie is known to be buried in Larch Wood (Railway Cutting) Cemetery, Ypres, although the exact location of his grave has been lost.

The Battalion was able to supply a copy of his memorial scroll which serves to eliminate the uncertainty as it shows the date of death as the 17th July. However it states killed in action although that could well just be a standard description.

Larch Wood (Railway Cutting) Cemetery
Zillebeke, alongside the Ypres/Comines Railway. 858 burials

Bertie Gowers' Headstone

Gv RI

HE whom this scroll commemorates was numbered among those who, at the call of King and Country, left all that was dear to them, endured hardness, faced danger, and finally passed out of the sight of men by the path of duty and self-sacrifice, giving up their own lives that others might live in freedom. Let those who come after see to it that his name be not forgotten.

41293, PRIVATE, Bertie GOWERS

9th Battalion.
Alexandra, Princess of Wales's Own (Yorkshire Regiment)
Killed in action, France & Flanders, 17/07/17
Born: Writtle, Essex, Enlisted: Chelmsford
FORMERLY 26292, ESSEX REGT.

Memorial Scroll

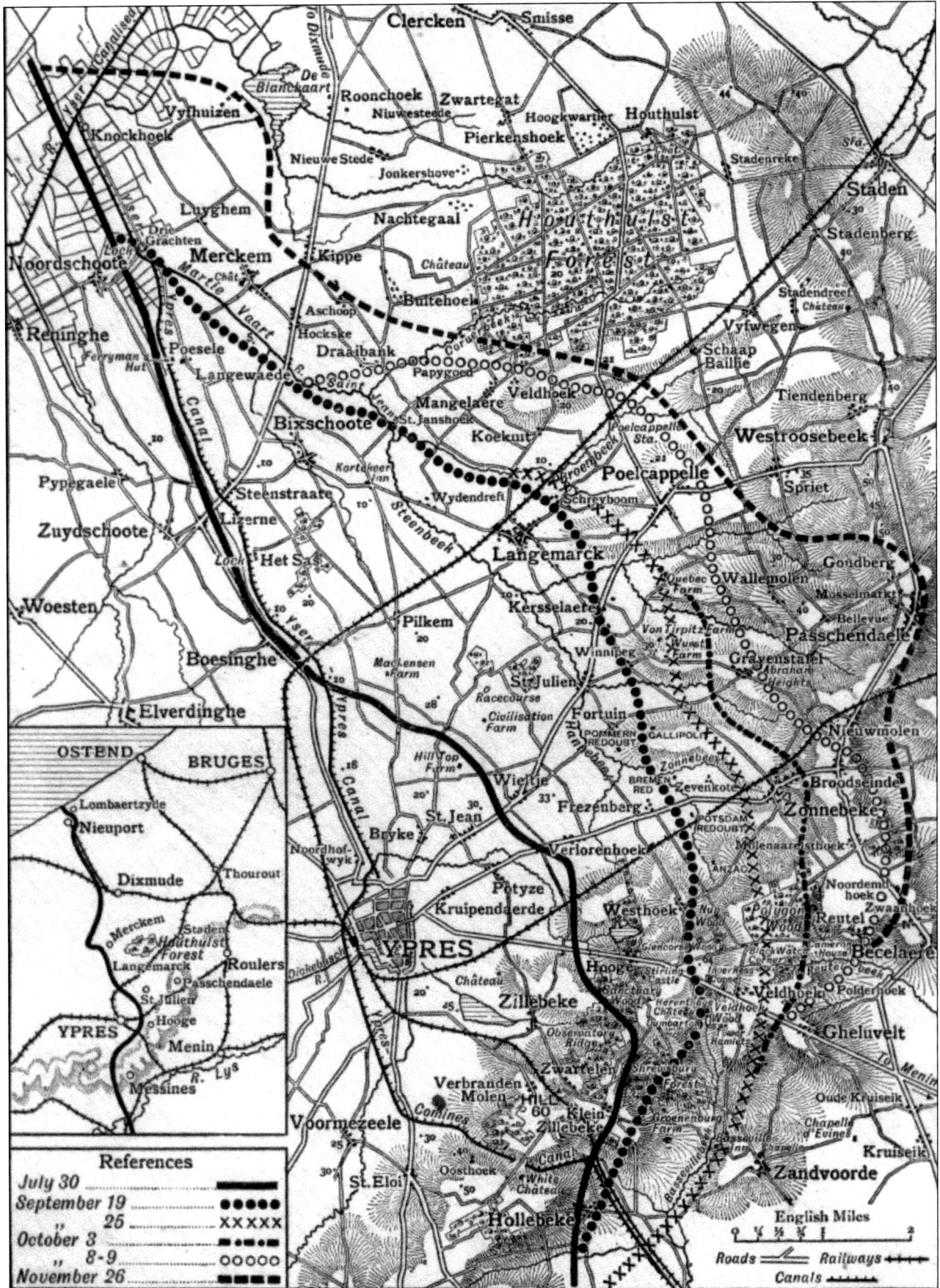

The Battle of Third Ypres 1917
(Passchendaele)

Perhaps the most evocative name from the First World War is that of **Passchendaele**. That name is but one part, the final stage, of The Third Battle of Ypres.

The Battle, and its execution, has been a cause of controversy. Field Marshall Sir Douglas Haig believed that the attack would clear the way to the Channel ports and lead to the long-hoped for breakthrough to open ground. But always the chances of that happening were unlikely.

The preceding years may not have seriously affected the morale of the British troops but the drain on manpower and equipment was such that another major assault was asking for almost superhuman qualities from the men. The crumbling of the Russians was already leading to the transfer of some German troops and equipment to the Western Front. The Germans had also perfected defence in depth with concrete pillboxes, enormously fortified bunkers, machine gun nests and the usual barriers of barbed wire.

Ziegler Blockhouse, Pilckem Ridge

There was no question of surprise and the usual bombardment lasting several days had the effect of simply destroying the already ruined landscape. All these negative factors were known or ought to have been known. And then to cap it all the summer of 1917 was one of the wettest in living memory, deluging the already marsh like ground and creating a sea of mud.

The plan was to take all the high ground surrounding Ypres, including Passchendaele, within a fortnight. As it turned out the horrendous conditions meant that some three and a half months elapsed before that goal was achieved at a cost of some 300,000 British casualties. Even then the break through never materialised and the final tragedy of Third Ypres was that in the next Spring the Germans swept through re-taking all the ground won at such a high price.

Stretcher bearers struggle in mud up to their knees
to carry a wounded man to safety; near
Boesinghe, 1st August 1917
(By kind permission of the Imperial War Museum)

The first Writtle casualty of 3rd Ypres was **Frank Pearson.** He was born in Writtle, about 1889, the son of George and Sarah of Chequers Lane. George was a journeyman baker. There were three brothers all older than Frank.

Originally Frank was with the Royal Army Service Corps but then switched to the Royal Welsh Fusiliers, the 17th Battalion. The Welsh Fusiliers were part of the 38th Division.

At 3.50am on the 31st July the 38th Division went into action just south of Artillery Wood. This was the first stage of the Battle – the Battle of Pilckem Ridge – which took place from the 31st July to the 2nd August.

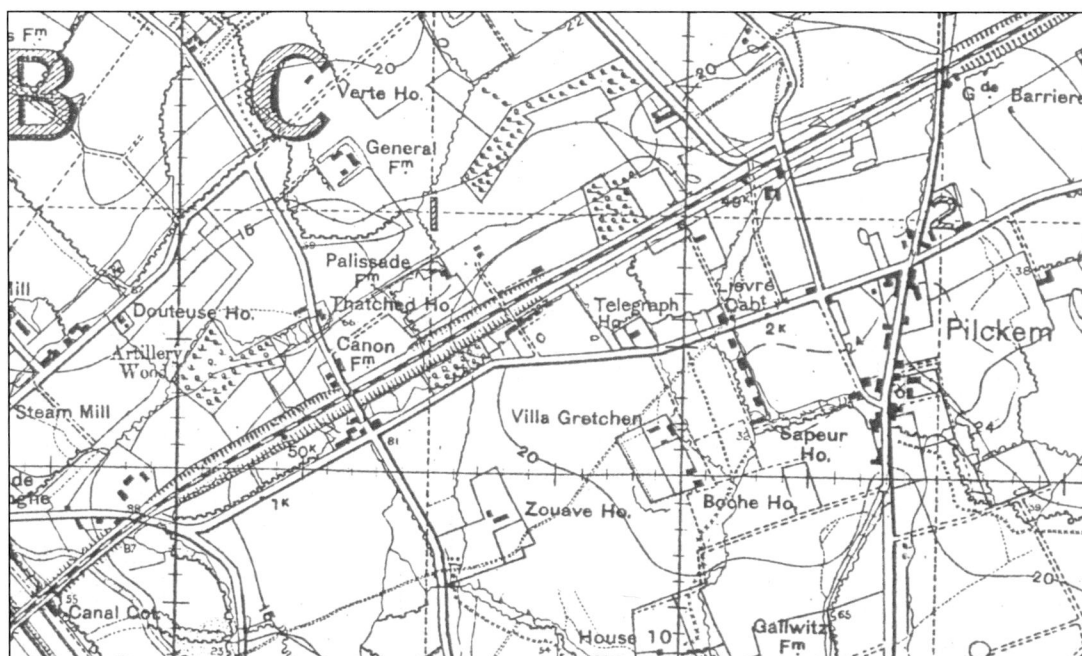

Trench Map of 1917, Artillery Wood left

The attack had been preceded by the usual lengthy bombardment. By the 31st July 4.3 million shells had been fired at the enemy lines. But even this was insufficient to destroy the German defences although what it did achieve was the final destruction of the surface of the ground - ground over which the troops would have to advance.

Individual shell-holes overlapped, each one a pool of foetid water. When the advance began the men were unable to move in any sort of order having to work round trying to find a dependable foothold. Groups of soldiers struggling in the mud were wiped out by machine gun fire. The wounded who fell could not rise and many of them drowned.

To make these horrendous conditions worse it began to rain heavily in the afternoon. Rain that fell in torrents. Shell-holes overflowed with foul stinking water, streams became torrents, mud clung voraciously to men and machines.

"Fierce, bloody fighting took place in the wet gloom and mud. In shell-holes, around pill-boxes and shattered woods, small groups of mud covered men hacked indecisively at one another as the rain poured down on the sodden landscape." John Giles "Flanders Then and Now".

Despite it all, the truly heroic efforts of the British soldiers achieved success on the 31st if success be measured in ground captured - 18 square miles, quite remarkable in view of all that had been thrown at them. The casualties for the day, some 27,000.

Menin Gate

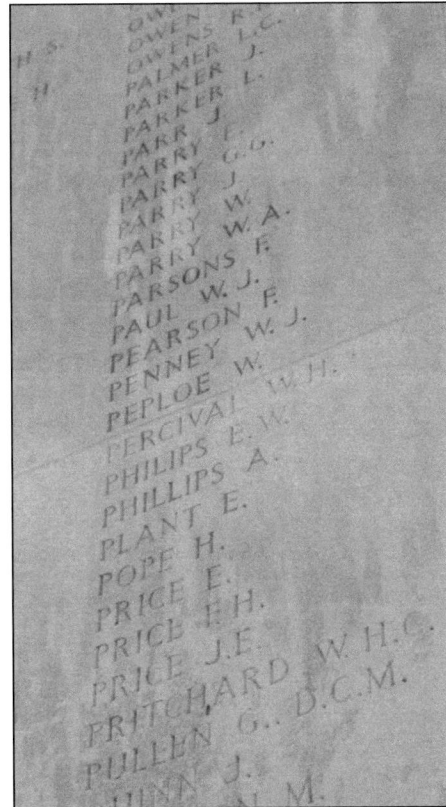

Frank Pearson's name

Frank was one of those killed in action on the 31st July but his body was never recovered and he is commemorated on the Menin Gate

3rd Ypres: Wounded at Pilckem Ridge 31st July. An Observation balloon is rising in the background.
(photo by kind permission of the Imperial War Museum.)

George Anstee was born in Writtle and was baptised at All Saints on the 26th May 1893. His father, George Frederick William Anstee was a butcher. He and his wife, Alice Ellen and their children lived at Heroffs, Writtle Green. It is reputed that Heroffs was built with stone from the collapsed tower of All Saints. The 1901 Census lists the children as Frederick, George, Edward, Hugh, Richard and Robert. Also living there was a 13 year old servant girl, Nellie Staines.

The Essex Regiment Museum records show that George was formerly with the 9th Reserve Cavalry Regt. Royal Fusiliers (City of London Regt) By the time of 3rd Ypres he was a private with the 1st Battalion Royal Fusiliers.

The War Diary of the Battalion gives a detailed account of their actions on the 31st July. They had taken over the trenches two days earlier but thunderstorms on the 29th had made the ground very wet and hampered all movement. On the night of the 30th/31st all ranks had a hot meal and a haversack ration comprising biscuits and chocolate was issued.

The four Companies of the Battalion left the Tunnel about 10.30pm and by 2am were formed up. At 3.20am the Officers commanding the Companies carried out a final check to see that all were in their places ready to move up under the barrage as soon as it started at Zero Hour. The night was very dark and the continuous rain had filled the shell holes with water making it very difficult to advance over the ground.

The German bunker known as Cheddar Villa, the remains of which have been incorporated into the farm buildings (2008). Cheddar Villa was captured in July 1917 and was a first aid post and then headquarters of the 4th Battalion Ox and Bucks who had been billeted in Writtle a long two years or more ago. The wide entrance of course faced the Germans and was the scene of a disastrous shelling on the night of 7th/8th April when a platoon of Ox and Bucks sheltering here sustained a direct shell hit. Many were killed and none escaped without injury.

There was great difficulty in getting information back to Headquarters owing to so many runners having been hit, situation reports were frequently sent down from the front, but never arrived.

More Rifle Grenades might be carried and less Bombs in future with advantage.

Great difficulty was experienced in evacuating wounded owing to the sudden state of the ground, and the distance they had to be carried.

It was heavy work for Regimental Stretcher Bearers as the casualties were very heavy and several Stretcher Bearers were knocked out, although we started off with 32. They had to be assisted by Fighting Troops.

CASUALTIES.

OFFICERS KILLED.

T/Captain W.A. BURDETT M.C.
T/Captain A.J. LEEMING.
2/Lieut. W.J. FIELD. M.C.

OFFICERS WOUNDED.

Lieut. J.R. WALLACE.
T/CAPTAIN C.A. QUIN. M.C.
T/Lieut. S.E. BARTON.
2/Lieut. N.F. MANLEY (ADJUTANT)
2/Lieut. E. GRADY. (Signal officer)
2/Lieut. H.A. JEFFRIES.
Lieut. P.H.S. HUTTON.

MISSING (BELIEVED KILLED).

Lieut. W.E. BRUCE.

WOUNDED (remains at Duty).

2/Lieut. K.S. SMITH.

OTHER RANKS.

Killed...............47
Wounded.............138
Missing..............77
Wounded (remain at
Duty)........9
                        271

TOTAL ALL RANKS....Killed   50
                 .....Wounded 145
                 .....Missing 78
                 .....Wounded at
                                10
                               283.

At ZERO HOUR 3.50 a.m. the Barrage started and the Companies moved up close under it, consequently there were no casualties from the enemy's retaliation barrage that he put up on our front line.

At the commencement of the advance the Companies moved forward and soon came under Machine Gun fire from LOWER STAR POST, this somehow caused the Battalion on our Right do to swerve to its Left and this made my Right Company do the same, and it lost direction advancing almost at N.E. This may have accounted for Captain Quin having been wounded early in the advance.

There were a lot of casualties caused by Machine Guns as they crossed the Valley in which is the SUNKEN ROAD at J.25.d.50.60.

Machine Guns were encountered at J.25.b.00.65. and J.25.b.05.85.; which caused casualties but the enemy managed to get them away before they could be captured.

The enemy did not attempt to make a stand until the STRONG POINT South of JEFFREY AVENUE was reached, where a party under Lieut. FLACK had some stiff fighting with Rifle Grenades and Rifle fire, they eventually captured the STRONG POINT including a Machine Gun which Lieut. FLACK personally knocked out with a Rifle Grenade. Enemy Snipers were very busy in this locality, accounting for a great many of our men.

Here "B" Company under Lieut. FLACK with a few men of "A" Coy. consolidated.

On the Left the right direction was maintained and "C" Company under Captain LEEMING reached a trench in BODMIN COPSE at J.19.d.38.41 where they consolidated, some of "A" Company's men were also with him.

Enemy's Snipers were very active around here and fired at our least movement. Here Captain LEEMING was killed. "D" Company under Captain HEPBURN had got into JEFFERY AVENUE where they consolidated and joined up with LIEUT. FLACK.

It was under the direction of these 2 Officers that consolidation was carried on. Their coolness and gallantr set a fine example to all ranks under them.

Lieut. K.S. SMITH of "A" Company got into a post, dug-ou at about J.19.d.00.45.

The 12th Battalion Royal Fusiliers came through my Battalion and some of them joined up with my men in the trench at about J.19.d.38.40 and South of it.

The 3rd Battalion Rifle Brigade, came up and also went through and occupied a line slightly in advance of us.

I was afterwards ordered to re-organise and withdraw and to occupy and consolidate STRONG POINTS on a line from J.25.a.93.43. to East corner of CLOMEL COPSE. "A" and "B" Coy's became No: 1 Company under Lieut.FLACK. "C" and "D" Coy's became No: 2 Company under Captain HEPBURN.

Extract from the War Diary

Zero hour came at 3.50 am. The Battalion Diary sets out the events of the day.

George Anstee's Grave
But ye shall die like men and fall like one of the princes.

Psalm 82

It emphasis the difficulties caused by the state of the ground.

The Diary concludes with details of the day's casualties. George was one of those wounded. He was taken by field ambulance to the line of huts strung along the road from Dickebusch to Brandhoek where wounded were given treatment. Initial treatment would be given to the wounded on the spot as much as time and circumstances would permit. Then the wounded were transferred back to the relative safety of a hospital behind the line such as this one. George's wounds were such that he died on the 1st August. He is buried in the Huts Cemetery which takes its name from those treatment huts.

Huts Cemetery - South west of Ypres
(Dickebusch, 1100 burials)

John W Bearup is, despite the unusual name, someone about whom information is sparse. The War Graves Commission list just one Bearup · namely John. He was born in East Yorkshire and his parents were William Henry and Elizabeth Ann Bearup of Patrington, Holderness. No other details are known but the 1920 Electoral Roll shows a Margaret Bearup living at Broseley Villa in Writtle.

John was a Quartermaster Serjeant with D Battery, 119th Brigade, Royal Field Artillery.

A Contemporary Postcard

He died on the 4th August 1917 aged 32. He is buried in Calais Southern Cemetery, near to Calais. This cemetery took in those from the various hospitals in Calais who had succumbed to their wounds.

Calais Southern Cemetery ·(718 burials)

John Bearup's grave
"The love that lingers over his name is
more than fame"

Royal Field Artillery Souvenir Silk Postcards

The next loss in 3rd Ypres - that part known as the Battle of Langemarck was **Alfred Charles Fayers** on the 16th August. Langemarck is a village four and a half miles north east of Ypres and had been captured by the Germans in Spring 1915 in the Battle of Second Ypres.

Alfred was born on the 6th January 1895 and baptised at All Saints on the 24th February. His parents were Herbert Charles and Bathsheba Rebecca. Alfred is shown in the 1901 Census as the eldest of three children. Herbert was a carpenter and the family lived at 3 Clifton Cottages, St Johns Green. Bathsheba died in 1902 aged just 27.

Alfred enlisted on the 4th December 1915. He was then aged 20 and gave his occupation as that of grinder. He joined the Essex Regiment but subsequently transferred to the Middlesex Regiment where he was a private in the 1st/8th Battalion. The Battalion formed part of the 167th Brigade.

The Attestation (part of the burnt records following Second World War bombing)

In the battle to be opened on the 16th August the 1/8th Middlesex were on the right with the 1st Londons on the left. The objective allotted to them was the high ground eastwards which lay between the Westhoek-Zonnebeke Road on the north and a line along the southern edge of Glencourse Wood. Thus Glencourse Wood and the Nonne Bosschen Wood lay in the line of advance and hard fighting was expected. Some 600 yards north west of Polygon Wood was the formidable German strong point – Iron Cross Redoubt.

To add to their burden, the ground over which they were to attack was in an appalling condition. The Woods had long since disappeared, only black and broken tree stumps remained. Shell holes full of water were everywhere and the rain on the soft ground had created sheets of water through which the soldiers were bound to founder. The Westhoek Ridge itself was 40 to 50 feet high and thick with mud.

3rd Ypres: Battle of Langemarck August1917
Shellbursts in the distance
(Photograph by kind permission of the Imperial War Museum)

On the night of the 14th August B & C Companies moved up, A and D Companies following them the next day. Whilst assembling, a heavy German barrage fell killing and wounding 28 men.

Zero hour on the 16th August arrived – 4.45 am. The men could see for themselves the conditions through which they would have to advance but the 1/8th set off with B Company in the first wave, followed by C and A with D in reserve.

Between the British and German trenches was a valley and as the troops reached the low ground they were brought to a halt – a broad belt of mud lay before them, about 30 yards across and 4 to 5 feet deep, an impossible barrier. Forced wide to try and find a way across, the various units lost touch with each other. B and C vainly tried to advance and, to counteract the fire being poured on them by the Germans, mortar teams were called up but were shot down before they could get into position.

By 10am with no support on the flanks, the first line of the Middlesex was withdrawn to a position about halfway between the initial start point and the eastern edge of Nonne Bosschen Wood. But there was no security here as at least a dozen German aeroplanes were active machine gunning the troops and then at 1 pm the enemy's artillery opened up and many casualties were suffered.

This continued until 3pm when the Germans were seen to be massing to the left and a counter attack was feared but it would have been as impossible for them to cross the sea of mud as it was for the Middlesex to advance across it.

Just before 6pm Lieut. Colonel Ingpen formed all the remaining men into two waves and they forced their way through to the line that they had originally achieved.

Next day the remnants of the 1/8th were relieved having suffered losses of 33 killed, 64 missing and 123 wounded including their Commanding Officer Lieut. Colonel Ingpen. Alfred, aged 22, was one of those killed, his body was not recovered and his name is recorded on the Memorial to the Missing at Tyne Cot Cemetery

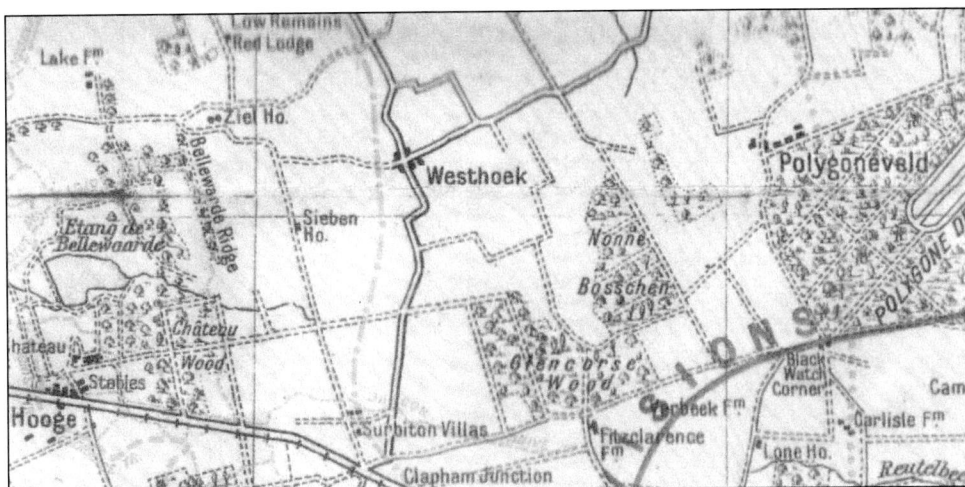
Centre; Nonne Bosschen Wood

Memorial to the Missing, Tyne Cot

Tyne Cot Cemetery, Passchendaele   contains 11,856 graves, 101 special memorials and the Memorial to the Missing which records the names of 34,888 men who fell in the Ypres Salient from 16th August 1917 until the end of the War and whose bodies were never found.

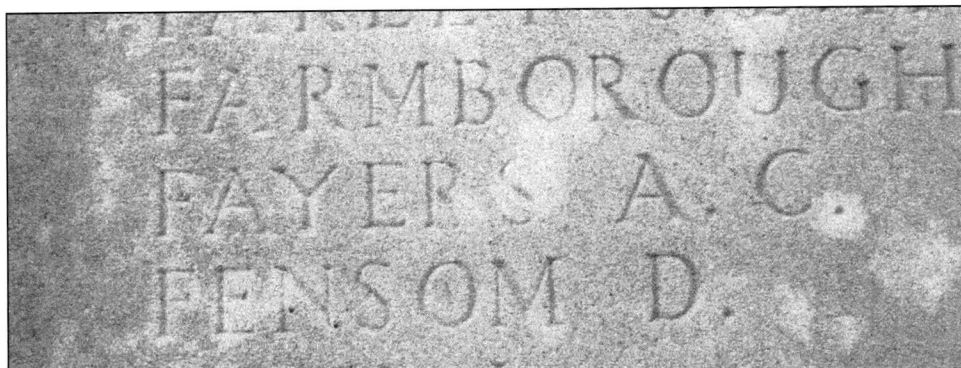
Alfred Fayer's name

William Ernest Poole – known as Dick – was the brother of John Poole who had been killed on the 4th May 1917. Dick was born in Writtle on the 21st February 1896 and his records describe him as the son of John and Elizabeth Poole of St. Johns Green. The records for his brother show mother's name as Esther. By the time of the War Dick's address is shown as Back Road.

Dick enlisted in the 4th Battalion the Bedfordshire Regiment – The Battalion's War Diary and their Official history detail their part in the Battle of Passchendaele 26th October to 10th November.

Troops walk along a duckboard through the remains of Chateau Wood (photograph by kind permission of the Imperial War Museum)

At the beginning of October the Battalion was in training. On the 24th the Battalion embussed to Danbury Camp, Pottenhook where it spent a very wet night under canvas. Next day it moved to the Canal Bank one mile north of Ypres, and settled into dugouts on the east bank. On the 27th the Battalion marched to an old trench near Cheddar Villa and two days later moved forward and on crossing the Poelcappelle – Wallemolen Road they came under heavy artillery fire which killed one of the NCO guides. This was unfortunate as the other NCO had no idea which way to go and so after a tiring struggle, they eventually reached the front line just after midnight although some of the men did not arrive until 2am.

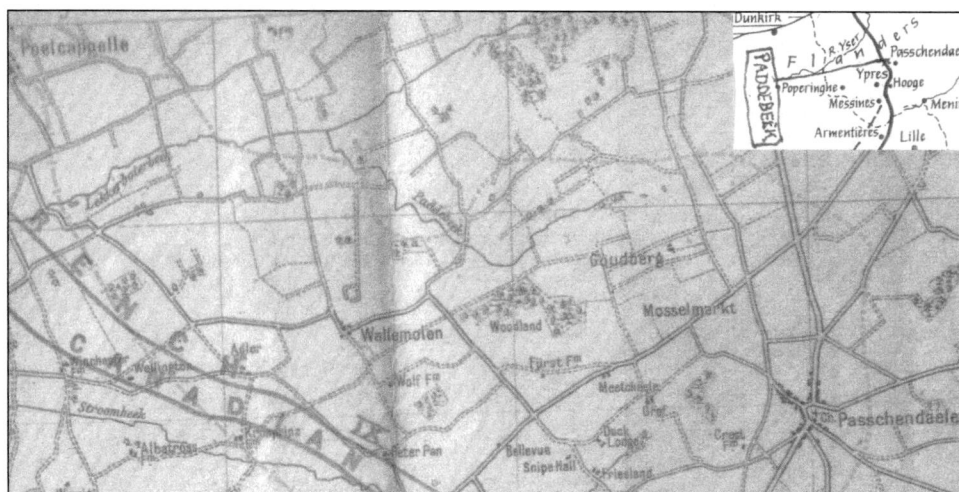

The Paddebeek (centre), Poelcappelle (top-left), Wallemolen (centre) and the elusive goal of Passchendaele (far right)

So on the 30th the Battalion was ready for the attack with the 7th Royal Fusiliers and 1st Artists Rifles on either side. Rain fell at 3am but cleared up later. At zero hour, 5.50am, every gun opened up a terrific barrage which fell ahead of the troops – a creeping barrage behind which the troops advanced. The advance commenced perfectly but then German counter-shelling fell on the assembly area killing several men there including Captain Gates.

Conditions were awful. Men up to their knees in mud and those who were not caught by shelling risked being sniped whilst stuck in the mud. But the advance continued slowly until the whole line reached the Paddebeek. This stream was reported to be five feet wide but it was actually ten feet wide and over seven feet deep in mud and water. One section attempted to wade through but sank and only three out of the seven men got back. All attempts to cross failed. German machine guns poured a deadly fire into the men as they got stuck in the awful morass. Many of the wounded simply sank into the mud.

Ground around the Paddebeek

Casualties under such conditions were naturally very heavy and by 9am all bar two of the officers and nearly all the senior NCOs had become casualties. At midday the Commanding Officer, Colonel Collings-Wells came up with his Adjutant and held a conference in a shell hole with his remaining two officers.

Then at 3pm the Germans counter attacked with infantry sweeping forward and backed by artillery fire. The British artillery however poured a deadly fire on the German soldiers. Fighting continued until about 5pm when the Germans were finally driven back.

Next day the situation became quieter but enemy shelling made the task of collecting the wounded extremely dangerous. The Battalion was relieved at 7pm. Total killed, wounded and missing 233 men. Dick was one of those missing on the 30th October and he is commemorated on the Tyne Cot Memorial to the Missing.

Dick Poole's name on the Tyne Cot Memorial

The Battle of 3rd Ypres came to an end in November at Passchendaele, by then merely a heap of rubble, but for the men of Essex there was a different battlefield. The Battle of 1st Gaza earlier in the year had turned into a stalemate. The Battle of 2nd Gaza in April was equally unsuccessful and so a further effort was to be made – the Battle of 3rd Gaza from 27th October to 7th November. Its aim was to break the Turkish defensive system from Gaza to Beersheba and was to be the prelude to the victorious advance into Jerusalem.

The Turks had been pre-occupied with reinforcing their troops in Baghdad and it was not until October that they hurried four divisions into Palestine.

On 27th October the bombardment of the Turkish defences began accompanied by a thunderstorm with vivid lightning. By 31st October everything was in readiness. The 5th Battalion of the Essex Regiment went into action on the 2nd November and on that day three men from Writtle were killed.

25 officers and 925 other ranks of the 5th went into action. Prior to the attack they had been briefed by their Commanding Officer Lieut.-Colonel Gibbons. At 4.30pm a short service was held and at 5pm they got some sleep. Then at 11pm a hot meal was served together with a pint of beer.

At 12.30am on the 2nd a move was made to the assembly point and two hours later all was ready. The tanks went in front and at 2.55am the Battalion advanced. The moon had disappeared and the light was very bad, smoke and dust from artillery bombardments reducing visibility still further.

A and D Companies were to take Rafah Junior Trench an offshoot of the Rafah Redoubt. B and C were to take Zowaiid Trench on the right. Unfortunately Lieut. Lancaster who was responsible for checking directions was killed as was Lieut. Evans. In the confusion all Companies ended up in the Rafah Redoubt. The telephone cable was cut by shellfire and runners got lost in the thick haze. The air was filled with fine sand and smoke which hung like thick fog.

Lieut.-Colonel Gibbons was determined to find out exactly what was happening and although hampered by machine gun fire made it through to the Redoubt. It appeared that in relying upon compasses B Company had got lost in the fog. The steel helmets were thought to have affected the compasses. Captain Deakin swiftly made up his mind and led an attack on Zowaiid Trench. The Turks were manning the Trench in strength but despite Captain Deakin going down with a broken leg the Essex fought their way in. They then moved forward to the Turks' second line but, with men falling rapidly, the low ground proved impossible to hold due to the fire from the enemy. However the front line trench was clung to with tenacity in spite of the enemy's attempts to force them out.

In all the trenches they had captured the Essex suffered severely from machine gun and shell fire. As the day wore on working parties were organised to clear the debris and to bury the dead. During the day Lieut.-Colonel Gibbons, who had been wounded in both hands, transferred command to Captain Franklin.

The casualties of the day were 2 officers killed and 6 wounded, 73 other ranks killed, 172 wounded and 9 missing.

Gaza War Cemetery

Stephen John Barker lived in Writtle and was educated in Chelmsford. He was a Private in the 5th Battalion. He was buried in Gaza War Cemetery joining the men from Essex buried there from the battles earlier in the year.

Stephen left a wife and 7 children. It is believed that his widow was E. Barker of Pitt Cottage.

Stephen Barker's grave in Gaza War Cemetery

Jack Marshall

Highwood Church with its original wooden cross

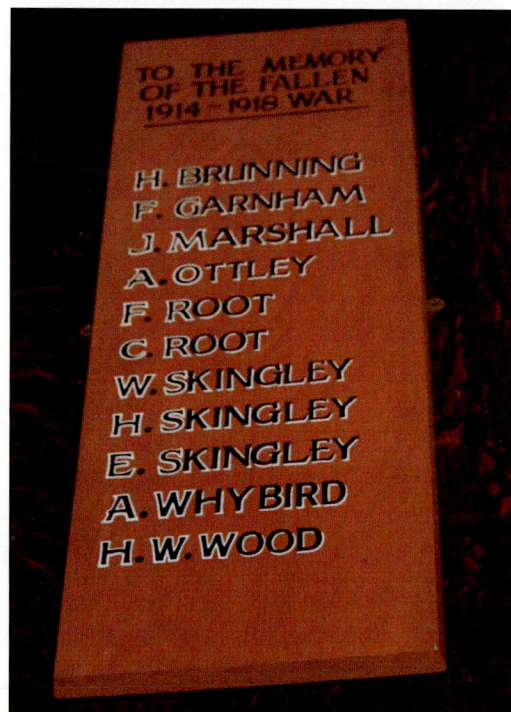

The Plaque in Highwood Church organ loft with the names of John Marshall and William Skingley

John Marshall – known as **Jack** - was also a Private in the 5th Battalion Essex Regiment. He had been born in Writtle and was baptised in All Saints on 19th January 1896. By 1917 he had moved to Hatfield Peverel. His family continued to live in Writtle and in 1914 he sent a postcard to Miss C Marshall at Oxney House. The reverse of the postcard was a photograph of himself.

After the Battle on the 2nd November his body was never traced and he is commemorated on the Jerusalem Memorial.

He is not recorded on the Writtle War Memorial but must have had a connection with Highwood as his name is on the plaque on the organ loft in Highwood Church.

Edward J Fitch was the son of Mrs Rachael Fitch of 3 Oxney Green.

Edward had been wounded in March 1917 but had recovered and was fit enough to take part in the attack on the 2nd November.

His body was never found and, aged 27, he is commemorated on the Jerusalem Memorial.

Jerusalem Memorial

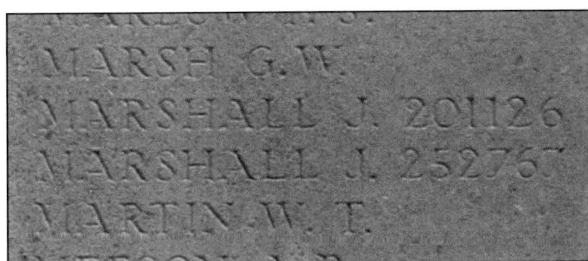

Jack Marshall's name

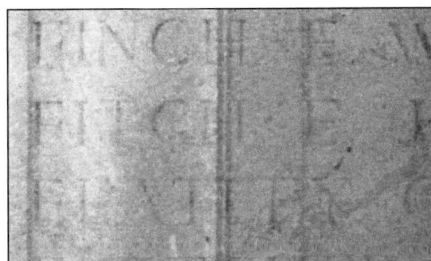

Edward Fitch's name

William S Skingley was the son of Henry and Lucy Skingley of Montpelier Cottages. At the time of the War he lived at Highwood.

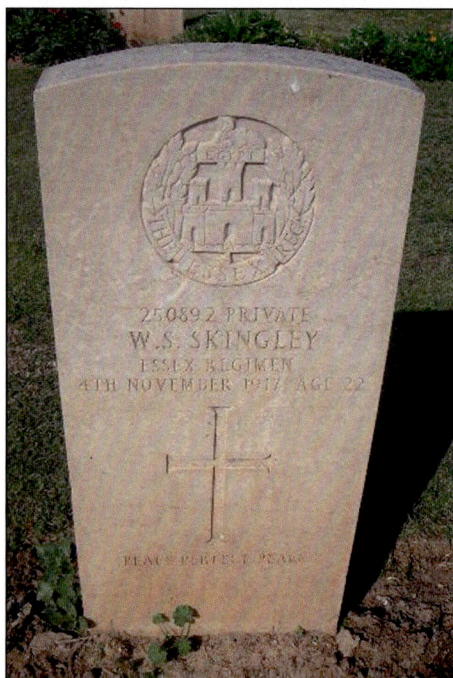

William Skingley's Grave
"Peace Perfect Peace"

He was a private in the 1st/5th Battalion of the Essex Regiment. Following the events of the 2nd and 3rd November the next two days were spent by the Battalion in consolidating their position on the Rafah Redoubt. During this time they were subjected to Turkish artillery fire until relieved by the 8th Hants on the evening of the 5th November.

The wounded had been brought in and tended but William was one of those who died from his wounds. He died on Sunday 4th November aged 22, and is buried in Deir el Belah Cemetery in the Palestine territory.

He is commemorated on the Writtle War Memorial and he too is named on the Highwood Church Organ Loft.

Deir el Belah Cemetery

By the 21st November the Egyptian Expeditionary Force had gained a line about 2 miles west of Jerusalem but the city was deliberately spared bombardment. Very severe fighting followed until the evening of the 8th December when all the city's defences were captured. Turkish troops left and next day the Turkish Governor sent a letter of surrender to the Allied lines. On the 11th December General Allenby formally entered the city.

Edwin Francis Page lived in Writtle although his name does not appear on the Memorial. He was a private in the 5th Battalion, Essex Regiment.

On the 28th November a raid was made by the 1st/5th on the Turkish position south of the river Auja. The Turks were guarding the bridge over the river and the aim of the raid was to destroy the bridge and, if possible, to capture the Turks who were thought to number about 12. Lieut. Keeling M.C. was to lead the raid with 40 NCOs and men.

The men got into position unobserved despite the fact that it was a bright moonlight night. The plan was to rush the position. Unfortunately as soon as they left the line the Turks spotted them and opened up with intense rifle and machine gun fire and Lieut. Keeling realised that they faced more than 12 of the enemy. The first man to lead the rush – Sergeant Upchurch – was killed instantly but the attack was pressed home. Some of the Turks jumped into the river, others were taken prisoner. The Turkish artillery then opened up and so it was necessary for Lieut. Keeling to get his men back. His subsequent report disclosed that they had killed at least 50 of the enemy and when the prisoners were interrogated it turned out that instead of the expected 12 the position had in fact been manned by over 200 men.

The British lost 7 men killed one of whom was Edwin. He has no known grave and his name is recorded on the Jerusalem Memorial.

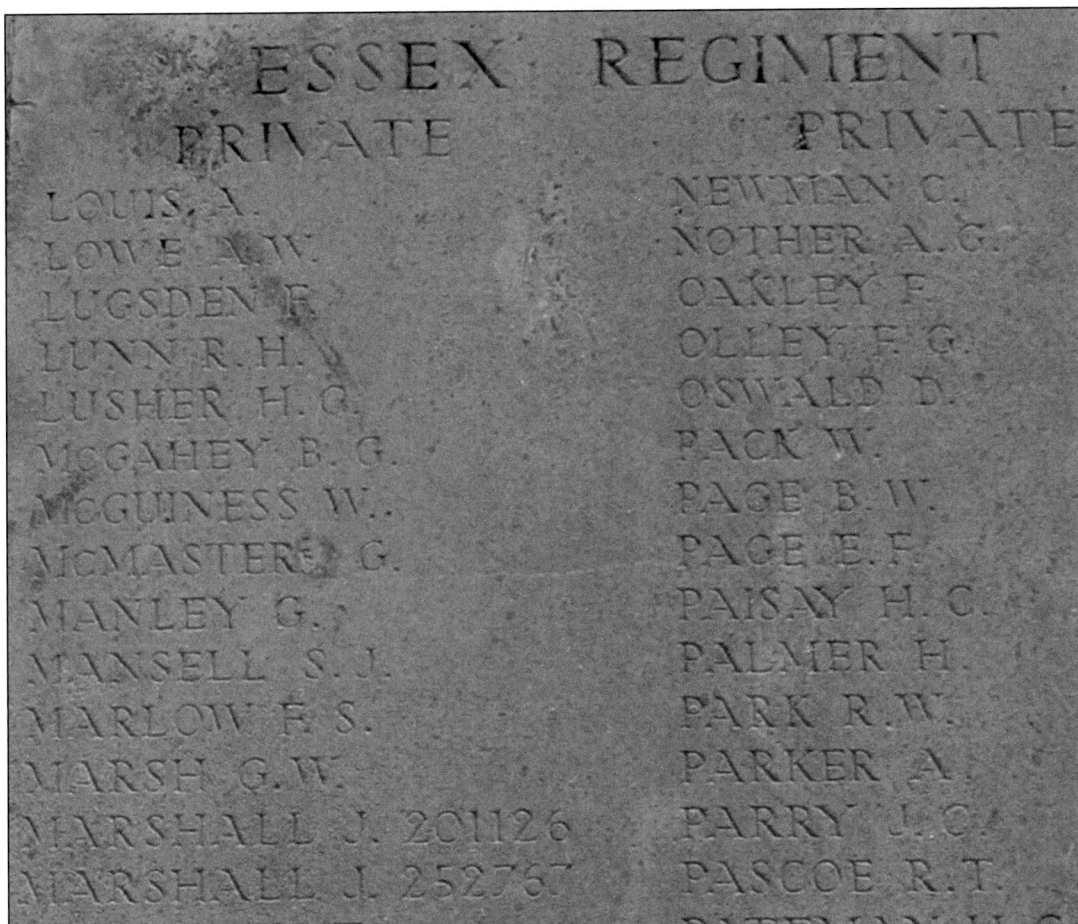

Edwin's name on the Memorial

The last death of 1917 is again someone not recorded on the Writtle War Memorial. **Ernest Edward Ellis** was born in Writtle. He was the son of James and Kate Ellis who at the time of the War lived at 11 Crompton Terrace, Writtle Road.

He enlisted in Chelmsford and was a member of B Company 1st/4th Battalion Norfolk Regiment. The 1st/4th Battalion was a Territorial Battalion and in 1915 served in Gallipoli, in 1916 in Egypt and in 1917 in Palestine.

Early in the morning of the 11th December a patrol of the 1st/4th found that the Turks were still holding Stone Heap Hill and the adjacent hills. At about the same time C Company holding Zephiziych Hill was being shelled by the Turks. By 9 am C Company was in great peril as some 300 to 400 of the enemy were within bombing distance and were working round the flank. Help arrived in the shape of B Company led by Captain Flatt. They charged with the bayonet and the Turks gave way and then ran, pursued by the men of B Company.

The rout of the Turks was not without cost to the Norfolks. Captain Jennings and 2nd Lieutenant Wood were killed, three other officers were wounded two of whom subsequently died from their wounds. Twelve other ranks were killed and of thirty six other ranks wounded, five died later. One man was missing.

Ernest Ellis' grave

Ernest aged 20 was killed in the action and is buried in Ramleh War Cemetery

Ramleh War Cemetery

CHAPTER 5 - 1918

The Final Year

The Central Powers' only chance of achieving any sort of victory was to defeat the British and French armies whilst the Germans had a superiority in numbers from the release of men from the Eastern front and before the Americans arrived in strength. Indeed 1918 had opened with the Allies very much on the defensive. Their offensives in 1917 had in reality achieved very little and the U boats were a constant threat to supply lines across the Atlantic.

But on the other hand the British naval blockade was taking its toll. Austria, always the weaker of the Central Powers, was nearly exhausted. Turkey was nearing collapse.

So everything pointed to a German Spring offensive which came at the end of March from the Oise to the Somme and on the Lys. The Germans achieved great success in many places storming through land that had been so painfully captured by the Allies. At the Somme they swept through towards Amiens; in Belgium almost to the gates of Ypres.

This gave rise to Field Marshall Haig's Order of the Day:-

"Many of us are now tired. To those I would say that victory will belong to the side which holds out the longest ... There is no other course open to us but to fight it out! Every position must be held to the last man ; there must be no retirement. With our backs to the wall and believing in the justice of our cause, each one of us must fight on to the end. The safety of our Homes and the Freedom of mankind alike depend upon the conduct of each one of us at this critical moment."

The decisive victory that the Germans needed never came. In addition, their advances outran their supply lines and in places troops abandoned their tasks and went looting.

The arrival in large numbers of American troops in the late Spring and early Summer was a welcome – if much belated – addition to the Allied force. By July and August the tide had turned and the Amiens offensive saw the Germans lose 100,000 men in casualties and prisoners. Civil unrest in Germany, the collapse of Austria-Hungary, mutiny in the fleet and the enforced retreat of the Army all led to the Germans having no option but to accept the terms imposed upon them and agree the Armistice.

Fighting went on in many places – the last Allied death being a Canadian at 10.58 am – but at 11 am on the 11th November the guns fell silent.

Ironically the British troops were at Mons at the time of the ceasefire – just where they had been when they fired the first shots 4 ½ years earlier.

During the year the deaths occurred of well known parishioners. Mrs E Clark, a keen exhibitor at Writtle horticultural shows. Louisa Hunt the wife of Mr Hunt, the postmaster. The Rev. J Buddell, aged 83, former pastor at the Congregational Church.

A more tragic death was reported in the Chronicle on the 4th January. Alice Digby aged 10, the daughter of Mr & Mrs George Digby of St Johns Green had been left in charge of the three younger children. She was leaning on the open stove to put the kettle on for hot water to wash the children when her clothing caught fire. A neighbour, Mr F Broyde, rushed in to try and save her but to no avail. A verdict of accidental death was recorded with a warning that guards should be used with open fires.

Throughout 1918 village life went on as normally as possible. The various organisations got on with life as usual or as usual as possible when everything was devoted to the war effort, or, if not directly for the war effort, then for self help.

On the 22nd February there was reported a meeting of gardeners and allotment holders when Mr Robson gave a talk on artificial manure. Mrs Bodell gave a talk to Writtle Women's Institute on fruit bottling and vegetable drying. At the February meeting of the Parish Council, with Mr A P Lindsell as Chairman, it was resolved that the Rural District Council should be asked to release more land for allotments to meet the ever growing demand. In March the Parish Council was faced with an application to graze goats on The Green; confusingly the newspaper reported this as approved whilst the Council Minutes say that it was an application to tether goats on The Green and that this was refused.

The Attwood Village Hall was the scene of an entertainment as reported on the 10th May where the sum of £13-5-6d (£13.27) was raised for the Red Cross. The Writtle and Widford Nursing Association raised £25 with its appeal.

In June the Parish Council was asked if it would take part in a Petition for a central fire station in Chelmsford complete with a motor fire engine. The Council resolved that it did not see its way to sign as the local arrangements better served the Parish.

The Empire Day programme was curtailed owing to inclement weather. In the Village Hall the Council School children rendered a selection of patriotic songs conducted by the Headmaster, Mr T Williams. The Blencoe Charity Grant of £3 was divided between seven boys and girls. The afternoon was rounded off with a wartime tea served by Mr C Russell. On the 24th July the children's sports which had been put off from Empire Day were held on The Green. The sports were organised by Mr Russell and School Staff assisted by wounded soldiers from the V A D Hospital.

January to November

Samuel William Adams is shown in 1901 as living with his family at Sycamore Cottages, Roxwell Road. The family comprised William aged 48, his wife Emily aged 35, her mother Emma Ellis a widow, and then Samuel aged 11, Emily 5, Lucy 3, Robert 2 and Frederick just 1 month old. By the time of the War the address of the family was Hoe Street Cottages, Roxwell.

Samuel had enlisted in the 13th Battalion of the Essex Regiment and had been promoted to Lance Corporal. The 13th had experienced a difficult time during the Battle of Cambrai at the end of 1917. At one stage it had been subjected to a determined assault where the men had virtually exhausted all their ammunition but they withstood it all. D Company received a special mention in dispatches. Two men escaped to tell of their last stand when, totally surrounded, the company fought on to the end. Total casualties of the 13th were 372 killed, wounded and captured.

On the 5th December the Battalion moved to Lebucquers and on the 8th relieved the 2nd Ox and Bucks at Derricourt. On the 23rd December it was back to the front line.

Extract from Caton Woodville's depiction of D Company 13th Essex (West Ham Battalion) who held a meeting and decided unanimously on no surrender and to hold their post to the last man; only two of their number made it back to the British lines

January 1918 started with bad weather. The 13th went into billets at Rocquigny. The cold and frost was succeeded by a quick thaw and then heavy rain turned the ground into a quagmire. On the 22nd January they took over the La Vacquerie sector.

On the 31st January the Battalion moved into support trenches at Villers Pluich, south west of Cambrai.

And it was here, in the wet and mud of a little chronicled aspect of the Western Front, that Samuel met his death, perhaps from a shell blast, perhaps on a trench raid. Whatever the circumstances the event does not even warrant any mention in the Official History; just one of so many thousands of unrecorded deaths.

Samuel died on the 5th February aged 29. He is buried in Fins New British Cemetery, Sorel-le-Grand in the Somme Region.

Samuel's Grave
"Gone from our home
But not our hearts"

Fins New British Cemetery
(1,511 burials)

William Henry Everard was the second Everard to die. He was baptised at All Saints on the 24th May 1896, and was one of the children of Frederick and Sarah. Frederick was a farm labourer. Two of the sons, Frederick and Charles, were maltsters' labourers. The other children were Dorothy and Bertie. The address of the family was at Writtle Green at the time of William's baptism but by 1901 the family had moved to St. Johns Green.

ST.JOHN'S GREEN. WRITTLE
H.Everard   H.Burr   -   -   F.Everard   -
S.Poole

William enlisted at the age of 20 years and 7 months at Chelmsford on the 17th November 1915. His medical was satisfactory – height 5 feet 10 inches, weight 146 pounds; health good. His occupation that of a grinder at Hoffmans, at the time one of Chelmsford's major employers. By this time the family had moved again as he gave his address and that of his father as Writtle Green once more.

William had originally enlisted in the Norfolk Regiment but transferred to the 25th Battalion Machine Gun Corps on the 13th March 1917.

Ten a Second: Nails for Prussia's Coffin

Practising with a man-mowing machine in Flanders.

Battle of Hazebrouck – manning a Lewis gun, rail line near Merris
(Photograph by kind permission of the Imperial War Museum)

William Everard's Attestation

The 25th Battalion joined the British Expeditionary Force in France on the 25th April 1917 and became part of the Army's 5th Division on the 14th September 1917. Early in March 1918 they were transferred to the Italian front but due to the German Spring offensive they were speedily recalled to France on the 21st March. They took part in the Battle of Hazebrouck and then the defence of Nieppe Forest - all part of the Battle of The Lys from the 9th to the 29th April.

On the 10th April Von Armin's Fourth Army launched its attack. Villages that had been fought over repeatedly in the past years changed hands yet again. The Germans got within 5 miles of Hazebrouck before the attack eventually ran out of steam on the 29th.

William suffered a gunshot wound to his leg on the 24th April and died on the 2nd May, aged 22. He is buried at Etaples Military Cemetery, Pas de Calais. He is commemorated on the Hoffmann Roll of Honour as well as the War Memorial.

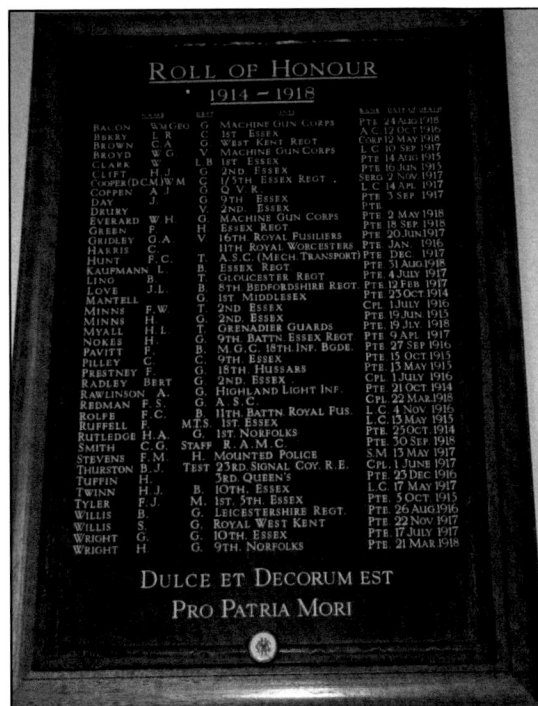

William's Grave

Etaples Military Cemetery

Etaples Military Cemetery

Etaples, next to Le Touquet and a few miles south of Boulogne was the site of immense British reinforcement camps and hospitals being remote from attack except by aircraft. Railway links were excellent. The hospitals could deal with 22,000 wounded or sick. The Cemetery contains 10,769 burials from the Great War.

Another well known Writtle name is that of Little. **Thomas Little** was the only son of William and Elizabeth Little of 7 Chequers Lane. He was baptised at All Saints on the 29th March 1896. William was shown in the 1901 Census as a general dealer but by 1918 Elizabeth alone was shown as Thomas' parent.

Thomas took the oath on attestation at Chelmsford on the 9th December 1915 and enlisted in the 3/1 Suffolk Yeomanry on the 27th April 1916. On enlistment he gave his occupation as greengrocer. The Suffolks left Folkestone and arrived in Boulogne on the 27th August. On the 7th September Thomas was posted to the 7th Battalion Royal West Kent Regiment – the Queens Own. Whilst with the West Kents he was awarded the Military Medal.

The West Kents had been engaged in bitter fighting in the Somme offensive of 1916. In the spring of 1918 the Germans stormed across the same battlefield. But in many ways it was their last throw of the dice and August saw a dramatic change of events. The British Army, which had been swept back to the outskirts of Amiens, now turned the tables. The 8th August was described by the German commander Ludendorff as being for the Germans "the black day of the war". The 7th Battalion was actively engaged in the day's success and although running into strong resistance held onto their gains.

Although ousted from Albert, the Germans still held Tara and Usna Hills and it was essential to dislodge them. On the 23rd August at 4.45 am the Battalion pushed forward and swiftly overcame resistance. The capture of the Hills rendered an advance on La Boisselle possible. This was tackled the next day and , pushing through, the Battalion linked up with the 10th Essex.

That evening the 7th returned to Albert for a brief rest. It had had three officers killed, five wounded and 142 other casualties but the gains made had been important. The next few days saw the advance moving forward until it reached Trones Wood, scene of the Battalion's epic fight in July 1916.

On the 27th August the 7th put in A Company to clear Bernafay Wood whilst D advanced between that Wood and Trones Wood. B Company was to establish itself just north of Bernafay.

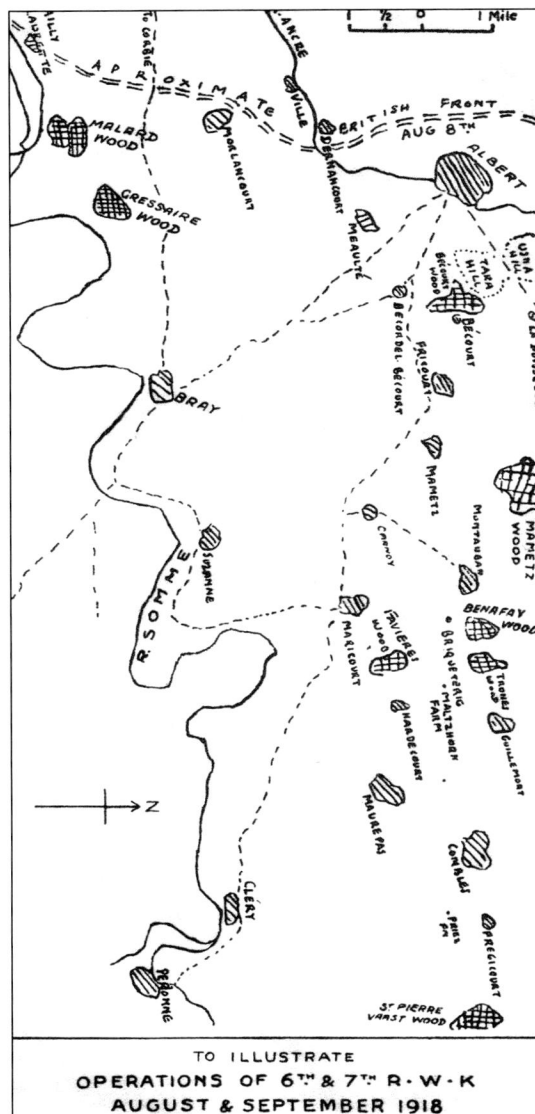

TO ILLUSTRATE
OPERATIONS OF 6TH & 7TH R·W·K
AUGUST & SEPTEMBER 1918

Operations of Royal West Kents, August and September

At about 6am the move forward began. A Company ran into some strong opposition but in the end cleared Bernafay Wood and joined up with D. B Company was held up by machine gun fire as Trones Wood had not been cleared. The Berkshires had been due to clear the Wood but they had suffered heavy losses.

Trones Wood, a contemporary postcard

Then at 8 am came a vigorous counter-attack by the Prussian Guard. D Company made a stand just west of Trones Wood but as the morning wore on the units became mixed up in the fierce fighting that ensued. Eventually the Germans were beaten back. The next day, the 28th, the 7th pushed further forward past Maricourt towards Hardecourt and A Company reached Maltzhorn Farm.

That night the Brigade, including the 7th Battalion was relieved. The 7th's losses, 90 in all were relatively light. Thomas was wounded during the fighting and at the age of 21 died of wounds on the 28th August.

The War Graves Commission are normally very reliable but their records and Thomas' headstone show the year of his death as 1916. This is not correct because all the Regimental records and the later correspondence relating to his death show the year as 1918.

Thomas is buried in Dartmoor Cemetery, Somme

The arrival of a telegram was something to be dreaded. In Elizabeth Little's case that telegram arrived on the 5th September. It regretted that Thomas had died at 56 Field Ambulance from a shell wound to his chest and left arm.

A.

POST OFFICE TELEGRAPHS.
(Inland Telegrams.)

Prefix_____ Code_____

Office of Origin and Service Instructions.

	Words.	Sent
		At_____ M.
	Charge.	To_____
		By_____

No. of Telegram_____

For Postage Stamps.
To be affixed by the Sender.

Any Stamp for which there is not room here should be affixed at the back of this form.

A Receipt for the Charges on this Telegram can be obtained, price One Penny.

When a reply is to be prepaid, write the words "Reply Paid" in the space below. These words are not charged for.

TO { Mrs E Little,
7 Chequers Lane, Writtle, Chelmsford

12 words, including the words in the address,

9 D.

Every additional word, 1/2 D.

FROM { Alliston, Hounslow.

The Name and Address of the Sender, IF NOT TO BE TELEGRAPHED, must be written in the Space provided at the back of the Form.

(This Paper Manufactured and Printed by McCORQUODALE & CO, Limited.)   A. Wt. 28897-8/026-027.   22,000,000.   10-12/15.   Sch. 2.

Telegram to Elizabeth Little

Forms B. 103/1.   86   Army Form B. 103.

Casualty Form—Active Service.

Regiment or Corps 3/ Suffolk Yeomanry

Regimental No. 2638   Rank Pte   Name Little P

Enlisted (a) 27-4-16   Terms of Service (a) D of W   Service reckons from (a) 27-4-16

Date of promotion to present rank ____   Date of appointment to lance rank ____   Numerical position on roll of N.C.Os. ____

Extended ____   Re-engaged ____   Qualification (b) ____

	Report	Record of promotions, reductions, transfers, etc., during active service, as reported on Army Form B. 213, Army Form A. 36, or in other official documents. The authority to be quoted in each case.	Place	Date	Remarks taken from Army Form B. 213, Army Form A. 36, or other official documents.
Date	From whom received				
		Embarked Folkestone	27.8.16		
		Disembkd. Boulogne	-do-		
		Arrived No 15 I B D 28;8;16 Posted to 1/4th Suff. Regt.			
		Transferred to 4th Reserve Bn R.W.Kent Regt. Posted to 7th Bn R.W.Kent Regt. 7-9-16. New No. Auth A.O.204/16 A.C.I.1499/16.			Lieut. For O. i/c T.F. Infantry Records G.H.Q. 3rd Echelon B.E.F.
		Proceeded to join 4th Batt	Etaples Field	18.12.16	list
		Wounded at duty	Field	3.10.17 28.1.18	list
		Awarded			
		Leave 26.9.16			
1918	C.B.	Died of Wounds	Field	28.8.18 list	Officer, i/c No 5 Infantry Section

(a) In the case of a man who has re-engaged for, or enlisted into Section D, Army Reserve, particulars of such re-engagement or enlistment will be entered.
(b) e.g., Signaller, Shoeing Smith, etc., etc., also special qualifications in technical Corps duties.

Casualty Form

- 213 -

Thomas Little's grave
"Kept by the Power of God"

The Military Medal

Dartmoor Cemetery
(Named Dartmoor at request of the Devon Regiment. Contains 768 burials)

In the Middle East there was a final push to defeat the Turks. Jerusalem had been captured the previous winter and the plan for autumn 1918 was based upon completely defeating the Turks before the rainy season in November

Once again the Essex Regiment was to play a leading role. A Private in B Company of the 5th Battalion was **William Blanks**. William was the son of Eliza and William Walter Blanks a maltster of Malting House, Church Lane. Earlier, Frederick and Charles Everard had as their occupations "maltsters labourers" – presumably employed by Mr. Blanks.

Young William was baptised on the 27th May 1888 and as the son of a prosperous brewer would have had a comfortable upbringing. His story then moves on to the War and his part in the closing stages of hostilities in Palestine.

Earlier in 1918 the 5th Battalion had enjoyed the relative comforts of the almond groves of Mulebbis. Water flow had improved and the campaign against the other enemy – mosquitoes – had been of some success. In June they moved to the River Auja and enjoyed bathing and fishing. Fishing was not of the traditional kind but the fish were shot at and, although rarely hit, they sustained shell shock and became easy prey making a much appreciated addition to the men's rations. They also found a healthy supplement to their diet from the oranges growing abundantly in the surrounding groves.

On the 9th July, thoroughly rested, the Battalion marched to Beit Nebola and although engaged in some road building work, this too was a pleasant camp. But their reason for being there was constantly present with patrols probing on both sides. Then in September everyone knew that an offensive, the Battle of Megiddo, was pending.

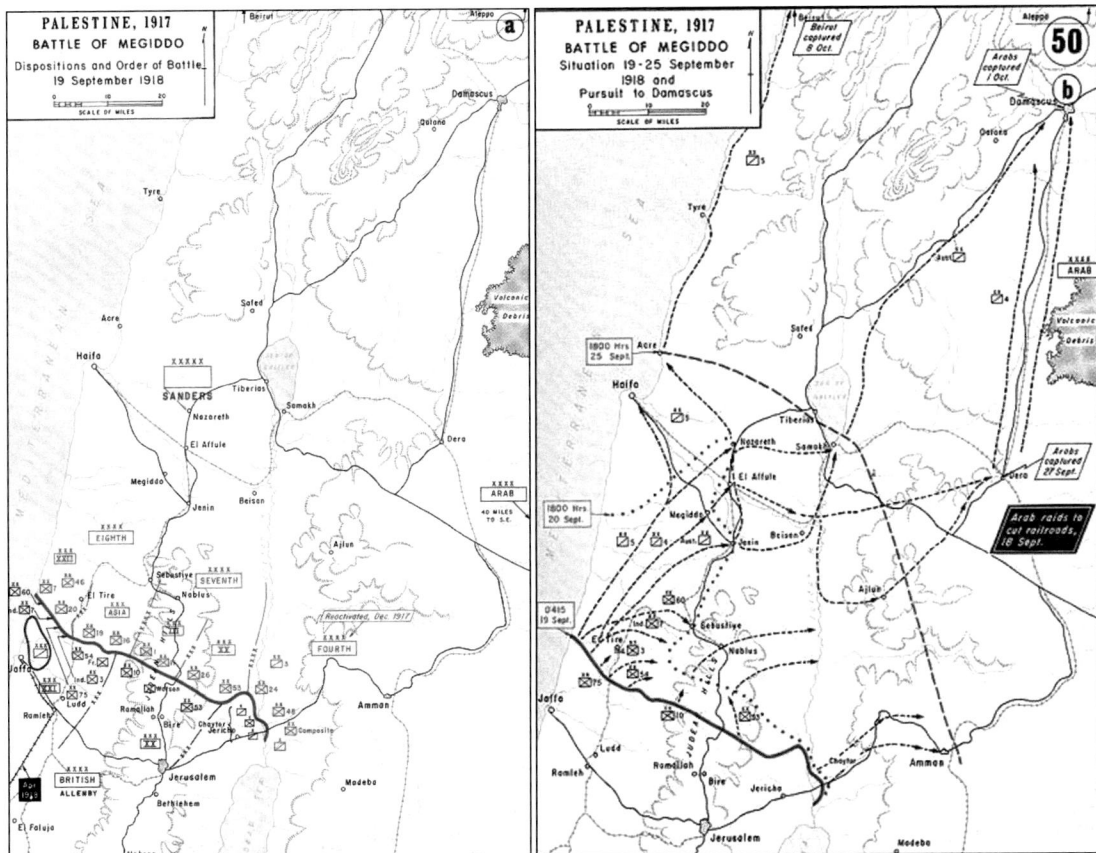

The Turkish force in Palestine was commanded by the vastly experienced Liman von Sanders, a German who had been with the Turkish troops for much of the War. However he was outnumbered by the British. Whilst von Sanders had some 29,000 men and 370 guns the British had 69,000 men and 540 guns, together with 8000 Arabs under Sherif Feisal.

A private of the Essex Regiment in Middle East uniform

The British plan was to force a gap in the Plain of Sharon through which the cavalry could pass to seize the Turkish line of communication whilst the Arab force would move against the enemy's rear.

On the evening of the 18th September the 161st Infantry Brigade, which included the 5th Essex, bivouacked at Muzier. The 5th and 7th Essex took up position. Shorts and jackets were worn by all ranks. Colonel Gibbons said "I voted for trousers but was over-ruled. Shorts give greater freedom of movement and are cooler, but the nature of the rocks and wiry grass we were to attack over was very rough on bare knees, as we found to our cost."

The enemy appeared to expect an attack and put down a considerable barrage on three occasions during the night, at 9pm on the 18th and then at 1am and 3am on the 19th. The Brigade started the attack punctually at 3.50am with the 5th and 4th Essex in the front line. The enemy continued to shell them. Colonel Gibbons had formed the Battalion up but some 250 yards behind the tape line and therefore this shelling only caused slight casualties. However amongst these was the officer commanding William's Company, Captain Portway M.C. who was wounded.

The enemy continued shelling and, after what must have seemed an age to the troops, the British Artillery replied, laying down a heavy bombardment. The Battalion passed on to Umm el Bureid which was not strongly held. However at Wadi Raba the Turks put up firmer resistance on the right at Hill 479 and B Company ran into barbed wire and machine gun fire. With the aid of Lewis guns three of the machine guns were silenced with two others captured.

Then it was over the next ridge with the intention of taking Kufr Qasim village, but here casualties were sustained through lack of cover. The village was captured and the time had come for the 7th Essex to take up the offensive. However, the Turks had rallied and the 7th sustained considerable casualties in attempting to cross the half a mile of flat ground.

At 10.35 the 5th Battalion received orders to take the Turks' rallying point of Sivri Wood and Hill 512. C and D Companies were in front with A and B in reserve. As they pressed on the Turks started to fall back from the Wood. D, A and B Companies were sent against the Hill, a difficult task but the measured artillery support covered them until the last minute and soon this formidable Hill was crowned by cheering men from the Battalion. They found , to great appreciation, two Turkish field kitchens with fires going and boiled lentils. Also some water bottles to replenish their own depleted reserves of water.

Battle of Megiddo; destroyed Turkish carts and gun carriages September 1918
(Photograph by kind permission of the Imperial War Museum)

For the Battalion the fighting was over. When the day's events were reviewed an officer wrote "Several years of war experience had made the British troops very highly disciplined and we went into battle as though going on parade."

Casualties for the 19th September were not heavy but however light each one represented a personal tragedy for the family. 2 officers and 5 other ranks were killed and 2 more died of wounds, 48 were wounded, 6 were missing. Amongst the missing was William then aged 30, who is commemorated on the Jerusalem Memorial.

William's name

The War had a liberating effect upon women. With the shortage of men they filled positions in factories and offices, drove buses, worked in postal deliveries and filled many other jobs usually the preserve of men. Traditionally nursing was a career for women but the difference now was that nurses could be ministering close to the areas of combat – indeed in some places they were to be found more or less in front line positions. Even at base hospitals they were not out of danger and many nurses fell victim to bombing raids and long range shelling.

Martha Townsend was a Staff Nurse with Queen Alexandra's Imperial Military Nursing Service. She was the daughter of James and Mary Townsend of "Redwalls" Rollestons Road.

The Service had been established in 1902 and was the successor to the Army Nursing Service formed in 1881. In turn that Service had come about due to the efforts of Florence Nightingale who had, after the Crimean War, succeeded in establishing an Army Training School for military nurses at the Royal Victoria Hospital at Netley.

Martha was born on the 11th February 1878. She was educated at a private school in Chelmsford and trained as a nurse at Lewisham Infirmary from July 1903 until July 1906 by which time she had attained the position of Staff Nurse. She was then engaged in private nursing until applying to join Queen Alexandra's Imperial Military Service in 1916.

After an interview on 1st November she was accepted on 3rd November. One of the particular questions asked was her experience in the nursing of enteric fever which she was able to confirm by virtue of her time at Lewisham. On the 13th November 1916 Martha was posted to the Military Hospital at Dartford. Then on the 6th May 1918 she embarked for Salonika to nurse the casualties from that theatre of war. She wrote to her mother from Southampton in a letter postmarked 11.30 am 7th May 1918

The War Hospital
Saturday   Dartford
Kent

Dear Mother and Father
Just a line to let you know I am leaving here tomorrow Sunday
afternoon & we stay the night in London & sail early Monday
morning we got the news yesterday. I am sending my bank
book on to you if anything happens to me the lot is yours,
but I hope I shall get back again alright.
X
with kind love to all
Your affect daughter

Martha, then aged 35, arrived in Salonika on the 25th May 1918 and took up her nursing duties.

Throughout the Salonika campaign disease was as much a problem as the enemy. The chief cause was malaria. One area, Macedonia, was just about the worst place in Europe for malaria. The lakes and rivers were huge breeding grounds for mosquitoes. Alongside malaria, the men of the British Salonika Force also faced dysentery and various enteric diseases. In July 1917 a specialised enteric hospital was opened near Hortiach.

During periods of action at the front the nature of hospital life could change to near chaos. For many nurses this was their first taste of war. Many of them had come from middle class homes and although their nursing experience meant that they were no shrinking violets this was something different altogether.

Daily life for hospital staff in the Balkans was tough. The mountainous terrain, poor transport, appalling winters and boiling summers coupled with often makeshift hospital buildings made for a challenging assignment. On the other hand there were compensations for nurses based not too far from Salonika as they were seldom short of attentive officers keen to take them to dinner.

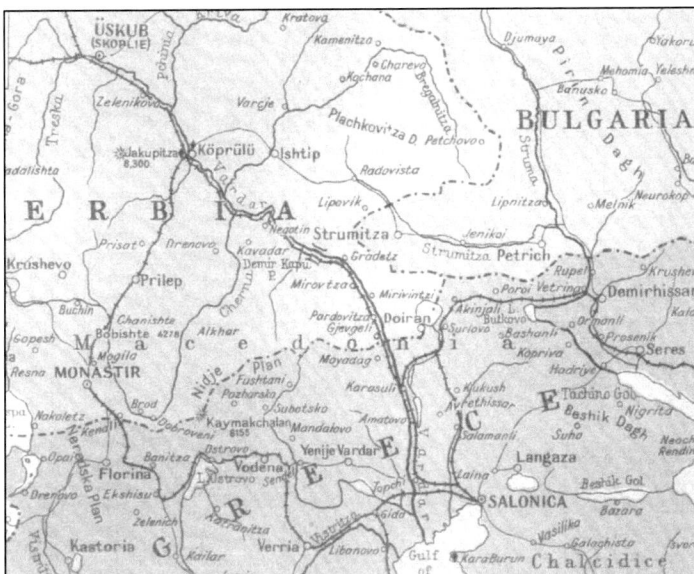

Map of Serbia and Greece

The end of the war in this part of Europe came in September 1918 when the Bulgarian Army was defeated. That the British Salonika Force was able to achieve this was in large measure due to the work of the men and women of the medical services.

On the 20th September Martha fell ill and as the Medical Case Sheet shows she rapidly deteriorated and, at 5.35 pm on the 21st September, died. The cause of death was given as broncho-pneumonia following the contraction of influenza.

Martha is buried in Mikra British Cemetery, Kalamaria, Greece.

Following her death a gratuity of £13·18·7d (£13.93) was paid and her personal belongings were then shipped back to her parents. She had not travelled light; her list of her clothes and other belongings ran to two columns on foolscap paper. In addition to clothing and other personal effects were articles described as being of sentimental or intrinsic value including a "Lusitania" medal. Is it possible that someone close to her was lost on that ship perhaps spurring her to enlist.

Martha Townsend's Grave
Her mother and father chose as the inscription "So soon passeth it away and we are gone".

Mikra Cemetery

MEDICAL CASE SHEET.*

Regimental No. | Rank. | Surname. | Christian Name.

Staff Nurse | Townsend | Martha

Unit. | Age. | Service.

Q.a.I.M.N.S.R (49 Gen. Hosp) | 36. | Salonika

Disease Influenza. Broncho-pneumonia.

Patient was quite well until 2.30 p.m yesterday when she complained of headache and pains in the back. T 103. P. 100. Respirations 26. at 5.0. p.m as her temperature had risen to 105° it was decided not to move her to No 43 General Hospital but to treat her here.

At 5.0. a.m this morning she developed capillary bronchitis & broncho-pneumonia which increased at an alarming rate.

The Consulting Physician came to see her at 6.45. a.m

At 4.0. p.m she became very cyanosed, the breathing became laboured, heart action very feeble and she died at 5.35 p.m

Disease was contracted on active service, subsequent to her joining the Q.a.I.M.N.S.R.

E.B. Riddick. Lt Col. R.a.M.c
O.C. 49 Gen Hosp.

* The first and last entries will be signed, and transfers from one Medical Officer to another, attested by their signatures.

Martha Townsend, medical case sheet

BLK/2/25585.

...of articles of sentimental or intrinsic value, the property
...Staff Nurse Townsend M., Q.A.I.M.N.S.R., 49th General Hospital,
A.M.C.

Bead Necklace in box (broken) | Silver chain with charm att'd
3 Brooches | Chain & pendant
Serviette ring | Silver pencil
Badge Q.A.I.M.N.S.R. | Eye glasses, chain & case
Bangle | 2 Charms
Tie Pin | Wrist Watch & strap
2 Identity Discs | 2 Albums
Silver Identity disc & chain | Travelling clock
Lusitania Medal | Book of prayers
Coin | Purse
Letters | 4 Farthings
Photos
Cards

List of Martha's articles of sentimental or intrinsic value

Little information has been forthcoming about **A.W. Wood**. He was married to Ellen and they lived at Town End. He enlisted in the Essex Regiment but subsequently transferred to the 12th Battalion Hampshire Regiment.

Soon after the opening of the Salonika campaign the XV1 Corps had its headquarters in January 1916 at Kirechkoi, Greece. In September 1918 the influenza epidemic raged across the country. Private Wood, aged 36, died on the 24th September and is buried in Kirechkoi – Hortakoi Cemetery. The cemetery is 15 kilometres north of Thessaloniki, Greece, on the outskirts of Kirechkoi, now known as Exohi. His name does not appear on the War Memorial.

It is possible that he died as a result of influenza as three quarters of the cemetery is filled with deaths from that cause.

However there was also a major offensive against the Bulgarians in September the Battle of Doiran. Training took place in August and early September but the outbreak of influenza proved so serious that the average strength of battalions was reduced by nearly a half.

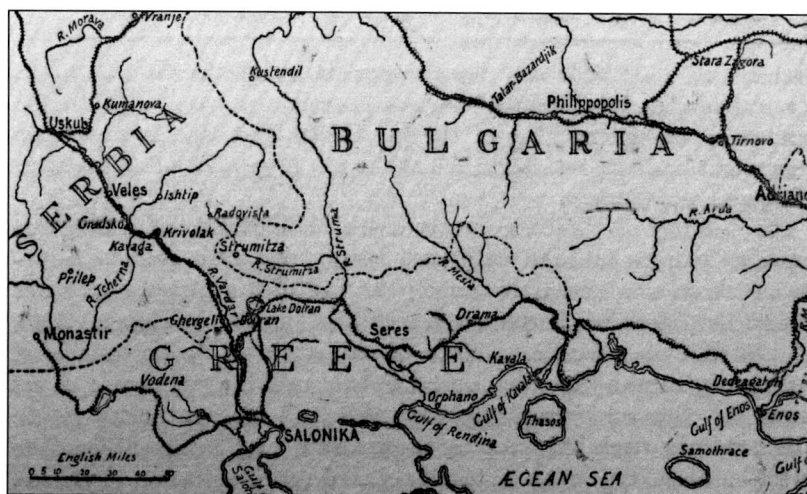

The Battle of Doiran

The attack began at dawn on the 18th September. The Greek contingent achieved some success but the British assault on that part of the Bulgarian defence known as Grand Couronne proved to be a tough proposition. The surrounding peaks were manned in strength and the British were met with a hail of bombs, rifle and machine gun fire. Hand to hand fighting ensued and some progress was made but at considerable cost and in places withdrawal had to be made.

So the renewed assault on the 19th September meant that the enemy would be found to be holding firm. Once again the Greek infantry fought well but the failure of the French Zouaves to advance caused difficulties for the British. Despite heavy casualties they forced their way forward but then were subject to such heavy fire from the sides that their position became untenable. The men were exhausted and ammunition was low. Then came the Bulgarian counter attack and there was no alternative but to retire. In doing so the shortage of ammunition saw the British having to make repeated bayonet charges.

But despite the Bulgarians holding off the assaults at Doiran their position generally was faltering. On 21st September their forces were in retreat but all was far from easy for the pursuing Allies. On the 24th September the advance was held up by a determined rear guard action.

The War, so far as this theatre was concerned, ended on the 29th September when an armistice was signed.

Kirechkoi - Hortakoi Cemetery
Containing 588 First War graves, also 58 Bulgarians, There are 17 graves of
British servicemen of the Second World War)

The grave of A.W. Wood
"Sleep on, beloved, sleep, and take thy rest"
Sleep on, beloved: Anon.

Amongst the War's casualties were those from families long established in Writtle. The Garwood family was one of these. In 1916 William, the son of Robert and Elizabeth Garwood had been killed. **George Frederick Garwood**, assumed to be his cousin, was the son of George and Catherine (also described as Kathleen) Garwood of Back Road, Oxney Green. George Senior was a farm horseman. In 1901, in addition to George, there were two younger children, Bertie, then 9, and Elizabeth, then 1.

George married Lilian and they set up home at 33 Nelson Road, Chelmsford.

In 1918 he was a Private in the 1st Battalion the Middlesex Regiment, The Duke of Cambridge's Own, the Regiment more commonly known as the Die-Hards.

Earlier that year the 1st Battalion had been in the front line at Ypres. Then at the end of August it headed south. Billets were at Pommera and after two weeks rest the Battalion marched to Equancourt and on the 19th September took up position in front of Villers-Guislain. Sporadic fighting occurred over the next few days but then it made ready for an attack on the German line.

On the night of the 23rd/24th September the 1st Battalion occupied a line south east of Villers-Guislain and whilst the 100th Brigade launched an attack the 1st bombed its way forward but the battalion that was supposed to link up with them was nowhere in sight and so the whole operation rather petered out.

Villers - Guislain south west of Cambrai

On the night of the 24th/25th they were subjected to a gas attack. Next day they moved back to support trenches.

The night of the 28th/29th the 1st Battalion made ready for an attack in the early hours. Their objectives ran from Derby Post to Villers Hill. The disposition was A company on the right, D Company in the centre and C on the left with B Company allotted a mopping up role.

The attack was launched at zero hour, 3.30 am. The 1st Middlesex together with the 4th Kings and the 2nd Argyll and Sutherland Highlanders initially made good progress but, although Villers-Guislain was stormed and taken, the enemy began to filter back into the village. D Company met with strong opposition whilst B found itself surrounded and cut off. By 1pm the Commanding Officer of the Battalion was obliged to report that what had happened to B, along with C Company, was unclear. Eventually, however, during the night the Germans were pushed back.

In the attack on the 29th September the 1st Middlesex had 4 officers and 71 other ranks killed, 3 officers and 159 other ranks wounded and 20 other ranks missing.

George was one of those killed. He was aged 31. He is buried in Villers Hill British Cemetery, Villers – Guislain, south west of Cambrai. Villers Hill Cemetery was begun as the Middlesex Cemetery and the original Cemetery (now Plot 1) contains 100 graves of which 50 belong to the 1st Middlesex.

Villers Hill Cemetery

George Garwood's Grave
"At Rest"
Flanked in death by companions "Known unto God".

The remaining two soldiers who died in 1918 are both buried in All Saints Cemetery. The first, **Frank Dale** originally came from Rugby and subsequently moved to Writtle.

He was a Gunner in the Royal Field Artillery. He died on the 8th November 1918 at the Military Hospital at Warley, aged 24 or 26 (both ages are given) and was buried just five days later at All Saints. It is likely that he was a victim of the influenza epidemic sweeping Europe which was responsible for millions more deaths. The exhausted state of the combatant nations no doubt contributed to the swift spread of the disease

Frank's name is not shown on the War Memorial

Frank's grave

Isaac John Everard is the third Everard commemorated on the War Memorial.

The 1901 Census gave the family details as Samuel, an agricultural labourer, aged 48, his wife Sarah aged 52 and their children Emily 18, Isaac 15, Thomas 13 and Minnie 10. The family lived at 10 Victoria Road, Oxney Green. Also in the household was a daughter, Alice Woodman aged 20 and her baby son of three months, George.

Descriptive Report on Enrolment

Isaac had enlisted in October 1916 in a part of the country somewhat removed from Writtle, namely Rugeley in Staffordshire. He gave his address as Causeway Cottages, Writtle, his age as 31 and trade that of a labourer. He passed his medical. Height 5 feet 6 inches, weight 123 pounds, physical development good apart from defective teeth.

He also gave as his next of kin his wife Rose Ella Everard, nee Day; they had married at Writtle on the 25th December 1909. It would appear that the Causeway Cottage address was her home as this is her address as a spinster.

Isaac was posted to the Royal Garrison Artillery on the 1st November 1916. He was a Gunner with 52 Siege Brigade and they left Southampton on the 25th April 1917 arriving in Le Havre a day later.

And there the story of Writtle's involvement in the Great War should have ended. The Armistice came into force at 11am on the 11th November 1918. But whilst on leave, starting on the 25th November 1918, Isaac was admitted to the Isolation Hospital at Roman Road, East Ham on the 5th December 1918 suffering from influenza with chest complications. He died there on the 28th November from pneumonia. He was buried on the 5th December at All Saints.

Isaac's headstone however is not of the usual War Graves Commission type and it will be seen that also buried with him is his wife Rose. She died just six days before him, on the 22nd November also at East Ham Isolation Hospital and also from influenza and pneumonia

Death certificate of Rose

The grave of Isaac and Rose Everard in All Saints Churchyard

Letter from the War Office

The War office received a letter from Isaac's sister Mrs G. Roberts of 10 Victoria Road, Oxney Green giving notice of death "on 12.11.18". The person dealing with this asked if this was a mistake - presumably querying the date of death and this resulted in his death certificate being produced showing his date of death correctly as the 28th November.

The War Office authorised the Artillery to release Isaac's effects to his father Samuel.

Declaration by Samuel Everard

In the last week of August 1914 the British retreated from Mons. The autumn of 1918 saw a series of British victories. But the German army was not yet broken. As the British advanced they came up against the Forest of Mormal, some forty square miles, its northern approaches guarded by the fortress of Le Quesnoy and with the German armies lined out in naturally strong positions.

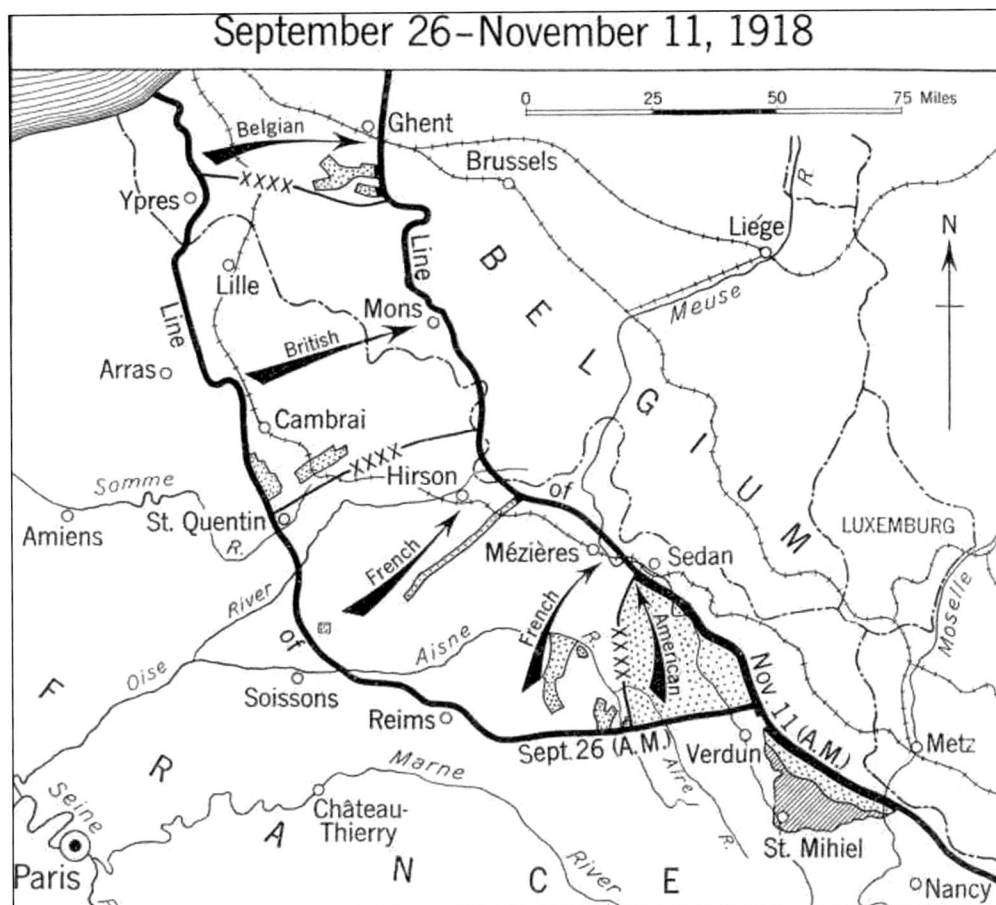

September 26–November 11, 1918

It was expected that the obstacle of the Forest, in which machine gun defence would be murderous, would be slowly turned along the north and south as the French and American armies had turned the obstacle of the Argonne Forest. But that was not the British way. The goal of Mons was the object of the British. The Germans were urgently seeking an armistice but the British soldiers wanted to stand victorious in the small city where the old Regular Expeditionary Force had opened the War against overwhelming odds.

So instead of working round the Forest the First, Third and Fourth Armies opened the Second Battle of Mons at dawn on the 4th November by a direct frontal assault. On a thirty mile front they went in straight and hard.

The New Zealanders cracked the tough nut of Le Quesnoy whilst the Fourth Army forced its way between Le Cateau and the Forest. All day the forest combat went on. When night fell it still went on with the British Divisions fighting over the wire entanglements, pits and barricades.

While the Third and Fourth Armies closed towards Mons from the south, the First Army advanced on Condé from where the canal stretched to Mons. Here the enemy retreated. In and around the Mormal Forest, where they attempted to resist, the Germans were wiped out.

Then against the German rear guard machine gunners the final phase began. Tournai fell to the British, then Maubeurge. And on Monday 11th November, before the ceasefire sounded, the successors of "the contemptible little army" fought their way into Mons. By the most remarkable coincidence in history the War for the British ended exactly where it had begun.

Although the formalities would not take place until 1919 the Armistice on the 11th hour of the 11th day of the 11th month brought to a finish "the war to end all wars".

AY, NOVEMBER 15, 1918.

PEACE AGAIN!

How the News was Received in Essex.

Great Public Rejoicings.

Some time in advance of other announcements, the Essex County Chronicle on Monday morning exhibited in its windows in the High Street, Chelmsford, the following statement:—

Peace—Official:
Armistice signed at 5 o'clock this morning; hostilities cease at 11.

Later came the following message:—
Press Bureau, 10.20.
The Prime Minister makes the following announcement:

The armistice was signed at 5 a.m. this morning, and hostilities are to cease on all fronts at 11 a.m. to-day.

The Essex County Chronicle message spread like wildfire, and in shorter time than it takes to write, High Street, Chelmsford, was ablaze with flags, processions, some small and some large, began to form and march through the town; Hoffmann's great works emptied themselves of the thousands of workpeople, and the Mayor, Ald. Cowell, issued a request notifying that he desired that the day should be considered a holiday in celebration of the signing of the armistice.

The Chronicle - 15th November 1918.

The Chronicle reported how Writtle celebrated the end of the War

WRITTLE.
The village went into general rejoicing and the shops closed. The V.A.D. wounded paraded the village with a tin-kettle and bath band. Flags were shown everywhere. A peal of bells was rung by the bellringers at the church.

And so Writtle, with the rest of the country, marked the end of the War with general rejoicing. For many there was no cause for celebration and for others there would still lie ahead much in the way of distress. Physical wounds and mental anguish would take their toll in the following years, the influenza epidemic had a long way to go before it ran its course and the fall out from the War caused further casualties, but for now, Writtle enjoyed the moment.

In Memoriam

In the aftermath of the War towns and villages all over the country sought ways of commemorating those who had lost their lives. Out of 16,000 villages in Great Britain there were just 32 (later adjusted to 41) who had no-one killed during the War – "the Thankful Villages". In Essex, the Parish of Strethall near Saffron Walden saw all their 15 men return. In a few villages memorials, for one reason or another, were not erected but in the vast majority of communities there was an overwhelming desire to mark the sacrifice made by their men, and women, in some permanent form.

On the 1st November 1919 the Chairman of Writtle Parish Council, Mr Lindsell, suggested a memorial to those from Writtle who had fallen in the War. It was resolved "that the Parish Council approves of a Memorial in the Village and that a public meeting be called to consider the question."

It was decided that the memorial should be the simple Cross favoured in many towns and villages. The Cross is made of Cornish granite and has on it 54 names (and later were added 23 names from the Second World War). It was dedicated on the 29th May 1920. The cost was £220 and the enclosure cost a further £51.10 shillings (£51-50p).

MEMORIAL AT WRITTLE

The memory of Writtle's heroic dead was perpetuated on Saturday by the unveiling of a handsome memorial cross, which has been erected in a commanding position on the pond end of the village green, 'in remembrance of those who gave their lives in the war. The monument, which cost about £230, is of cornish granite and the octagonal column, standing on two steps, bears the inscription, "To the glory of God and in honour of all who went forth from this parish in answer to the call of duty, and in lasting memory of those who gave their lives in the cause of freedom and right." At the base of the column is inscribed the names of 58 Writtle men who made the supreme sacrifice. The task of collecting subscriptions to defray the cost was undertaken by members of the Parish Council, supported by interested ladies and gentlemen of the parish, having Mr. A. P. Lindsell as chairman, and Mr. T. Williams (schoolmaster) as hon. sec.

A large gathering of relatives, ex-Service men, and friends witnessed the unveiling ceremony, which was presided over by Mr. A. P. Lindsell. Messages were received from the Vicar, the Rev. E. S. Grover, and Mr. E. A. Hunt, J.P., both of whom are away on holiday.—The chairman said there was nothing greater in the life of man than duty, and they wanted to acknowledge the undying debt of gratitude they owed to the brave men who gave all in the cause of others, and to show that those at home were not unmindful of those sacrifices. Addressing the children, Mr. Lindsell pointed to the greatness of service for others.

Miss M. A. Usborne then released the Union Jack that enfolded the memorial.—Dr. R. N. Arnold-Wallinger, on behalf of the subscribers, committed the custody of the monument to the Parish Council. The cross, he said, stood as a visible bond of unity among every class in the parish, all of whom were represented in the names it bore.—The Chairman, in accepting the care of the monument on behalf of the Parish Council, said it would not only be their duty but their privilege to preserve it.

During the service the Rev. W. Peoples, curate, read Scriptural passages, and the hymns, "O God, our help in ages past," and "For all the saints," etc., were feelingly sung, music being supplied by Hoffmann's band, under Mr. Geo. Lee. The Rev. W. Peoples curate-in-charge, pronounced the Benediction.

A beautiful collection of floral tributes was placed on the steps of the monument by relatives of the fallen, during which the "Last Post" was sounded. Ex-Service men of the parish laid two wreaths at the foot of the memorial, "In remembrance of our comrades, gone but not forgotten," and "From comrades of those whose memory will always be before us by this memorial."

The Parish Magazine of April 1921 in reporting the financial cost then continued "Standing in the very heart of the village it serves a double purpose as a faithful remembrance of those who laid down their lives in the cause of Freedom and Right and as a constant reminder that we too, one and all, must be prepared to uphold those high principles for which they made the supreme sacrifice".

On the Armistice Day following the dedication of the Memorial the Parish Magazine reported that a service was held there with 300 village school children forming a semi-circle around the Memorial. The sale of poppies had raised the sum of £12-1-6d (£12.07½p). Prayers were said and then the bells were rung, half muffled, to the memory of the fallen.

The Armistice had taken place on the 11th November 1918 but the influenza epidemic that swept Europe in the dying days of the War caused numerous deaths.

To take just one day, 8th November 1918, the Weekly News had a long list of those who had succumbed to the disease.

"Master Cecil Nicholls, aged 15; the wives of three Bishop Stortford soldiers; Clara Weston, widowed when her husband was killed in France; Corporal Sidney Bowman while home on leave; Raymond Jarvis and his wife - Raymond, who was the son of the Mayor and Mayoress of Colchester, had been invalided out of the Army after being gassed."

And the list continued.

In Writtle, the death of Edward Betts, aged 12, was reported on the 13th December. He was a Boy Scout and died following attending the funeral of another Scout. His coffin was draped with the Union Flag and the bearers were soldiers, recovering from wounds, members of the V.A.D. Edward was described as very musical and had played at events at the Hospital. The Reverend Peoples officiated and the last Post was sounded by Robert Gardener.

The families of Edward and Robert had both lost loved ones. Ernest Betts had died on the "Alcantara" on the 29th February 1916. Charles Gardener had died of dysentery on the 9th November 1915. Robert Gardener and his brother Edward lived with their mother, Bertha, the widow of Charles Gardener although their address was now shown as Waterloo Street, not Road. Living with them was Charles' father, Robert.

The families of those who had died got on with their lives, no doubt each remembering in their own way. A few might have visited the grave of a husband, son or brother. In May 1920 the Weekly News carried the following advertisement… "Battlefield Tour including travel and accommodation. Motor Tour Bruges, Ypres, Passchendaele, etc. £9." Some commissioned memorials, most would simply have their loved ones' names shown on the War Memorial. Forms had to be completed to obtain medals and personal effects.

Edward Harvey died on the 10th January 1917. His widow, Britannia, received the standard letter telling her she would be sent a commemorative plaque upon completion of a Declaration.

Declaration signed by Britannia

It would seem to us today a cruel exchange; a young wife with toddlers of 3 ½ and 2 ½ gets a plaque and a scroll in place of a husband. And of course no Welfare State in existence.

Leonard Moss died on the 1st April 1917. The Statement was completed on 5th July 1919 by his father Frederick. By then two of his sisters had emigrated, one to Australia and one to Canada. The Declaration was witnessed by the congregational minster at The Manse.

There appears to have been some confusion concerning William Everard who died on the 2nd May 1918. In 1921 his mother wrote enquiring about his medals.

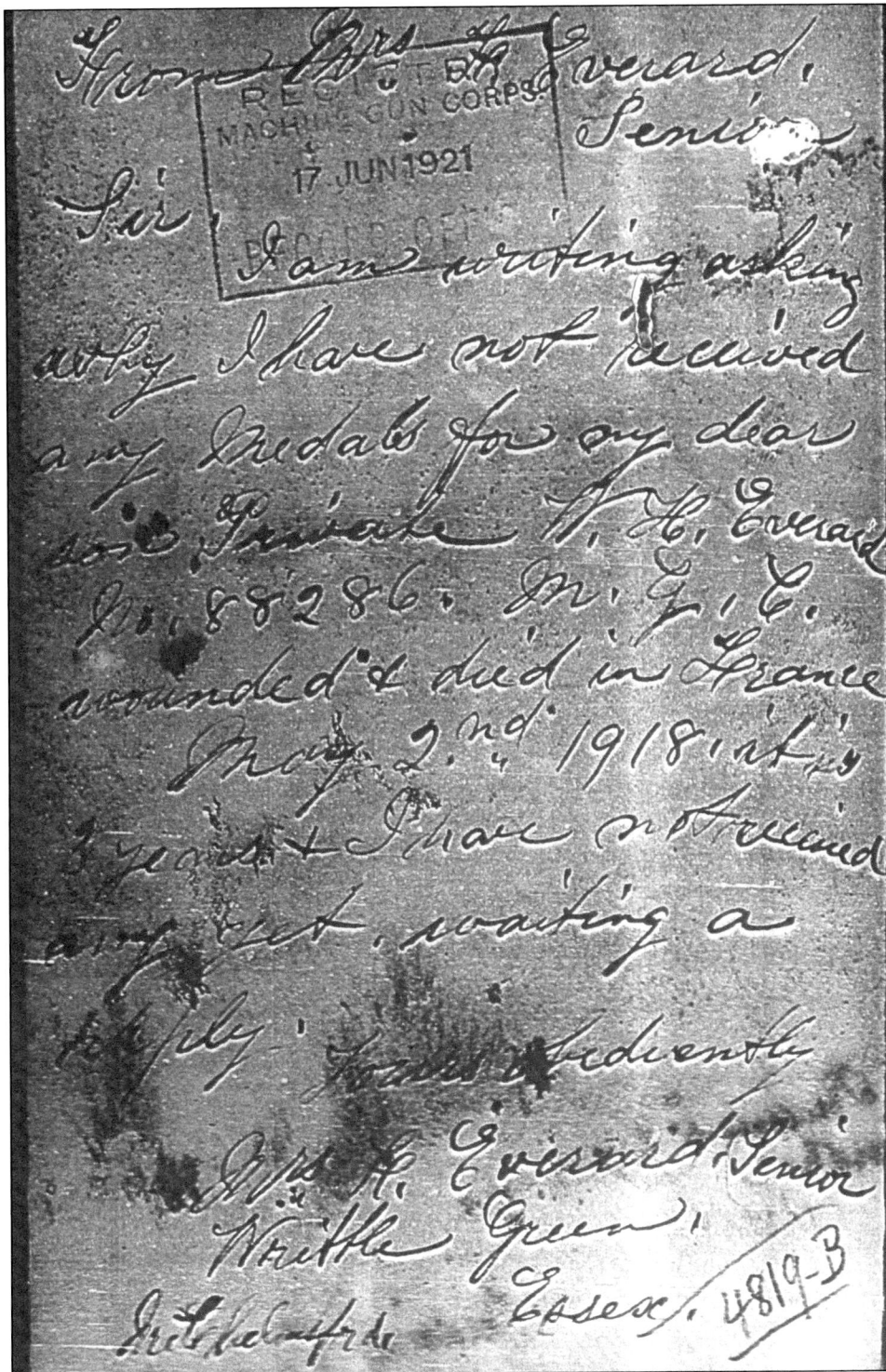

"I am writing asking why I have not received any medals for my dear son Private W.H. Everard No. 88286 M.G.C. wounded and died in France May 2nd 1918 it is 3 years and I have not received any yet. Waiting a reply".

She was informed that the medals would be issued to the only person authorised to receive them, Mr Everard. He had completed the appropriate Declaration in 1919.

Regiment MACHINE GUN CORPS

Army Form W. 5080

To be filled in by Officer in Charge of Records.

88286 Pte Everard W H ... deceased

STATEMENT of the Names and Addresses of all the Relatives of the above-named deceased Soldier in each of the degrees specified below that are now living.

NOTE.—Against those degrees of relationship in which there is no relative now living the word "none" is to be inserted. If the answers are not filled in much correspondence and delay may be occasioned by the neglect.

Degree of relationship		NAME IN FULL of every relative now living in each degree enquired for (see note above).	ADDRESS IN FULL of each surviving relative opposite his or her name.
Widow of the Soldier		None	
Children of the Soldier and dates of their births... ...		None	
Father of the Soldier		Frederick Everard	Whittle Green
Mother of the Soldier		Sarah Everard	Whittle Green
Brothers of the Soldier	Full Blood ...	Frederick Everard 38	Whittle Green
		Charles Joseph Everard 36	Bridge Street Whittle
	Half blood ...	None	
Sisters of the Soldier	Full blood ...	Dorothy Jane Stevens 25	Whittle Green
	Half blood ...	None	

DECLARATION.

I hereby declare that the above is a true and complete Statement of all the Relatives of the late Soldier now living in the degrees enquired for.

Frederick Everard .... Signature of the Declarant.

Relationship to the Soldier Father

Address in full Whittle Green

I hereby certify that the above Statement and Declaration made by Frederick Everard and signed in my presence is complete and correct, to the best of my knowledge and belief.

Dated at Whittle this 3 day of June 1919

Signature Edmund A Hunt

Qualification

Address Whittle

Declaration signed by Mr Frederick Everard

In fact it was to Mrs Sarah Everard that the medals were issued in 1922.

I hereby acknowledge the receipt of the British War Medal and Victory Medal granted in respect of the service of No 88286 Private William Henry Everard M G Corps

Mrs S Everard Whittle Green

Date Nov 13th 1922.

Signature Sarah Everard

Sir I am sorry I could not answer before I have been away. Sarah Everard

The Officer in Charge of Records wrote to Herbert Fayers at 3 Clifton Cottages, St Johns Green requesting that the Declaration be completed in respect of his son Alfred who died on the 16th August 1917. Herbert completed the Declaration so that the plaque and scroll could be sent to him.

Herbert Fayers' Declaration
(damaged by fire as a result of enemy bombing in the Second World War)

The medals and commemorative plaque were sent to Mr Fayers. All families received a commemorative plaque (known as "the death penny") in addition to the medals and personal effects.

Elizabeth Little, the mother of Thomas Little who had been killed on the 28th August 1918, was shown upon his enlistment as next of kin, in fact his only kin. She received a letter stamped 20th March 1919 together with his personal effects. They included 6 marks – no doubt in readiness for an anticipated entrance into Germany.

List of Thomas' personal effects

A month later, 9th May 1919, approval was given to the release of Thomas' Military Medal to his mother.

Somewhat strangely a year later Mrs Little wrote to the Army asking if she had been named as Thomas' next of kin or, if someone else had been named, who that was. Perhaps a fear he had secretly married? The Records Office confirmed that there was no other person and that she was the next of kin.

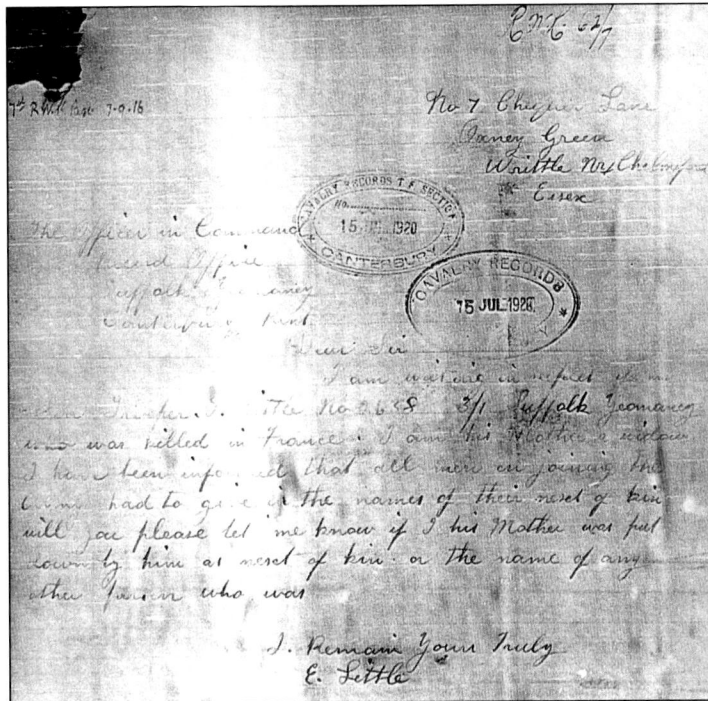

"I am writing in respect of my son Trooper T. Little No. 2638 3/1 Suffolk Yeomanry who was killed in France. I am his mother a widow. I have been informed that all men on joining the Army had to give in the names of their next of kin will you please let me know if I his mother was put down by him as next of kin or the name of any other person who was."

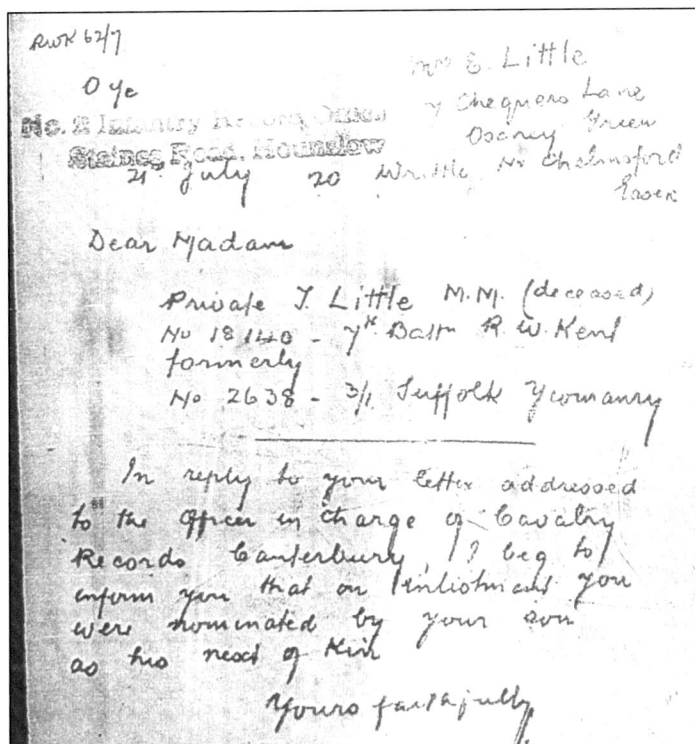

Reply

- 239 -

The Last of the Fallen

There are two further graves of Writtle servicemen in All Saints Churchyard.

The mammoth task of clearing the Battlefield

George Bennett Fitch, is not recorded on the Writtle War Memorial. He lived at Little Oxney Green. He enlisted in the Essex Yeomanry but then transferred to the Suffolk Regiment. His final transfer was to the Labour Corps.

George's grave in All Saints Churchyard

At the beginning of the War, labour – of which there was an ever growing need – had been organised on a fairly haphazard basis. In 1916 the Army Labour Corps was formed. In August 1917 the various companies in the Army Labour Corps were formed into the Labour Corps. Towards the end of the War the number of men making up the workforce for the massive task of clearing the debris and in salvage work was huge. Some soldiers switched to the Labour Corps where trained men were needed to supervise a collection of labourers of different nationalities and of varying degrees of competence.

There is little else readily known about George Fitch. He died on the 11th February 1919 aged 28 and was buried six days later in Writtle Churchyard.

James Rumsey comes from another well known Writtle family but although commemorated on the War Memorial there is not a lot known about his service. The War Graves Commission has no details about him.

James was born on the 24th February 1892 and was baptised at All Saints on the 15th May. His parents were George James and Alice Rumsey and George's occupation was given as a wheelwright.

By 1901 the Census showed the Rumsey family, of some considerable size, living at Oxney Green. George was then a beer retailer and Alice a landlady. The children; George 17, Sarah 16, Frances 14, Bertha 12, James 9, Blanche Alice 6 and Percy 5. Subsequently George took over as Landlord of the Rose and Crown.

When Blanche Alice died in 1916, James and another brother Percy were unable to attend being on active service in France. Eldest brother George was also in the Army and it is believed that he suffered a shrapnel wound. Percy was in the Royal Flying Corps.

The Rumsey family grave

It is understood that James suffered from being gassed in France and was discharged from the Army in 1918. He died on the 17th August 1919 and is buried in the family grave in the Churchyard

Although 1919 had seen the formal ending of the War with the signing of the Treaty of Versailles on the 28th June 1919 the turmoil created during those years created conflicts which rumbled on and none more so than in Russia where the White Russians endeavoured to overthrow the Bolsheviks.

The civil war in Russia was probably of small importance to the villagers in Writtle welcoming back the soldiers and sailors who returned home and mourning those who did not. But a son of Writtle was to be involved in an audacious and immensely courageous action in August 1919 and, although he had moved away from Writtle by then and is not named on the War Memorial, he is commemorated by a plaque in the Church.

He is **Thomas Richard Guy Usborne** the son of Edward Francis and Edith Constance Usborne who lived at "Motts" in 1901. Edward was director of the Writtle Brewery. In 1901 Thomas was six months old, his date of birth the 9th October 1900. Also living there was his sister Hermione, aged 3, and three servants. Subsequently the family moved to Burlesdon in Hampshire.

Thomas entered a Naval Training Establishment on the 15th September 1913 just a couple of weeks short of his 13th birthday. He passed out on the 1st January 1917 and that month joined the "Royal Sovereign" as a midshipman. He was described as "intelligent and keen" but failed his navigation examination due to "Temp'y Exam fright". Subsequently he passed and on 28th April 1919, as Acting Sub Lieutenant, he was sent to Osea Island for training on Coastal Motor Boats.

A prohibition order forbidding unauthorised persons coming near the base was published on the 5th July 1918.

The Order published in the Chronicle

The base could accommodate 52 boats and included supply and maintenance facilities. The existing hotel had been converted into senior officers' quarters and the sanatorium provided the junior officers' quarters. The boats were hauled up the slipway by means of a capstan and thence on to a traverser which ran in a pit. The boats were then stored in two lines of berths.

Some of the facilities built in this area specifically for the war effort have survived to this day. The massive concrete traverser pit appears as a dry dock or inland harbour. Parts of the slipway, up which boats were hauled, can still be seen and much of the pier survives. The former hotel and senior officers' quarters is now a private house as is the sanatorium/junior officers' quarters. A number of the other buildings and huts also remain.

(Heritage Conservation at Essex County Council)

On the 15th July Thomas was promoted to sub Lieutenant and the following day joined, in a fateful choice, CMB 79 at Greenwich.

The events of 1918 and 1919 in the Baltic that led to the Kronstadt raid were a response to the fear of the spread of Bolshevism. The British Government embarked upon a show of strength in the Baltic both to help the White Russians fighting the Bolsheviks and to support the independence of the Baltic States. Some British troops were dispatched to the area and fans of the 1970's series "When the boat comes in" will recall that James Bolam's character, Serjeant Jack Ford, was not demobbed at the end of the War but had been sent to Russia.

But it was on the naval force that hope was pinned to contain the Red tide. A number of clashes with the Bolshevik fleet led to the plan of attacking the formidable naval base at Kronstadt and putting out of action its two battleships. The base was heavily protected and the only chance of getting through would be a fast attack, impossible for warships having to negotiate the minefields and other obstacles, but achievable by the use of Coastal Motor Boats with their high speeds and shallow draughts. The CMBs were 40 feet long and their petrol engines allowed a top speed of 35 knots. They carried machine guns and an 18 inch torpedo – later two torpedoes.

At 10 pm on Sunday 17th August 1919 seven CMBs set out from Biorko, Finland. Each had a captain, a second in command whose main task was to fire the torpedoes, a motor mechanic and a crew of ratings. No 79's captain was Lieutenant Bremner, his second in command, at just 19, Sub Lieutenant Thomas Usborne.

They entered the North Channel about two hours later, running the gauntlet of the forts guarding Petrograd Bay. At about the same time the RAF mounted a diversionary bombing raid which caused little actual damage but lots of confusion.

The lead group of CMBs, Nos 79,31 and 88, throttled back their engines and glided past the guardship at the harbour entrance. Then they roared into the middle harbour and Thomas on No. 79 fired at the depot ship "Pamyat Azova". The torpedo struck home and she quickly sank. The next target needed a difficult manoeuvre by 31 but again the torpedoes found their mark, the dreadnought "Petropavlovsk", which blew up and sank.

These explosions brought the garrison from their shelters and fire was opened up on the boats from all directions. No. 88's captain was shot through the head but her second in command was able to re-gain control and fired the torpedo which resulted in an explosion on board the other battleship the pre-dreadnought "Andrei Pervozvanni". Her flames lit up the whole basin.

The Petropavlovsk

CMB No 24 was to deal with the guardship "Gavriil" but unfortunately the torpedo missed. The Russian crew retaliated and a shell split 24 in half and sank her.

In the meantime 86, 72 and 62 had followed the lead boats. Nos 86 and 72 had hoped to deal with the cruiser "Rurik" but 86 had engine problems whilst 72 had her torpedo firing mechanism damaged by a shell splinter. In a fine piece of seamanship the captain of 72, though under fire, was able to tow the other boat away.

The three lead boats were now racing back from the middle harbour but No 79 had the bad luck to collide with the back up boat, 62. The captain of 62 displaying great presence of mind, went full speed ahead with both boats locked together until they came to a boom guarding part of the harbour which they destroyed by exploding against it the crippled 79. With both crews on board No 62 her captain made for the main channel and in doing so fired torpedoes at the guardship "Gavriil" but missed. Again the Russians returned fire with shells and machine guns and unfortunately No 62 was hit and sunk.

As dawn was breaking on the morning of the 18th August the remaining CMBs, 31 and 88 and 72 with 86 in tow made for the safety of the open sea pursued by a hail of shellfire.

The raid was a success. At the cost of three CMB's the Russian surface fleet had been reduced to a few destroyers and there was no longer a significant threat to the British Baltic Force nor a seaward threat to the smaller Baltic States.

But the human cost was considerable. There had been three officers and six ratings rescued by the Russians when 62 and 79 collided; they were imprisoned but subsequently released. Six officers, including Thomas Usborne, and nine ratings had been killed. For his part Thomas was awarded a mention in Dispatches. In the light of what he, and all those taking part, went through it does not seem enough albeit that no honour could replace them in the hearts of their families.

Thomas' Naval Record

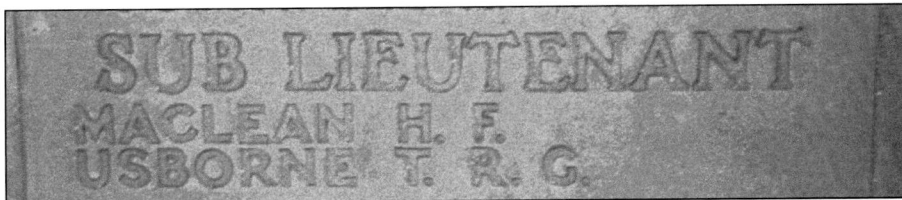

Thomas' name on the Portsmouth Memorial

The Plaque in All Saints

Changes

Village life returned to a normality. People moved, people died, the world moved on.

George Anstee had died on 31st July 1917 but his two brothers both survived. Fred was wounded in Gallipoli and subsequently became the village postman. Edward lived in Ongar Road and his daughter became a senior United Nations official and was created a Dame.

Sir Daniel and Lady Gooch left Hylands in 1920. Their leaving was a cause of much regret. In the same edition of the Parish Magazine the death of Lady Gooch was announced and her interment was in the same grave as their son Lancelot who had died on the 4th October 1915. Sir Daniel died a few years later in 1926.

---

iv.   WRITTLE PARISH MAGAZINE.

WOMEN'S INSTITUTE WORKING PARTY.

Mrs. Burbidge hopes to meet the members of the W.W.I. Working Party on Wednesday, Oct. 5th, at 2.15, in the Iron Room. Will all the members make a special effort to be present?

There will be a discussion about the work for the W.W.I. Show in November.

GIRL GUIDES.

On their return home from a very enjoyable holiday the girls found themselves welcomed very hospitably to tea by Mrs. Lodge.

A prize had been offered for the best essay on their week's outing. This was won by Ivy Cuthbertson with a very good account, but too long to insert here, as had been suggested.

On Wednesday, Oct. 5th, it is proposed to hold Social Evening in the Village Hall, from 7 till 9.

BROWNIE PACK.

On Saturday, September 10th, the 1st Writtle Brownie Pack, under Brown Owl Miss M. Sparrow, and Tawny Owl Miss G. Roffey, went for a day's camp on Galleywood Common. They all spent a jolly day playing games and gathering blackberries, and after camp-fire yarn, they made for home. Mr. C. Russell kindly provided conveyances.

THE PASSING OF HYLANDS.
II.

The two Churches, Widford built in 1861, and Galleywood in 1873, are a noble monument to Mr. Arthur Pryor's sense of what was due from the owner of a great estate to the Church to which he belonged.

His son, Mr. Arthur Vickris Pryor, sold the estate in 1908 to Sir Daniel Fulthorpe Gooch, Bart., who has, after holding it for 13 years, in turn sold it to a local resident.

During the time that Sir Daniel and Lady Gooch resided at Hylands the use of the Park has always been allowed for good causes, and a fête held in 1912 on behalf of the funds of Church schools realized over £500.

Hylands was the first War Hospital opened in Essex, and Lady Gooch became its superintendent. About one thousand exceptionally serious cases were dealt with during the time it was used for this purpose. It must have cost the generous donors many thousands of pounds to maintain the Hospital.

Two fêtes, held in the Park on behalf of the Essex Regiment Prisoners of War, resulted in the sum of one thousand pounds being handed over to the funds.

King George held a Review of the Troops of the South Midland Division on October 11th, 1914; and it was here that Lord Kitchener inspected the troops shortly before he met his tragic death in the "Hampshire."

The family left Hylands to take up their residence at Tatchbury Mount, Totton, at Christmas last.

Many of the farms have since been resold to the tenants and others. What the future of the beautiful mansion and gardens will be is a matter of speculation.

It is with sincere regret that we have to record the death of Lady Gooch, which occured on Tuesday, July 26th, at Totton. The funeral took place at Widford on the Friday following; the interment being made in the same grave as that of her eldest son, Lancelot Daniel Edward, who died while on service as a Midshipman in the late war.

BAPTISMS.
"Suffer the little children to come unto Me."
September 25, Joyce Alma King.
    ,,   25, Leslie Alfred Eve.

MARRIAGE.
"Love never faileth."
September 10, Joseph William Coe and Elizabeth Mabel Campen.

CHURCH COLLECTIONS.

SEPTEMBER 1ST—30TH.	£	s.	d.
Church Expenses	7	1	6
Parochial Fund	2	6	6
District Visitors' Fund	2	3	1
Chelmsford Hospital	4	10	0
Royal Agricultural Benevolent Institution	4	10	0
Total ...	20	11	1

William Bowtell died on the 16th July 1916 and his father died in the same year. His widow, Maria, took over as landlady of The Prince of Wales. Their grave is in All Saints Churchyard.

Many Writtle families rarely moved. For instance Henry Richard Malyon the father of Frederick Malyon - who had died on the 26th March 1917 - carried on living at 31 St Johns Green until his death in 1962; his wife lived on for another 30 years dying in 1992 aged 89. Thomas Little's mother Elizabeth (Lizzie on the Funeral records) carried on living at 7 Chequers Lane until her death on the 12th August 1949 at the age of 84.

In September 1921 the Parish Magazine reported that there was great sadness at the impending departure from the village of Mr Jeayes, his wife and their daughter. Their son, Henry, had died in Palestine on the 26th March 1917. The Magazine report stated how active Mr & Mrs Jeayes had been in Church and Parish Life.

The Bowtell grave

On the 4th January 1918 the death of Robert Woodhouse was reported.

Death of Robert Woodhouse

The death of his grandson Robert on the 14th August 1915 was understandably "a heavy loss" to him. How much more so when he had been the one exhorting, in no uncertain terms, young men to enlist at the meeting on The Green in September 1914. And how long ago that must have seemed.

The 1901 Census had shown the Woodhouse home, Longmeads, as a place of life, a true family home. By 1920 the only family members left there were Mrs Ellen Woodhouse and her eldest daughter Mary.

A stained glass window was erected in 1918 to commemorate Dorothy Woodhouse and Robert. It depicts Christ Triumphant and on the left St Dorothea and on the right St George.

In July 1921 the Writtle Parish Magazine reported the death of Mrs Woodhouse, the widow of Robert Woodhouse JP, at the age of 88.

The Woodhouse family sold Longmeads in 1930 to the Seabrook family. Mr Seabrook created many imaginative features in the gardens which were opened to the villagers on occasions throughout the year. By the 1950s much of the land had been sold and the house was used as a hostel. Today it houses the Community Association.

The Grave of Robert and Ellen Woodhouse, All Saints Churchyard

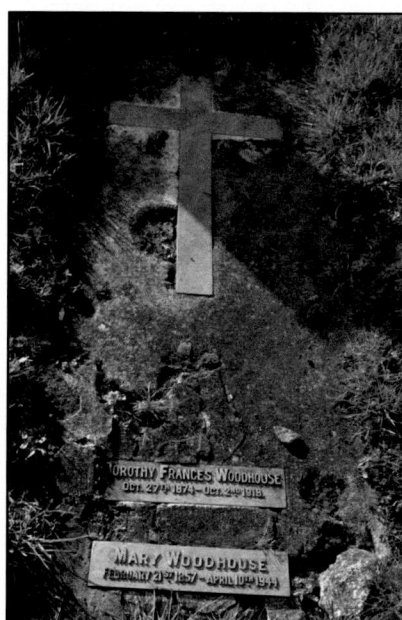

The grave of Dorothy Woodhouse and Mary Woodhouse, All Saints Churchyard

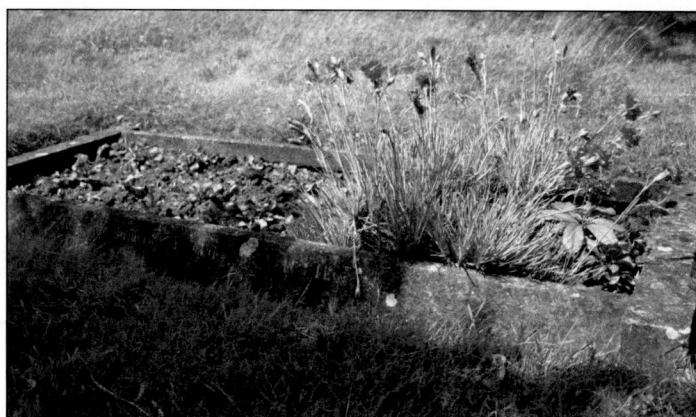

William Cresswell died on the 1st July 1916. His parents grave in All Saints bears the inscription "In Loving memory of Willie killed in the Somme."

One of the memorials in All Saints was a screen across the South Aisle given by Margaret Usborne in memory of her brother Guy, killed in the Kronstadt raid on the 18th August 1919.

Thomas Usborne's widow Florence and her daughter Phyllis were presented at Court in 1923. Florence died in 1958 aged 90. Both she and Thomas are buried in the All Saints Churchyard.

The Usborne's property, Writtle House, was demolished in 1920

Writtle House

Martha Townsend's parents died within two months of each other in 1924. They were buried in the Churchyard of All Saints and their headstone also commemorates their daughter

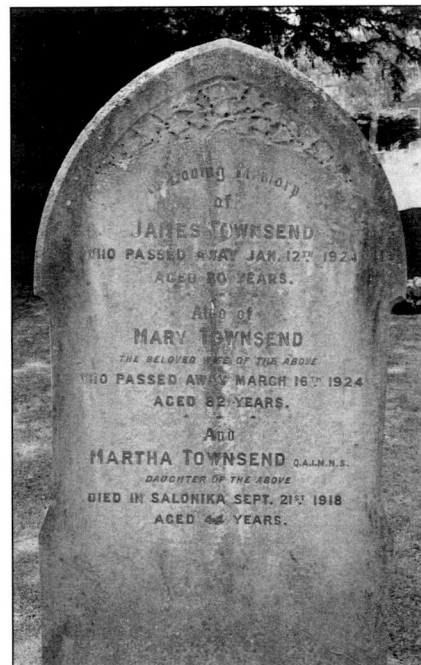

The Townsend Headstone

William Poole – Dick –died on the 30th October 1917. On the 31st October 1922 a memoriam appeared in the Essex Herald

"In everlasting memory of our dear Dick wounded and missing at Passchendaele Ridge October 30th 1917

No loving hand clasped yours that day
No home voice said goodbye
You fell in battle's dread array
But God himself was nigh

From father, mother, sisters and brothers
St Johns Green Writtle
'Peace Perfect Peace' "

That could equally serve as a memoriam to all those who died.

Lest We Forget

In the wider arena, the end of the War was the beginning of the decline of the British Empire – the greatest Empire the world had ever seen. The financial cost to Britain, the loss of so much of her shipping and the loss of the ordered pre War way of life, all lessened her power over the Empire. The War also marked the Coming of Age of the colonies such as Canada and Australia who saw themselves as countries in their own right.

In Britain itself the old hierarchy would no longer be accepted unquestioningly. The "homes fit for heroes" failed to materialise and men who had fought for their country were no longer prepared to go back to the old ways. A social revolution had begun which in this country was largely peaceful. Perhaps disillusionment, coupled with the Depression and the failure of the General Strike, knocked the stuffing out of the workingmen's organisations and meant that the sudden, often violent, changes seen in some countries were not witnessed here.

In places like Writtle much of the pre-war working population had been engaged in labouring whether agricultural or industrial for men and domestic service for women. All wars are catalysts for change and the First World War caused a vast explosion in mechanisation which was then adapted for peace time use. The increase in mechanical and technical invention marked the beginning of a trend towards a reduction in man power and, in time, spurred on by the further developments seen during the Second World War, created the conditions where many traditional forms of employment began to disappear.

The decline in Britain of manufacturing started in the aftermath of the First World War. The Second World War truly was this nation's "finest hour" but the country emerged with much of its economy ruined and deeply in debt to the U.S.A.

The great factories of Chelmsford - Hoffmann, Marconi, Crompton - where so many Writtle people worked, have all gone. And whilst some villagers still work on the land certainly far, far fewer than at the beginning of the last century.

On the closure of the Hoffmann factory in 1989 its War memorials were transferred to the Cathedral.

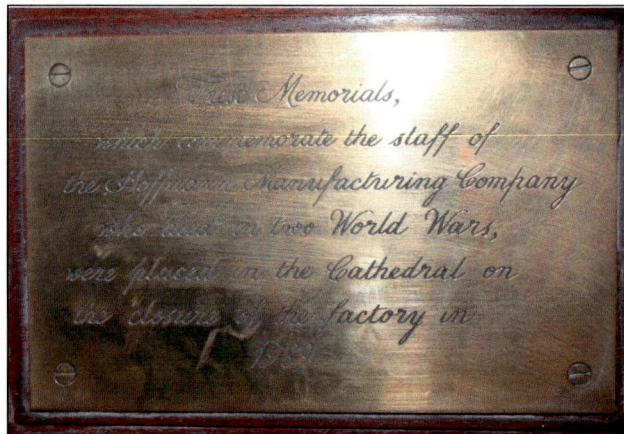

Almost universal car ownership and the seemingly unstoppable growth of the supermarkets has for many villages meant the death of small shops. The Writtle Archives' publications are essential reading to chart the differences in the life of commercial Writtle.

The changes in Writtle itself are all around us. The population has greatly increased, many of the old families have gone, but some still remain bearing the names of those who died and who are commemorated on our memorial.

The Ox and Bucks returned once more to Writtle in September 1949 for the dedication of a bench on The Green. The presentation was by the Old Comrades Association of the 1st/4th Ox and Bucks. A large crowd was present for the presentation ceremony.

Members of the Oxford & Bucks at unveiling ceremony
seat which was donated by them in September 1949

The Presentation

The Bench 1949

How many people read the plaque or even know the reason that the bench is there. It is largely forgotten, like the men of the Ox and Bucks themselves and like those of Writtle who gave their lives, perhaps remembered just once a year by some, ignored by many. Thus our history slips away. In a changing society will future generations care?

Not just a quick coach tour as part of an examination syllabus or a diversion from a trip to stock up on drink and cigarettes but proper respect.

All one can hope is that the words on the Memorial "in lasting memory of those who gave their lives in the cause of freedom and right" will be understood by future generations. Let those who come after us honour the villagers who answered their country's call and who did not return.

The Future